The Shadow of the Tsunami

ஐ

The Shadow of the Tsunami

and the Growth of the Relational Mind

ⳍ

Philip M. Bromberg

With a Foreword by Allan Schore

Routledge
Taylor & Francis Group

NEW YORK AND LONDON

Routledge
Taylor & Francis Group
711 Third Avenue
New York, NY 10017

Routledge
Taylor & Francis Group
2 Park Square
Milton Park, Abingdon
Oxon OX14 4RN

International Standard Book Number: 978-0-415-88694-9 (Hardcover)

Library of Congress Cataloging-in-Publication Data

Bromberg, Philip M., 1931–
  The shadow of the tsunami and the growth of the relational mind / Philip M. Bromberg ; with a foreword by Allan Schore.
    p. cm.
  Includes bibliographical references and index.
  ISBN 978-0-415-88694-9 (hbk. : alk. paper) — ISBN 978-0-203-83495-4 (e-book) 1. Psychoanalysis. 2. Dissociation (Psychology) 3. Psychotherapist and patient. I. Title.
  RC509.B756 2011
  616.89′17–dc22   2011002612

Visit the Taylor & Francis Web site at
http://www.taylorandfrancis.com

and the Routledge Web site at
http://www.routledgementalhealth.com

CONTENTS

Acknowledgments

CR The route of my clinical writing that led to this book's topic took shape during the 5 years following the publication of *Awakening the Dreamer: Clinical Journeys* (2006a). Throughout that period I was blessed with the ongoing friendship and professional collaboration of many colleagues, some of whom were acknowledged in the previous volume and whose names certainly deserve to be reiterated here. Regrettably it isn't possible for me to thank most of them individually a second time, and I offer both gratitude and apology to those here unnamed, whose enduring presence in my life remains a treasured gift.

There are, however, certain colleagues who have contributed so centrally and concretely to the gestation of my current thinking that the opportunity to finally thank each of them personally is an expression of gratitude long overdue. The nature of what they have given to me is varied. Many have enriched this volume through the exciting interaction between their own writing and mine; others have stirred me in spontaneously new ways as we shared joint ventures such as scientific conferences or co-teaching; and without exception, all of them have made this book possible by their support and comradeship during this half-decade. To: Tony Bass, Jessica Benjamin, Robbie Bosnak, Larry Brown, Wilma Bucci, Velleda Ceccoli, Rich Chefetz, Adrienne Harris, Anita Herron, Hazel Ipp, Robert Langan, Edgar Levenson, Pat Ogden, Lois Oppenheim, Jean Petrucelli, Allan Schore, Don Stern.

To acknowledge my patients has come to feel almost unnecessary because they are equal partners in an adventure that is the wellspring of my wish to write. It is perhaps enough to express my special gratitude to those patients, necessarily disguised, who have not only entrusted me with their private experience but have allowed me also to draw in detail upon the give-and-take of our relationship for illustrative use in this book.

During the phase in which I worked with my editor, John Kerr, his penetrating wisdom and understanding of my vision increased my ability to elucidate, across chapters, the coherent perspective on healing and growth which underlies the book's title. As with my first two books, his guidance and input was again invaluable, and once again I consider myself fortunate to have had him at my side.

I am grateful to Kate Hawes, Routledge's Publisher, for her faith in my work, and to the staff of skilled professionals who allowed the process of designing and producing the book to be so wonderfully collaborative. I especially want to thank Kristopher Spring, Associate Editor at Routledge, whose determination to overcome my ambivalence about undertaking a third book was the deciding factor in my choosing to do it. Kristopher's official title does not begin to convey the uniqueness of his dedication, the creative range of his mind, or the level of expertise he has provided in readying this book for its entrance into the world.

Foreword[1]

Allan Schore

❧ This new book from Philip Bromberg is the third of a trilogy, following what have now become classics, *Standing in the Spaces* (1998a) and *Awakening the Dreamer* (2006a). These books have enhanced our understanding of trauma and illuminated its powerful interface with the mind/brain process of dissociation in shaping the relationship through which the deepest and most enduring healing and self-growth is achieved in treatment. In an even broader sense, Bromberg has enhanced our recognition that dissociation is intrinsic to the development of what is normal as well as pathological in being human. In the following pages the reader will note a significant expansion of Bromberg's ideas from these earlier volumes. This takes the form of not only a further clarification of the concepts he developed over the body of his earlier writings, but an even more extensive elaboration of the ways he uses these in his clinical work. Indeed the book is chock-full of rich clinical vignettes, written in an experience-near style that has gained him a reputation as perhaps the most evocative clinical writer of our times. But in addition, Bromberg has dramatically progressed in integrating psychology and biology into relational mind/brain/body conceptualizations of treatment. The subtitle of the very last chapter of his 2006a book was "Where psychoanalysis, cognitive science, and neuroscience overlap." There he began to incorporate contemporary neuroscience, including my own work, into the core of his clinical model. As you will soon see each and every chapter of this book contains relevant information from neuroscience.

The reader who is already familiar with not only Bromberg's previous work but also with my own will note there is a remarkable overlap

---

[1]Allan Schore, Ph.D., is on the clinical faculty of the Department of Psychiatry and Biobehavioral Science, UCLA David Geffen School of Medicine, and at the UCLA Center for Culture, Brain, and Development.

between Bromberg's contributions to clinical psychoanalysis and mine in developmental neuropsychoanalysis, a deep resonance between his theoretical concepts and my own work in Regulation Theory. A common theme of both of our writings is the problem of early developmental trauma and dissociation and their enduring impact on the mind/brain/body's capacity to interpersonally regulate affect, referred to in this book as "the shadow of the tsunami." On the surface, it may appear that we're exploring these problems from different perspectives, but at a deeper level we're both interested in the science *and* the art of psychotherapy (which happens to be the title of my next book). This common focus on the centrality of trauma and affect, which are both intrinsically biological phenomena, allows for a convergence of our perspectives on development, psychopathogenesis, and treatment. But we share more than just an intellectual commonality of our theories. In my review of his last book (Schore, 2007) I admitted a personal bias to his clinical style of working with patients, since it is so similar to my own. Since that time, our ongoing rich dialogues in a series of annual Affect Regulation conferences in New York City has significantly increased the interpenetration of our ideas into each other's work, and more importantly, has intensified a deep friendship.

This book is more than just a further elaboration of Bromberg's groundbreaking work on trauma and dissociation. Here he expands and broadens his clinical model and defines what he sees as the relational mechanism of therapeutic action common to the treatment of all patients. In fact he argues that we are now experiencing a paradigm shift in psychotherapy: from the primacy of cognition to the primacy of affect, from the primacy of content to the primacy of process and context, and thereby a shift away from the concept of "technique." In my writings and presentations I have described the same shift in paradigm (Schore, 2009d, 2011). My neuropsychoanalytic perspective views the shift from conscious cognition to unconscious affect, and asserts that the relational change mechanism embedded in the therapeutic alliance acts not through the therapist's left brain explicitly delivering *content* interpretations to the patient's right brain, but through right-brain to right-brain affect communication and regulation *processes*. This book is dedicated to what that shift looks and feels like clinically, from the experience-near perspective of a relational model of treatment that impacts both the conscious and especially unconscious mind/brain/ bodies of both members of the therapeutic relationship. Although it uses the terminology of contemporary psychoanalysis, this volume will be appreciated by the broader audience of psychodynamic clinicians and indeed all psychologists, psychiatrists, social workers, and counselors practicing psychotherapy.

In his invitation to write this foreword Philip noted, "The length is up to you." He said this knowing that I am anything but brief in my writings. And so this foreword will contain four sections: the first on development, the next two on psychopathogenesis, and the last on psychotherapy. Following the format of my review of his last book I will describe in some detail not only his but my own work in these areas, including points of direct connections between his clinical model and my work in interpersonal neurobiology. In the last section on psychotherapy I shall discuss in more detail the neurobiological correlates of two major themes of this book: unconscious relational communications, and the psychotherapeutic change mechanism of "shrinking the shadow of the tsunami." In addition to acting as a commentary on Bromberg's ideas, this foreword also serves as a reader's guide of interpersonal neurobiology that can be accessed after reading Bromberg's remarkably evocative clinical descriptions.

Development: Attachment and the Early Evolution of the Right Brain Core Self

In my review of *Awakening the Dreamer* (Schore, 2007) I noted Bromberg's active incorporation of advances in attachment theory and affective science into the core of his clinical model; he asserted:

> The developmental achievement of a sense of self that is simultaneously fluid and robust depends on how well the capacity for affect regulation and affective competency has been achieved.... When these early patterns of interpersonal interaction are relatively successful, they create a stable foundation for relational affect regulation that is internalized as nonverbal and unconscious. Thus, further successful negotiation of interpersonal transactions at increasingly higher levels of self-development and interpersonal maturity is made possible. (Bromberg, 2006a, p. 32)

This developmental model appears in every chapter of this book, and it lies at the core of Bromberg's model of psychotherapeutic change. In this work he moves even more deeply into not only the affective dynamics of attachment, but into the interpersonal neurobiology of attachment. In chapter 5 he concludes:

The development of a mature capacity for affect regulation rests on a utilization of the natural dialectic, always operative, between auto-regulation and relational regulation. Schore (2003a, 2003b) makes it clear that the degree to which early relational bonds are internalized as stable and secure actually determines significant aspects of the brain's structure, especially in the right hemisphere. This in turn determines whether later in life an individual can utilize interactive regulation, such as in a psychotherapeutic relationship, when his own auto-regulatory mechanisms are not available.

In a number of works on Regulation Theory I have integrated current research, developmental data, and clinical observations to offer an interpersonal neurobiological model of attachment (Schore, 1994, 2001, 2002, 2003a, 2003b, 2009a, 2009b, 2009c, 2010, 2011). To summarize modern attachment theory (Schore & Schore, 2008), the essential task of the first year of human life is the creation of a secure attachment bond of emotional communication between the infant and the primary caregiver, and the subsequent expanded capacity for affect regulation. During spontaneous right-brain to right-brain visual-facial, auditory-prosodic, and tactile-proprioceptive emotionally charged attachment communications, the sensitive, psychobiologically attuned caregiver regulates, at an implicit level, the infant's states of arousal (Schore, 1994).

In order to enter into this communication, the mother must be psychobiologically attuned to the dynamic crescendos and decrescendos of the infant's bodily-based internal states of arousal. To effectively accomplish this interactive regulation, the mother must modulate nonoptimal high or low levels of stimulation which would induce supra-heightened or extremely reduced levels of arousal in the infant. In this mutually synchronized attunement of emotionally driven facial expression, prosodic vocalization, and kinesic behaviors, dynamically fluctuating moment-to-moment "state-sharing" represents an organized dialogue occurring within milliseconds, and it acts as an interactive matrix in which both partners match states and then simultaneously adjust their social attention, stimulation, and accelerating arousal in response to the partner's signals. Throughout this book Bromberg refers to "what Allan Schore calls right-brain to right-brain 'state-sharing'."

It is important to note that developmental research shows frequent moments of misattunement in the dyad, ruptures of the attachment bond (what Bromberg calls *intersubjective collisions*). In early development, an adult provides much of the modulation of infant states, especially after a state disruption or a transition between states, and this intervention allows for the development of self-regulation. The key to this beneficial interaction is the caregiver's capacity to monitor and regulate her own (especially negative) affect. In this essential regulatory pattern of "rupture and repair," the attuned "good enough" caregiver who induces a rupture of the attachment bond and thereby a stress response in her infant through a misattunement remedies the situation and helps her infant regulate his or her negative affect via her coparticipation in "interactive repair" (Bromberg's *intersubjective negotiations*). The process of re-experiencing positive affect following negative experience allows the child to learn that negative affect can be tolerated and that relational stress can be regulated.

At the end of the first year right lateralized cortical-subcortical circuits imprint, in implicit-procedural memory, an internal working model of attachment which encodes strategies of affect regulation that nonconsciously guide the individual through interpersonal contexts. Thus, emotion is initially externally regulated by the primary caregiver, but over the course of infancy it becomes increasingly internally regulated as a result of neurophysiological development. These adaptive capacities are central to self-regulation i.e., the ability to flexibly regulate the psychobiological states of emotions through interactions with other humans, interactive regulation in interconnected contexts, and without other humans, autoregulation in autonomous contexts. Attachment, the outcome of the child's genetically encoded biological (temperamental) predisposition and the particular caregiver environment, thus represents the regulation of biological synchronicity between and within organisms.

These nonverbal attachment interactions with the social environment are occurring during the human brain growth spurt (Dobbing & Sands, 1973) of infancy. This developmental stage also represents a critical period of maturation of the early developing right hemisphere (Chiron et al., 1997; Gupta et al., 2005; Sun et al., 2005). Almost two decades ago I proposed:

> The infant's early maturing right hemisphere, which is dominant for the child's processing of visual emotional information, the infant's recognition of the mother's face, and the *perception* of arousal-inducing maternal facial expressions, is psychobiologically attuned to the output of the mother's right hemisphere, which is involved in the expression and processing of emotional information and in nonverbal communication. (Schore, 1994, p. 63, emphasis added)

A large body of experimental data now supports the developmental principle that implicit affective attachment interactions directly impact the experience-dependent maturation of "the emotional brain," the right hemisphere (Ammaniti & Trentini, 2009; Schore, 1994, 2003a, 2003b, 2010; Siegel, 1999).

As Bromberg notes, bodily-based attachment transactions represent "a conversation between limbic systems" (Buck, 1994). These emotional communications imprint cortical-subcortical connections of the developing right brain, which is deeply connected into the emotion processing limbic system (see Figure F.1, vertical axis on right side). Basic research in developmental neuroscience now demonstrates: "The functional maturation of limbic circuits is significantly influenced by early socio-emotional experience" (Helmeke et al., 2001, p. 717). In addition, prenatal and postnatal interpersonal events also wire the connectivity of structures in the developing central nervous system (CNS) with the energy-expending sympathetic and energy-conserving parasympathetic branches of the evolving autonomic nervous system (ANS). There is now consensus that the right brain plays a greater role than the left in autonomic arousal and therefore the somatic aspects of

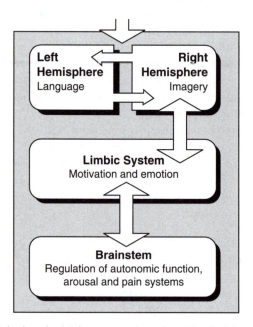

Figure F.1 Right hemispheric connections into the limbic and autonomic nervous systems. Note the vertical axis on the right side of the figure.

emotional states. Confirming this interpersonal neurobiological model, a near-infrared spectroscopy study of infant–mother attachment at 12 months concludes: "Our results are in agreement with that of Schore (2000) who addressed the importance of the right hemisphere in the attachment system" (Minagawa-Kawai et al., 2009, p. 289).

Attachment transactions leave an enduring imprint of the developmental trajectory of the right brain, the locus of the core self. Neuroscientists now contend that throughout the lifespan: "The neural substrates of the *perception of voices, faces, gestures, smells and pheromones,* as evidenced by modern neuroimaging techniques, are characterized by a general pattern of right-hemispheric functional asymmetry" (Brancucci et al., 2009, p. 895, emphasis added). These adaptive perceptual processes are critical in all intimate contexts, including psychotherapy. At numerous points in this book Bromberg refers to the essential function of the *perception of state switches* in intersubjective communications, and the clinician's "overarching attunement is to his contextualized perceptual experience." He states that "perception is a relational process–a personal interaction between the mind of the individual and what is 'out there'." This "perception" is a rapid, implicit, nonconscious right brain function.

The highest corticolimbic centers of the right hemisphere, especially the orbitofrontal cortex, the locus of Bowlby's attachment system, act as the brain's most complex affect and stress regulatory system (Cerqueira et al., 2008; Schore, 1994, 2000). The regulatory system of the right orbitofrontal (ventromedial) cortex is known to have direct synaptic connections with the sympathetic and parasympathetic branches of the ANS that is responsible for the somatic aspects of affects (Hansel & von Kanel, 2008), with the right amygdala, the major subcortical fear center of the brain (Morris & Dolan, 2004), what Bromberg refers to as an affective "smoke detector" and an "early warning system," and with the hypothalamus, and thereby the hypothalamic-pituitary-adrenal axis that controls stress. It is now accepted that via a right lateralized vagal circuit of emotion regulation, "the right hemisphere–including the right cortical and subcortical structures–would promote the efficient regulation of autonomic function via the source nuclei of the brain stem" (Porges et al., 1994, p. 175). Basic research also now establishes that optimal stress regulation is dependent on "right hemispheric specialization in regulating stress- and emotion-related processes" (Sullivan & Dufresne, 2006, p. 55). Describing the essential survival functions of this lateralized system Schutz (2005) notes:

The right hemisphere operates a distributed network for rapid responding to danger and other urgent problems. It preferentially processes environmental challenge, stress and pain and manages self-protective responses such as avoidance and escape. Emotionality is thus the right brain's "red phone," compelling the mind to handle urgent matters without delay. (p. 15)

Psychopathogenesis: Negative Impact of Attachment Trauma and Dissociation on Developing Right Brain

In the very first chapter of this book Bromberg reintroduces the reader to a theme that runs throughout his previous writings: the negative impact of relational trauma on the developmental trajectory described above. In his last book he noted: "The reason that developmental trauma (also termed relational trauma) is of such significance is that it shapes the attachment patterns that establish what is to become a stable or unstable core self" (2006a, p. 6). In that work he linked trauma specifically to autonomic hyperarousal, "a chaotic and terrifying flooding of affect that can threaten to overwhelm sanity and imperil psychological survival" (p. 33), and described how dissociation is then automatically and immediately triggered as the fundamental defense to the arousal dysregulation of overwhelming affective states. Indeed, Bromberg's longstanding clinical explorations of the survival defense of dissociation have significantly altered the practice of psychoanalytic psychotherapy.

This psychopathological model appears as a central theme of the present volume. In the second chapter he states:

When the original "other" is a primary attachment figure, a parent or an other whose significance is interpersonally similar to a parent's, that person holds the power to destabilize the child's mental state by rupturing a relational connection that organizes the child's sense of self-continuity. In order to preserve the attachment connection and protect mental stability, the mind triggers a survival solution, dissociation, that allows the person to bypass the mentally disorganizing struggle to self-reflect without hope of relieving the pain and fear caused by the destabilization of selfhood.

Returning to my own work in this area, in contrast to the optimal growth-facilitating attachment scenario outlined above, in a relational growth-inhibiting early environment the primary caregiver induces traumatic states of enduring negative affect in the child. This caregiver is inaccessible and reacts to her infant's expressions of emotions and stress inappropriately and/or rejectingly, and therefore shows minimal or unpredictable participation in the various types of arousal regulating processes. Instead of modulating she induces extreme levels of stimulation and arousal, very high in abuse and/or very low in neglect. And because she provides no interactive repair the infant's intense negative affective states last for long periods of time.

Interdisciplinary evidence now indicates that the infant's psychobiological reaction to trauma is comprised of two separate response patterns: hyperarousal and dissociation. In the initial hyperarousal stage, the maternal haven of safety suddenly becomes a source of threat, triggering an alarm or startle reaction of the infant's right hemisphere, the locus of both the attachment system and the fear motivational system. The maternal stressor activates the hypothalamic-pituitary-adrenal (HPA) stress axis, thereby eliciting a sudden increase of the energy-expending sympathetic component of the infant's autonomic nervous system, resulting in significantly elevated heart rate, blood pressure, and respiration, the somatic expressions of a dysregulated hypermetabolic psychobiological state of fear-terror.

But a second, later forming reaction to relational trauma is dissociation, in which the child disengages from stimuli in the external world—traumatized infants are observed to be "staring off into space with a glazed look." This parasympathetic dominant state of conservation-withdrawal occurs in helpless and hopeless stressful situations in which the individual becomes inhibited and strives to avoid attention in order to become "unseen" (Schore, 1994, 2001). The dissociative metabolic shutdown state is a primary regulatory process, used throughout the life span, in which the stressed individual passively disengages in order to conserve energies, foster survival by the risky posture of "feigning death," and allow restitution of depleted resources by immobility. In this passive hypometabolic state heart rate, blood pressure, and respiration are decreased, while pain numbing and blunting endogenous opiates are elevated. It is this energy-conserving parasympathetic (vagal) mechanism that mediates the "profound detachment" of dissociation.

It is now established that there are in fact two parasympathetic vagal systems in the brainstem medulla. The ventral vagal complex rapidly regulates cardiac output to foster fluid engagement and disengagement with the social environment, and exhibits rapid and transitory patterns associated with perceptive pain and unpleasantness, all aspects of a secure attachment bond of emotional communication. On the other hand, activity of the dorsal vagal complex is associated with intense emotional states and immobilization, and is responsible for the severe hypoarousal and pain blunting of dissociation. The traumatized infant's sudden state switch from sympathetic hyperarousal into parasympathetic dissociation is described by Porges (1997) as "the sudden and rapid transition from an unsuccessful strategy of struggling requiring massive sympathetic activation to the metabolically conservative immobilized state mimicking death associated with the dorsal vagal complex" (p. 75). This work in psychophysiology nicely fits with Bromberg's assertion that trauma is associated with autonomic sympathetic hyperarousal, and that dissociation is a response to hyperarousal.

Porges (1997) describes the involuntary and often prolonged characteristic pattern of vagal outflow from the dorsal vagal nucleus. This state of dorsal vagal parasympathetic activation accounts for the extensive duration of "dead spots" in the infant's subjective experience (Kestenberg, 1985), "void" states associated with pathological dissociative detachment (Allen et al., 1999), and for what Bromberg calls dissociative "gaps" in subjective reality, "spaces" that surround self-states and thereby disrupt coherence among highly affectively charged states. These "gaps" are also discussed in the developmental psychoanalytic literature. Winnicott (1958) notes that a particular failure of the maternal holding environment causes a discontinuity in the baby's need for "going-on-being."

Hesse and Main (1999) point out that the disorganization and disorientation of type "D" attachment associated with abuse and neglect phenotypically resemble dissociative states. The underlying mechanism of this can only be understood in neurobiological terms. During episodes of the intergenerational transmission of attachment trauma the infant is matching the rhythmic structures of the mother's dysregulated arousal states. This synchronization is registered in the firing patterns of the stress-sensitive corticolimbic regions of the right brain, dominant for the human stress response and survival (Wittling, 1997; Wittling & Schweiger, 1993). These right hemispheric structures are in a critical period of growth during the early stages of human development (Allman et al., 2005; Bogolepeva & Maolfeeva, 2001; Chiron et al., 1997; Schore, 1994).

In light of the fact that many of these mothers have suffered from unresolved trauma themselves, this spatiotemporal imprinting of the chaotic alterations of the mother's dysregulated state facilitates the downloading of programs of psychopathogenesis. This growth-inhibiting relational environment is a context for the real-time inter-generational transmission of an enduring susceptibility to attachment trauma and to the unconscious use of a dissociative defense against overwhelming and dysregulating affective states. In a recent prospective study Dutra et al. (2009) observe that maternal disrupted affective communications and lack of involvement in the regulation of stressful arousal are associated with the child's use of dissociation, "one of the few available means for achieving a modicum of relief from fearful arousal." This in turn leads the child "not to acknowledge pain and distress within a set of caregiving relationships that are vital for survival" (p. 388).

The chronic, massive psychobiological misattunement of attachment trauma between the infant and primary caregiver sets the stage for the characterological use of right brain pathological dissociation over all subsequent stages of development. Describing the use of this defense by certain personality structures, Allen and Coyne (1995) observe: "Although initially they may have used dissociation to cope with traumatic events, they subsequently dissociate to defend against a broad range of daily stressors, including their own posttraumatic symptoms, pervasively undermining the continuity of their experience" (p. 620). Attachment studies reveal that individuals with a history of relational trauma utilize dissociative behaviors in later life—hypoarousal and heart rate deceleration has been found in dissociating infants, adolescents, and adults (see Schore, 2003a). These psychobiological events are not only intrasubjectively experienced but implicitly communicated in intimate contexts (including right-brain to right-brain transference/countertransference transactions).

Psychopathogenesis: Clinical Manifestations of Pathological Dissociation

The enduring negative impact of the characterological use of pathological dissociation in individuals with a history of relational attachment trauma is a major theme of this book. In the very first chapter Bromberg notes:

> The affect evoked by trauma is not merely unpleasant but is a disorganizing hyperarousal that threatens to overwhelm the mind's ability to think, reflect, and process experience cognitively.

Affective dysregulation so great that it carries the person to the edge of depersonalization and sometimes self-annihilation is not describable by the term anxiety. Continuity of selfhood is at stake.

And later in the book (chapter 5) he asserts:

One could even suggest that the impact of trauma leads to the most rigid dissociative mental structure when one of the resulting disjunctive states is highly organized by the *attachment-related core-self*, and the trauma threatens its violation. In such instances, the threat of affective destabilization carries with it a potential identity crisis.

Consonant with these clinical observations I have cited neurobiological research that now clearly demonstrates continuity over the course of the lifespan of the expression of the primitive autoregulation defense of pathological dissociation in patients with a history of relational trauma. It is now well established that early childhood abuse specifically alters right lateralized limbic system maturation, producing neurobiological alterations that act as a biological substrate for a variety of psychiatric consequences, including affective instability, inefficient stress tolerance, memory impairment, and dissociative disturbances (Schore, 2002). In a transcranial magnetic stimulation study Spitzer et al. (2004) report: "In dissociation-prone individuals, a trauma that is perceived and processed by the right hemisphere will lead to a 'disruption in the usually integrated functions of consciousness'" (p. 168). In functional magnetic resonance imaging research Lanius et al. (2005) show predominantly right-hemispheric activation in post-traumatic stress disorders (PTSD) patients while they are dissociating, and conclude that patients dissociate in order to escape from the overwhelming emotions associated with the traumatic memory, and that dissociation can be interpreted as representing a nonverbal response to the traumatic memory. Two recent studies also demonstrate that dissociation is associated with an impaired competence of right hemisphere emotion processing, especially when it becomes loaded with high arousal, negatively valenced emotional stimuli (Enriquez & Bernabeu, 2008; Helton et al., 2010).

These and other studies are now exploring the evolution of a developmentally impaired regulatory system over all stages of life, and provide evidence that prefrontal cortical and subcortical limbic-autonomic areas of the right brain are centrally involved in the dissociative response. The right cerebral hemisphere, more so than the left, is densely reciprocally interconnected with emotion processing limbic regions, as well as with subcortical areas that generate both the brainstem arousal and autonomic (sympathetic and parasympathetic) bodily-based aspect of emotions (see right lateralized vertical axis of Figure F.1). There is now agreement that sympathetic nervous system activity is manifest in tight engagement with the external environment and high level of energy mobilization and utilization, while the parasympathetic component drives disengagement from the external environment and utilizes low levels of internal energy (Recordati, 2003). The stress regulating dynamic uncoupling of the two components of the ANS underlies the description that "Dissociation is conceptualized as a basic part of the psychobiology of the human trauma response: a protective activation of altered states of consciousness in reaction to overwhelming psychological trauma" (Loewenstein, 1996, p. 312).

Pathological dissociative detachment thus represents a bottom-line defensive state driven by fear-terror, in which the stressed individual copes by pervasively and diffusely disengaging attention "from both the outer *and* inner worlds" (Allen et al., 1999, p. 164, emphasis added). I have suggested that the "inner world" is more than cognitions, the realm of bodily processes, central components of emotional states (Schore, 1994). This conceptualization bears directly upon Bromberg's assertion in this volume (chapter 8) that dissociation underlies the mechanism by which "the mind/brain tries to avoid self-annihilation by protecting the inner world from the existence of the outside."

In line with the current shift from cold cognition to the primacy of bodily-based affect, clinical research on dissociation is now focusing on "somatoform dissociation." According to Nijenhuis (2000), somatoform dissociation is an outcome of early onset traumatization, expressed as a lack of integration of sensorimotor experiences, reactions, and functions of the individual and his/her self-representation. Thus, "dissociatively detached individuals are not only detached from the environment, but also from the self–their body, their own actions, and their sense of identity" (Allen et al., 1999, p. 165). This observation describes impaired functions of the right hemisphere, the locus of the "emotional" or "corporeal self." Van der Kolk and his colleagues (1996) conclude: "Dissociation refers to a compartmentalization of experience: Elements of a trauma are not integrated into a unitary whole or an integrated sense of self" (p. 306).

In a number of works I have offered interdisciplinary evidence which indicates that the implicit self, equated with Freud's system *Ucs*, is located in the right brain (Schore, 1994, 2003b, 2009b). The lower subcortical levels of the right brain (the deep unconscious) contain all the major motivational systems (including attachment, fear, sexuality, aggression, etc.) and generate the somatic autonomic expressions and arousal intensities of all emotional states. On the other hand, higher orbitofrontal-limbic levels of the right hemisphere generate a conscious emotional state that expresses the affective output of these motivational systems (see Figure F.1). Neuroanatomical research now demonstrates:

> Descending pathways from orbitofrontal and medial prefrontal cortices, which are linked with the amygdala, provide the means for speedy influence of the prefrontal cortex on the autonomic system, in processes underlying appreciation and expression of emotions.... Repetitive activation of the remarkably specific and bidirectional pathways linking the amygdala with the orbitofrontal cortex may be necessary for conscious appreciation of the emotional significance of events. (Barbas et al., 2003)

This right lateralized cortical-subcortical system is the neurobiological processor of Bucci's (1997a) symbolic-subsymbolic communications. The higher right cortical hemisphere is involved in symbolization and imagery functions; the lower right subcortical areas (e.g., amygdala, hippocampus, hypothalamic-pituitary-adrenal axis, brainstem arousal systems, etc.) in unprocessed, unformulated affective experience. Thus: "The right hemisphere is ... more closely in touch with emotion and the body (therefore with the neurologically 'inferior' and more ancient regions of the central nervous system)" (McGilchrist, 2009, p. 437).

The hierarchical apex of this right lateralized cortical-subcortical system, the orbitofrontal cortex—the senior executive of the emotional brain—functions as a dynamic filter of emotional stimuli (Rule, Shimamura, & Knight, 2002), provides a panoramic view of the entire external environment, as well as the internal environment associated with motivational factors (Barbas, 2007, p. 239), and intuitively formulates a theory of mind, now defined as "a kind of affective-decision making" (Happeney et al., 2004, p. 4). The orbitofrontal cortex, which I equate with Freud's system *Pcs*, performs an essential adaptive motivational function—the relatively fluid switching of internal bodily-based states in response to changes in the external environment that are nonconsciously appraised to be personally meaningful. I suggest that in optimal contexts this right brain system allows for what Bromberg describes in chapter 7 as "a mind–brain mechanism that is intrinsic to everyday mental functioning," one that flexibly and seamlessly "attempts to select a self-state configuration that is most immediately adaptive within the constraints of self-coherence. This flexibility is what gives a person the remarkable capacity to negotiate character stability and change simultaneously–to stay the same while changing (chapter 5)."

On the other hand, pathological dissociation, an enduring outcome of early relational trauma, is manifest in a maladaptive highly rigid, closed right brain system. This system's implicit visual, auditory, and tactile perceptual functions, performed by the temporoparietal areas of the posterior right cortical hemisphere that "plays a key role in perception and awareness" (Papeo et al., 2010, p. 129), are radically altered in trauma. In chapter 3 Bromberg observes: "The ordinary links between symbolic and subsymbolic communication have been broken–at least for a while. The essence of dissociation is that it alters perceptual experience–and thereby drains the interpersonal context of personal meaning." In addition, this closed system responds to even low levels of intersubjective stress with the survival response of defensive parasympathetic dorsal vagal parasympathetic hypoarousal and heart rate deceleration. This results in moments of "psychic death" and an inability to sustain an inner sense of "aliveness". McGilchrist (2009) describes dissociation as "a relative hypofunction of the right hemisphere" (p. 235)

Neurobiologically, dissociation reflects the inability of the right brain cortical-subcortical implicit self-system to recognize and process the perception of external stimuli (exteroceptive information coming from the relational environment) and on a moment-to-moment basis integrate them with internal stimuli (interoceptive information from the body, somatic markers, the "felt experience"). This failure of integration of the higher right hemisphere with the lower right brain and disconnection of the central nervous system from the autonomic nervous system induces an instant collapse of both subjectivity and intersubjectivity. Stressful affects, especially those associated with emotional pain are thus not experienced in consciousness (Bromberg's "not-me" self-states).

It is important to emphasize that dissociation involves more than an alteration of mental processes, but rather mind–body disconnections. It ruptures the integration of psychic and somatic experience, what Winnicott (1949) called *psyche-soma*, and thereby self-wholeness. Kalsched (2005) describes operations of defensive dissociative processes used by the child during traumatic experience by which "Affect in the body is severed from its corresponding images in the mind and thereby an unbearably painful meaning is obliterated" (p. 174). There is now agreement that "traumatic stress in childhood could lead to self-modulation of painful affect by directing attention away from internal emotional states" (Lane et al., 1997, p. 840). The right hemisphere is dominant not only for regulating affects, but also for maintaining a coherent sense of one's body (Tsakiris et al., 2008), for attention (Raz, 2004), and for pain processing (Symonds et al., 2006), and so the right brain strategy of dissociation represents the ultimate defense for blocking emotional bodily-based pain. The endpoint of chronically experiencing catastrophic states of relational trauma in early life is therefore a progressive impairment of the ability to adjust, take defensive action, or act on one's own behalf, and a blocking of the capacity to register affect and pain, all critical to survival.

At all points of the life span, although dissociation represents an effective short-term strategy, it is detrimental to long-term functioning, specifically by preventing exposure to potential relational learning experiences embedded in intimate intersubjective contexts that are necessary for emotional growth. As Bromberg notes, the function of pathological dissociation is to act as an "early warning system" that anticipates potential affect dysregulation by anticipating trauma before it arrives. If early trauma is experienced as "psychic catastrophe," dissociation represents "detachment from an unbearable situation," "the escape when there is no escape," "a submission and resignation to the inevitability of overwhelming, even psychically deadening danger," and "a last resort defensive strategy" (see references in Schore, 2003a, 2009a). This psychobiological survival defense becomes characterological in personalities who experience attachment trauma in early development.

The fragile unconscious system of such personalities is susceptible to not only hypermetabolic hyperarousal, but also mind–body hypometabolic collapse. The latter is manifest in a sudden a loss of energy-dependent synaptic connectivity within the right brain, expressed in a sudden implosion of the implicit self, a rupture of self-continuity, and a loss of an ability to experience a particular conscious affect. This collapse of the implicit self is signaled by the amplification of the affects of shame and disgust, and by the cognitions of hopelessness and helplessness. Because the right hemisphere mediates the communication and regulation of emotional states, the rupture of intersubjectivity is accompanied by an instant dissipation of safety and trust, a common occurrence in the treatment of the right brain deficits of severe personality disorders (Schore, 2003a, 2009b). Current research shows that insecurely attached dissociative patients dissociate as a response to negative emotions arising in psychodynamic psychotherapy, leading to a less favorable treatment outcome (Spitzer et al., 2007). Both Bromberg and I have argued that this bottom-line defense represents the major counterforce to the emotional-motivational aspects of the change process in psychotherapy.

Psychotherapy: Critical Role of Enactments in Affective Change Processes

I would like now to focus more directly upon this book's valuable clinical contributions to a deeper understanding of the essential mechanisms of psychotherapy, that is, "therapeutic action." A major theme of the upcoming chapters is the problem of clinical enactments, a challenging clinical phenomenon that is also a focus of my own recent work (Schore, 2011). Bromberg argues: "Clinically, the phenomenon of dissociation, though observable at many points in every treatment, comes into highest relief during enactments, requiring an analyst's close attunement to unacknowledged affective shifts in his own and his patient's self-states (chapter 7)." In my earlier review of *Awakening the Dreamer*, I concluded that the book's major accomplishment was in convincingly demonstrating, both clinically and theoretically, that attending to dissociative processes in enactments is essential to the treatment of patients with a history of relational trauma (Schore, 2007). Indeed, clinical research now shows that pathological dissociation, a primitive defense against overwhelming affects, is a key feature of reactive attachment disorder of infants, pediatric maltreatment disorder, dissociative identity disorder, posttraumatic stress disorder, psychotic disorders, eating disorders, substance abuse and alcoholism, somatoform disorders, and borderline and antisocial personality disorders.

In this volume Bromberg expands his trauma-dissociation model ("shrinking the shadow of the tsunami") to the treatment of all patients, and in chapter 7 suggests that therapeutic joint processing of enactments

allows one's work with so-called "good" analytic patients to become more powerful because it provides a more experience-near perspective from which to engage clinical phenomena that are immune to interpretation, such as "intractable resistance" and "therapeutic stalemate." Further, it puts to rest the notion of "ana-lyzability," and allows analysts to use their expertise with a wide spectrum of personality disorders often considered "difficult" or "unanalyzable," such as individuals diagnosed as borderline, schizoid, narcissistic, and dissociative.

That said, the focus of the following chapters is on patients with a history of relational trauma and pathological dissociation. He states: "The big difference between people is the extent to which the sudden affective hyperarousal touches an area of unprocessed developmen-tal trauma and is not only unpleasant, but mentally unbearable and thus unavailable to cognition. The risk of this happening is a central aspect of working with enactments." Reflecting his developmental and neurobiological clinical perspective, Bromberg argues (chapter 5) that: "Enactments, to the degree they relive aspects of attachment-related developmental trauma in a patient's past, activate the brain's 'fear sys-tem'." Recall the previous discussion of the subcortical right amygdala, the brain system that processes "unseen fear" (Morris et al., 1999). This volume's numerous clinical vignettes offer almost poetic descriptions of the dialogical unconscious attachment processes that are intersub-jectively activated in enactments. In this last section of the foreword I utilize the neuropsychoanalytic perspective of Regulation Theory to discuss two major processes embedded in enactments: unconscious relational communications, and the psychotherapeutic change mecha-nism of "shrinking the shadow of the tsunami."

Unconscious Relational Communications

Throughout this book Bromberg repeatedly asserts that enactment is an unconscious communication process that reflects those areas of the patient's self-experience where trauma has compromised the capacity for affect regulation. The enactment is a dyadic dissociative process that is transmitted not through symbolic but subsymbolic commu-nication that is "deadened to reflective functioning." In this dyadic process, if the therapist is "too long listening to the 'material' without being alive to his own internal experience of the relationship itself, a dissociative process often begins to develop in the therapist that may have started in the patient but quickly becomes a cocoon that envelops both patient and therapist (chapter 2)." He further proposes that the phenomenon of enactment (subsymbolic communication of "not-me") and the phenomenon of intersubjectivity (symbolic communication of a relational "me") represent discrete communication channels. These communications take place in a "transference/countertransference field" that is characterized by "its vividness and its immediacy." How does the clinician receive these dissociated communications? Bromberg suggests that the clinician must adopt an interpersonal/relational listening stance in which his "overarching state of mind is attuned to his fluctuating, moment-to-moment experience of what it is like for him to be with his patient and for his patient to be with him during the course of a session.... His 'material' is an ever-shifting experiential context, the most powerful element of which first reaches him perceptually, not cognitively" (chapter 6).

Within this listening stance the focus of the therapist's attention is on the shifting states of mind that organize the content at any given moment, not on content per se. In this intersubjective context "verbal content is only one ingredient of a here-and-now field, a field that is shaped by an ever-changing affective dialectic between what is being enacted and what is being said." In order to attain this stance of "open-ended listening" the clinician must "leave rational thought behind." In support of this enactment communication model he cites Seymour Epstein's (1994) work on "Integration of the cognitive and the dynamic unconscious" that describes "the existence of two parallel, interacting modes of information processing: a rational system and an emotionally driven system" (p. 709). In line with this conceptualization, Bromberg concludes that in enactments, heightened affective moments of the treatment, what matters is the "therapist's affective honesty" that is "rarely communicated through content or through language per se. It is primarily communicated through a relational bond that Schore and others including myself believe is mediated neurobiologically by right-brain to right-brain state sharing." In the previous sections of this foreword I discussed the developmental interpersonal neurobiology of right brain state-sharing.

Indeed, my work in Regulation Theory describes in some detail these right brain unconscious relational communications, and so I will offer a brief summary of this work. A major tenet of my studies dictates that the relevance of developmental attachment studies to the treatment process lies in the commonality of implicit right-brain to right-brain affect communicating and regulating mechanisms in the caregiver–infant and the therapist–patient relationship (the therapeutic alliance). Within the therapeutic dyad, not left brain verbal explicit patient–therapist rational discourse but right brain implicit nonverbal emotion-laden communication directly expresses the attachment dynamic. Just as the left brain communicates its states to other left brains via conscious linguistic behaviors so the right nonverbally communicates its unconscious states to other right brains that are tuned to receive these communications.

Recent neuroscientific information about the emotion processing right brain is directly applicable to models of patient–therapist affective communications. Decety and Chaminade (2003) describe right brain operations essential for adaptive interpersonal functioning, ones specifically expressed in the therapeutic alliance: "Mental states that are in essence private to the self may be shared between individuals ... self-awareness, empathy, identification with others, and more generally intersubjective processes, are largely dependent upon ... right hemisphere resources, which are the first to develop" (p. 591). And with respect to the receptive relational mechanism within the therapeutic alliance, Keenan and his colleagues (2005) assert: "The right hemisphere, in fact, truly interprets the mental state not only of its own brain, but the brains (and minds) of others" (p. 702).

The quintessential clinical context for a right brain transferential/countertransferential implicit communication of a dysregulated emotional state is the heightened affective moment of a clinical enactment. Spontaneous nonverbal transference/countertransference interactions at preconscious-unconscious levels represent implicit right-brain to right-brain nonverbal communications of fast acting, automatic, regulated and especially dysregulated bodily-based stressful emotional states between patient and therapist (Schore, 1994). Transference is an activation of right brain autobiographical memory, as autobiographical negatively valenced, high intensity emotions are retrieved from specifically the right (and not left) medial temporal lobe (Buchanan et al., 2006). Transference can be described as "an established pattern of relating and emotional responding that is cued by something in the present, but oftentimes calls up both an affective state and thoughts that may have more to do with past experience than present ones" (Maroda, 2005, p. 134). Writing on unconscious emotional memories Gainotti (2006) asserts: "The right hemisphere may be crucially involved in those emotional memories which must be reactivated and reworked during the psychoanalytical treatment" (p. 167). It is now well established that the right hemisphere is dominant for nonverbal (Benowitz et al., 1983) and emotional (Blonder et al., 1991) communication.

Earlier I discussed how attachment states are transmitted in spontaneous, implicit, regulated and dysregulated right-brain to right-brain
visual-facial, tactile-proprioceptive, and auditory-prosodic emotionally charged communications. In a number of contributions I have
offered interdisciplinary evidence which indicates that these nonverbal communications are rapidly expressed within an enactment.
With reference to auditory nonspeech communications Hutterer and
Liss (2006) point out that nonverbal variables, such as tone, tempo,
rhythm, timbre, prosody, and amplitude of speech, as well as body
language signals, act as essential aspects of therapeutic technique. In
a recent review of the neurobiology of affective prosody Ross and
Monnot (2008) assert: "Thus, the traditional concept that language is a
dominant and lateralized function of the left hemisphere is no longer
tenable" (p. 51). They conclude:

> Over the last three decades, there has been growing realization
> that the right hemisphere is essential for language and communi-
> cation competency and psychological well-being through its abil-
> ity to modulate affective prosody and gestural behavior, decode
> connotative (non-standard) word meanings, make thematic infer-
> ences, and process metaphor, complex linguistic relationships
> and non-literal (idiomatic) types of expressions. (p. 51)

Interestingly, basic research indicates that prosodic emotional communications are more efficiently processed in the left ear, and thereby
the right hemisphere (Sim & Martinez, 2005). This means that in an
optimal listening stance the clinician's left ear (right hemisphere) and
not right ear (left hemisphere) processes the patient's subtle prosodic
changes in state. Recall, the right hemisphere is dominant for "perception of voices" (Brancucci et al., 2009). Indeed, later in this book
Bromberg postulates, "One's clinical ear hears the voice of another
part of self."

Importantly, this neuropsychoanalytic perspective also dictates that
the clinician's stress-inducing misattunements are processed in the
patient's left ear. During mutual enactments these right hemispheric
nonconsciously processed nonverbal auditory threat cues (and not
the clinician's left hemispheric verbalizations) instantly trigger fear-
induced self-state changes in the patient. In support of this model I
direct the reader to the enactment in the case of Martha in chapter 4,
where Bromberg describes "a listening stance that detects a switch in
self-states." But in this context of mutuality and intersubjective collision

he observes that on the other side of the dyad the patient's perceptual processing focused on his prosodic output:

> Nevertheless, there was enough displeasure in my voice about what I perceived as her effort to distract us from our "task" to trigger her early warning system. Martha's self-state switched. Not only had her laughter disappeared, but everything about her that went with it seemed gone also. Her entire physical being had become that of a scared, unhappy, little girl.

As a result of his subsequent correction, interactive repair, and his own self-state switch he notes, "I was now a bit recovered from my shock, and I'm sure that my tone of voice reflected the tenderness I was feeling."

In addition to offering a number of poignant clinical descriptions of enactments, Bromberg also speculates about their underlying neurobiology. In an upcoming chapter he specifies not only cortical but subcortical areas of the right brain in unconscious relational communications. He states: "The secret that is being revealed through an enactment is that while your patient is telling you one thing in words, to which you are responding in some way, there is a second 'conversation' going on between the two of you. Buck (1994, p. 266, cited in Schore, 2003b, p. 49) refers to this as 'a conversation between limbic systems.'" Here he directly involves the right lateralized cortical-subcortical limbic-autonomic axis in "symbolic" and especially "subsymbolic" implicit communications (see earlier discussion). Again, I present the reader with a brief synopsis of my work in this area.

In *Affect Regulation and the Repair of the Self* (2003b) I offered a chapter, "Clinical implications of a psychoneurobiological model of projective identification." According to Bromberg (2006a), projective identification is "a core element in the process of enactment" (p. 185). My entire chapter focused on the moment-to-moment implicit nonverbal communications within an enactment that takes place in "a moment," literally a split second. Here I argued that Freud's (1915a) dictum, "It is a very remarkable thing that the *Ucs* of one human being can react upon that of another, *without passing through the Cs*" (p. 194, emphasis added), can be neuropsychoanalytically understood as a right-brain to right-brain communication from one relational unconscious to another.

The "conversation between limbic systems" that occurs during enactments is more precisely a conversation between right lateralized limbic and autonomic nervous systems. In chapter 7 of that same volume I suggested:

> [F]acially-mediated right brain-to-right brain communications, at levels beneath awareness, can instigate the regulation (or dysregulation) of autonomic function.... It is now well established that the autonomic nervous system reacts to *perceptual stimuli that may never enter consciousness* (Lazarus & McCleary, 1951) and that it is involved in the generation of nonconscious affect that is triggered by the visual perception of an emotionally expressive face.... This unconscious process ... may be expressed as "primitive emotional contagion" (Hatfield et al., 1992). I also suggest that this transfer of nonconscious affect is mediated by a *right amygdala to right amygdala communication.* (Schore, 2003b, p. 227, emphasis added)

Thus subsymbolic communications of "not-me" states (mutual deep projective identifications) are subcortical nonconscious communications between the right amygdala, right insula, and right lateralized sympathetic and dorsal vagal parasympathetic autonomic nervous systems of the patient and therapist. These unconscious relational communications are not mental but psychobiological and bodily-based, and they are received in the therapist's somatic countertransference.

As a result of the cocreation of a more or less efficient right brain communication system, the therapist can now act as an affect regulator of the patient's conscious and unconscious (dissociated) dysregulated affective states. In chapter 5 here, Bromberg observes, "Schore... stresses the dual role of the analyst as psychobiological regulator and coparticipant, and that this duality is especially vital during heightened affective moments. In other words, the analyst's role is therapeutic because his regulating function is not independent of his coparticipation." This therapeutic attachment mechanism supports an "affectively alive interpersonal engagement with the shifting self-states that organize the internal object worlds of both patient and analyst" what Bromberg calls a "coconstructed royal road." This same right-brain to right-brain system of unconscious relational communication and regulation is also centrally involved in "negotiations between collisions and safety." These interpersonal experiences of being "safe but both too safe" allow for novelty and surprise, which facilitate "the enhanced spontaneity and flexibility of a patient's personality structure." Bromberg observes that as the treatment progresses "there occurs a transformation of unthinkable 'not-me' self-states into enacted here-and-now events that are played out interpersonally, processed together with the analyst's subjective experience of the same event, and so become part of the patient's overarching configuration of 'me.'"

Psychotherapeutic Change Mechanism of Shrinking the Shadow of the Tsunami

In this final section I offer some thoughts about this volume's important contributions towards explicating the essential change mechanisms of psychotherapy. Each chapter contains hypotheses on "therapeutic action," but here I will focus only on what Bromberg sees as the psychological and biological consequences of effective psychotherapeutic treatment of "the shadow of the tsunami," dissociation and the patient's fear of potentially traumatic affect dysregulation. This neuropsychoanalytic perspective will refer back to the earlier sections of this foreword. For more neurobiological commentaries on Bromberg's proposals on intersubjective collisions and negotiations, safe surprises and novelty, and limitations of interpretations see Schore (2007, 2011). In the upcoming very first chapter Bromberg proposes:

> I argue that for all patients, regardless of how minimal the scope or duration of the vulnerability, enduring personality growth in analytic treatment is interwoven with the ability of the patient–analyst relationship to increase a patient's threshold for affective hyperarousal. This use of the patient–analyst relationship takes place through the nonlinear joint processing of an enacted (dissociated) communication channel in which the patient's fear of affect dysregulation (the shadow of the tsunami) is "shrunk" by the broader ability to safely distinguish the likelihood of mental shock that could indeed be affectively overwhelming from the kind of excitingly "edgy" experiences that are always interwoven with the risk of spontaneity. The patient's fear of dysregulation, as it is relived in the enacted present, becomes increasingly containable as a cognitive event, thus enabling the mind/brain to diminish its automatic reliance on dissociation as an affective "smoke-detector."

Later in chapter 4 he speculates further upon the neurobiological change mechanism:

> Through ... shared minding of the dissociative gap, the automatic neurosynaptic warning signal that triggers immediate dissociation as a protection against potentially destabilizing hyperarousal becomes more selective at the brain level and, through a feedback loop, allows the patient's mind to support increased development of intersubjectivity. Little by little, the patient's potential to bear internal conflict is increased by easing the mental struggle to hold it cognitively.

In a very recent contribution that specifically integrates my work and Bromberg's (Schore, 2011), I describe the neurobiological underpinnings of the psychotherapeutic change mechanism that both of us are exploring. In that work I suggest that recent clinical relational models and interdisciplinary scientific data indicate that effective psychotherapy of early forming attachment pathologies and severe personality disorders must focus on unconscious affect and the survival defense of pathological dissociation, "a structured separation of mental processes (e.g., thoughts, emotions, conation, memory, and identity) that are ordinarily *integrated*" (Spiegel & Cardeña, 1991, p. 367, emphasis added). The clinical precept that unregulated overwhelming traumatic feelings associated with hyperarousal can not be adaptively integrated into the patient's emotional life is the expression of a dysfunction of "the right hemispheric specialization in regulating stress- and emotion-related processes" (Sullivan & Dufresne, 2006, p. 55). As described earlier this dissociative deficit specifically results from a lack of integration of the right lateralized limbic-autonomic circuits of the emotional brain (see Figure F.1).

A general clinical principle of working in enactments with traumatic affects and the defense of dissociation is that the sensitive psychobiologically attuned therapist allows the patient to re-experience dysregulating affects in affectively tolerable doses in the context of a safe environment, so that overwhelming traumatic feelings can be regulated and integrated into the patient's emotional life. Bromberg points out that in these heightened affective moments the therapeutic relationship must "feel safe but not perfectly safe." These therapeutic affective transactions occur at the edges of the regulatory boundaries of the windows of affect tolerance (Schore, 2009c), or what Bromberg terms as a relational space bordering on overwhelming hyperarousal and "edgy experiences."

In ongoing intersubjective attunements, collisions, and negotiated repairs, therapeutic interactive regulation of affective arousal impacts the patient's threshold of activation of a right brain stress response to a social stressor. In earlier writings Bromberg (2006a) observed:

> The patient's threshold for "triggering" increases, allowing her increasingly to hold on to the ongoing relational experience (the full complexity of the here and now with the therapist) as it is happening, with less and less need to dissociate; as the processing of the here and now becomes more and more immediate, it becomes more and more experientially connectable to her past. (p. 69)

Effective work at the regulatory boundaries of right brain high and low arousal psychobiological states ultimately broadens the windows of affect tolerance, thereby increasing the patient's ability to consciously experience and communicate a broader range of more intense and more complex emotions that result from the simultaneous blending of affects.

In this manner regulated therapeutic enactments positively alter the developmental growth trajectory of the right brain and facilitate the top-down and bottom-up integration of its cortical and subcortical systems. This structural maturational progression allows for a functional expansion of the ability to regulate (by both autoregulation and interactive regulation) and thereby tolerate a broader range of high and low arousal negative and positive affects. More specifically effective affectively-focused psychotherapy facilitates an increase of interconnectivity within the right brain, especially between the orbitofrontal cortex, anterior cingulate, insula, amygdala, and the (HPA) axis. This experience-dependent maturation of right lateralized limbic-autonomic stress-regulating circuits also promotes the complexity of defenses, right brain strategies for coping with stressful bodily-based affects that are more flexible and adaptive than pathological dissociation. This developmental advance is expressed in the emergence of the capacity to experience more than one conscious affect at a time, and thereby to adaptively tolerate intrapsychic conflict.

These neurobiological alterations of the right-lateralized vertical axis is expressed in further development of the right brain core of the self and its central involvement in "patterns of affect regulation that *integrate* a sense of self across state transitions, thereby allowing for a continuity of inner experience" (Schore, 1994, p. 33, emphasis added). Recent neuroscience research indicates that "the right hemisphere is significantly more efficient and interconnected than the left hemisphere," and thereby it plays a "leading role" for "*integration* tasks" (Iturria-Medina et al., 2011, p. 56, emphasis added). This therapeutic expansion of the right brain thus supports the integration of what Bromberg (2006) calls dissociated "not-me" states into right lateralized autobiographical memory and a relational "me." The affectively-focused psychotherapy described in the following pages thereby facilitates an expansion not only of the explicit self and the conscious mind, but the implicit self and the unconscious mind. Current neuroscience is seriously disputing the earlier claim that the left hemisphere is dominant in humans. This right-lateralized cortical-subcortical system is dominant not for verbal functions and voluntary motor behavior, but for more essential abilities: nonverbal communication, affect regulation, coping with stress, maintaining homeostasis, and survival!

A major theme of this remarkable book and indeed of Bromberg's entire career is the exploration of an effective relational treatment of the right brain "bottom-line" survival of defense pathological dissociation, an outcome of early relational trauma. According to McGilchrist (2009): "Dissociation is ... the fragmentation of what should be experienced as a whole–the mental separation of components of experience that would ordinarily be processed together ... suggesting a right hemisphere problem" (p. 236). The essential functions of the right brain, the biological substrate of the human unconscious described by Freud are now thought to include:

> [E]mpathy and intersubjectivity as the ground of consciousness; the importance of an open, patient attention to the world, as opposed to a willful, grasping attention; the implicit or hidden nature of truth; the emphasis on process rather than stasis, the journey being more important than the arrival; the primacy of perception; the importance of the body in constituting reality; an emphasis on uniqueness; the objectifying nature of vision; the irreducibility of all value to utility; and creativity as an unveiling (no-saying) process rather than a willfully constructive process. (McGilchrist, 2009, p. 177)

For almost a century psychoanalysis, and indeed all forms of "the talking cure" neglected the fundamental problem of mind–body trauma, a fundamental aspect of so many severe psychiatric disorders. Partly due to this avoidance the psychotherapeutic techniques of clinical psychoanalysis changed little over the last century. But in the 1990s trauma, bodily-based emotion, and the brain/mind interface finally became a focus of both intense scientific and clinical inquiry. In this seminal period the mental health field's repressive and indeed dissociative defenses against the darker sides of the human condition finally lifted. Bromberg's pioneering work has blazed the trail for clinicians around the world to formulate a deeper understanding of their patients with a history of early relational trauma. In his highly acclaimed books on these subjects, *Standing in the Spaces* (1999), *Awakening the Dreamer* (2006a), and now this one, *The Shadow of the Tsunami,* he powerfully demonstrates how this recent developmental and neurobiological information about trauma and dissociation has qualitatively transformed our clinical models and altered our conceptions of therapeutic action.

Indeed, like myself (Schore, 2009d), Bromberg here contends that we are now experiencing not just an advance in the field of mental health but a paradigm shift. In an upcoming chapter he asserts:

> Interpersonal and relational writers largely have endorsed the idea that we are in fact confronted with a paradigm change and have conceptualized it as a transformation from a one-person to a two-person psychology. I feel that this formulation is accurate, and that three central clinical shifts are intrinsic to the conceptual shift: A shift from the primacy of content to the primacy of context, a shift from the primacy of cognition to the primacy of affect, and a shift away from (but not yet an abandonment of) the concept of "technique."

He further concludes that this paradigm change in psychotherapy involves "the replacement of a focus on *content* with a focus on *process.*"

In my neuropsychoanalytic writings I have described the same shift in paradigm: from conscious cognition to unconscious affect. Regulation Theory asserts that the relational change mechanism embedded in the therapeutic alliance acts not through the therapist's left brain explicitly delivering *content* interpretations to the patient's right brain, but through mutual bidirectional right-brain to right-brain affect communication and regulation *processes* (Schore, 2011). In the beginning of this foreword I noted the similarities between Bromberg and myself in not only our theoretical understandings, but in our clinical style of working relationally and affectively with patients. This book is dedicated to what that paradigm shift looks like from the experience-near perspective of a relational model of treatment that impacts both the conscious and unconscious, especially dissociated processes in both members of the therapeutic dyad.

Over the course of his career Philip Bromberg has deservedly earned an international reputation for eloquently describing the subtle yet essential intersubjective events that occur at the interface of the patient's and therapist's internal worlds. As opposed to the usual case presentation in terms of left brain detached linear verbal exchanges, he has created a new form of description of the therapeutic dialogue—evocative multisensory portraits of the moment-to-moment nonlinear encounters between his and the patient's conscious and especially unconscious minds in a language that is saturated with right brain nonverbal visual and auditory images, metaphors, and indeed poetry. As this foreword ends, it is my pleasure to now hand you over to the creative mind of my dear friend and colleague. You're in for a rich amalgam of psychoanalysis, literature, philosophy, popular music, neuroscience, trauma theory, and biology from a master of the art of psychotherapy.

Preface

The Shadow of the Tsunami

℞ A book's preface is typically written when the chapters are almost completed and the author is at least somewhat aware that the book is soon to be sent into the world on its own. A moment of subtle stress, this. An author's most reliable context for negotiating between his own subjectivity and the imagined subjectivity of an "other"–his reader–is about to be thwarted at the moment it is most needed. For his book is almost done. His readers are about to have unimpeded freedom to dislike what he has written, to find him uninteresting, to find him wrongheaded, and worst of all–*to not understand him.* The author is losing his ability to imagine being recognized "as who he is." By the time the preface is being written, the book has no power to reduce this source of anxiety because the book and the author are no longer one.

Hearteningly, there is usually another internal voice in the author besides the one experiencing diminished control over being understood, and for this voice it is exciting when a *reader* has the right to think for himself. Here is where writing a preface can become interesting. Because it is yet to be written, perhaps it can be made tantalizing enough to inspire a reader to believe that, if he hangs in, some really good stuff might be found in the chapters ahead. The real challenge for the author is in doing this with honesty.

With these anxieties and hopes in mind, I have chosen to forego the easy, almost automatized format of here foreshadowing the content of each chapter. My reasoning is twofold: For readers already familiar with my overarching perspective who want to discover where my continuing clinical explorations have led me since the publication of *Awakening the Dreamer* in 2006, I felt that a chapter-by-chapter preview was unwarranted because my frame of reference is by now so embedded in my writing that it is inherently communicated in each chapter's specific content. I am at the same time aware that this preface must

1

meet the needs of other readers for whom the present volume is a first introduction to my work, and I suspect that they, too, will appreciate not knowing in advance what to expect. My belief is that by giving *all* readers maximum freedom to engage each chapter without prior "assistance" as to how I prefer it to be understood, their self-states as readers will more spontaneously interact with mine as author, and for any given reader, the process of *understanding* a chapter will entail a relational engagement between us more than a direct assimilation of my ideas. What I hope to evoke between the reader and myself is a form of "state-sharing" (Schore, 2003a, pp. 94–97)–the right-brain to right-brain communication process through which each person's states of mind are known to the other implicitly. To inaugurate the process, this preface will invoke, rather than summarize, what lies ahead.

In what should come as no shock to previous readers of my work, I am going to turn first to literature, a domain of human creativity that is close to my heart in many ways, including its ability to affectively evoke the aspect of a psychoanalytic relationship that is most difficult to capture in words–the part that is "lost in translation," a phrase famously attributed to Robert Frost. I say "attributed" because it is not to be found in any of his published works, poetry or prose–but this doesn't mean he did not say it. In literature, as in psychoanalysis, lack of "hard data" does not make something less real, and in this regard, a bit of internet research on my part has paid off. In a posting on a literary blog, Luba V. Zakharov (March 8, 2008) disclosed the original source of Frost's aphorism: Louis Untermeyer's (1964) memoir of his relationship with Frost.

According to Untermeyer, during the course of an interview with Frost while they were discussing a remark a critic had made about Frost's poetry, Frost remarked: "You've often heard me say–perhaps too often–that poetry is what is lost in translation." Trusting Untermayer's memory, we can safely assume that Frost said it. But what caught my eye was what Frost said next, according to Untermayer: "It is also what is lost in interpretation." Also what is lost in interpretation! What a find for a psychoanalytic writer who believes that the concept of interpretation is in need of serious revisiting.

Untermeyer was a long-time friend and a great admirer of Frost. It is not far-fetched to imagine that they achieved their own measure of "state-sharing" in their conversation. And what he reports is consistent with a comment Frost made in an interview with John Ciardi (1959). That comment, in turn, takes me to my dilemma in this preface–and in this book. If what analyst and patient achieve in their work together

defies "translation" and "interpretation" alike, then why write about
it? If it is a "mess"—and I contend that it is—then why bother trying
to be orderly about it afterward? If cocreated process is inherently
unpredictable, then why have chapters with definite themes, and why
arrange them in a definite order? And why have a preface introducing
the lot? Frost's comment goes to the heart of my hopes. Here is what
Frost said to Ciardi:

> *"A poem is an arrest of disorder."*

Frost's commitment to order is a paradoxical, almost limited, one.
He speaks only of an arrest of disorder—not a breathtaking illumination
that puts everything straight. I have done no better in these pages—and
I have not attempted anything so difficult as poetry—and will do no
better in this preface. And yet—let me appeal to another passage from
Frost, this time in prose (though, as the reader will see, it is hard for
Frost to write anything that is not poetry). It captures well my feeling
for my own process as a psychoanalytic writer, though, again, I remain
mindful that however impossible it is to capture analytic process, it is
surely not so hard as writing a decent poem.

In the passage, Frost (1939) is addressing not a poem's formal qualities but the affective bond *between poet and poem* that is shaped during
the ongoing process of a poem's cocreation. He terms this bond "the
figure a poem makes":

> If it is a wild tune, it is a poem. Our problem then is, as modern
> abstractionists, to have the wildness pure; to be wild with nothing
> to be wild about. *We bring up as aberrationists, giving way to undi-*
> *rected associations and kicking ourselves from one chance suggestion to*
> *another in all directions as of a hot afternoon in the life of a grasshopper.*
> Theme alone can steady us down. Just as the first mystery was
> how a poem could have a tune in such a straightness as meter, so
> the second mystery is how a poem can have wildness and at the
> same time a subject that shall be fulfilled. *It should be the pleasure of*
> *a poem to tell us how it can. The figure a poem makes.*[1]

---

[1] The psychologist William James in 1892 (cited in Meares, 2001, p. 757)
wrote something almost identical in describing the essence of inner life as its
spontaneous movement: "The train of imagery wanders its own sweet will,
now trudging on sober graves of habit, now with a hop, skip and jump, darting
across the whole field of time and space" (p. 271).

Frost goes on:

> It begins in delight, it inclines to the impulse, it assumes direction with the first line laid down, it runs a course of lucky events, and ends in a clarification of life—not necessarily a great clarification, such as sects and cults are founded on, but in a *momentary stay against confusion*. ... It is but a trick poem and no poem at all if the best of it was thought of first and saved for the last. (p. 440, emphasis added)

Enough with my dilemmas as an analytic writer. Time for me to deal with my "first" and my "last." The reader may have noticed that the chapter titles of this book begin with "Shrinking the Tsunami" and end with "The Nearness of You," and that the others do not reveal the nature of the *path* between the "book-ends." So, too, the psychoanalytic relationship: It moves two unrelated people along a path that bit by bit shrinks the tsunami, the dissociated emotional disasters of early life that always seem to lie just around the corner, and bit by bit brings the participants closer and closer to "the nearness of you." The beginning and end placement of these two chapters, my way of situating what I hold to be the two interlocking achievements in a successful treatment, is in this sense my attempt to name them—a way of acknowledging, individually, the reward of "healing" and the reward of "growth." But their linear separateness is meaningful in that context only. In both book and treatment, there is no true beginning chapter nor a linear path along which a final chapter is reached. What comes to be increasingly understood by both partners, and perhaps most deeply as the "final" chapter of the analytic relationship approaches, is that their nearness survives the ending of the "book," and that what took place along the path did not happen because "this" led to "that," but rather because the path has been its own destination.

Perhaps I should say a bit more about both achievements, beginning with the shadow of the tsunami. If early in life the disruption of human relatedness is experienced for the most part as interpersonally reparable, then the impact of developmental trauma on adult living, including one's vulnerability to "adult-onset" trauma, tends to be largely containable as internal conflict and available to self-reflection and potential healing as part of the give-and-take of a good relationship.

But for others the impact of developmental trauma leads to something very different. When a child suffers consistent nonrecognition and disconfirmation of her self-experience—the cumulative nonrecognition of entire aspects of self as existing–what happens is that developmental trauma and vulnerability to massive trauma become interwoven. In adulthood, the capacity to then live a life that is creative, spontaneous, stable, and relationally authentic requires an extraordinary natural endowment, and probably, a healing relationship with some person who enables the adult to *use* her natural endowment. This other person is often a therapist but need not be.

What such a relationship offers is the restoration of felt legitimacy in the right to exist as more than an object in the mind of another, and release from torment by the illegitimatized "not-me" parts of self that haunt the corridors of the mind as a dissociated affective tsunami and take possession of life. Wherever a developmental tsunami has hit, if left unhealed it has left a shadow. One lives with the shadow and, to one degree or another, it follows the person along the path to adulthood. Sometimes it accompanies the person throughout life, held as part of a dissociative mental structure. The price paid for the protection afforded by a dissociative mental structure–the brain's proactive effort to foreclose the potential return of affect dysregulation associated with the residue of the relationally unprocessed trauma–is huge.

The person's present and future are plundered by an overly rigid sequestering of "me" and "not-me" self-states that is the legacy of developmental trauma too relationally barren to allow cognitive symbolization and self-reflection. As I have elaborated elsewhere (Bromberg, 2010), the dissociative nature of this duality makes traversing the path through adulthood not simply a voyage but two voyages: one accessible to consciousness and choice, and the other a shadowy presence within the first–a voyage with a life of its own that channels each choice toward a variation of the same, seemingly predestined outcome. The outcome of one's "best" intentions is most often characterized by unanticipated failures, and destructive patterns of living that feel "sort-of" familiar, but are recognized always too late.

Such patients' "presenting problems" notwithstanding, the unmet longing for release from this hauntedness is what finally brings them to therapy. Why? Because no matter how hard one tries, "not-me" self-states are never anaesthetized completely or indefinitely nor, for many, is the dread of the destabilizing flood they may bring. Though they may feel ghostly they can't be exorcised, and even when these part of self seem to have "disappeared" from overt participation in human relationships, sooner or later the pain of relational emptiness exceeds the mind's capacity to bear it and these self-states break out of their dissociated captivity and create enough internal dysregulation to make someone think about seeking help, no matter how reluctantly. I say "reluctantly," because someone who suffers this way and who uses dissociation as the only sure way of protecting herself, tends to be "of several minds" about the wisdom of entering psychotherapy. Whether or not the patient recognizes it explicitly, at least one part of her is pretty certain that her unilateral system of self-protection is being put at risk by the very nature of this relationship.

And indeed she is right in her supposition. Sooner or later, "the shadow of the tsunami" will be evoked, bringing with it an enacted reliving of the original relational context that led to its existence, and for more individuals than one might imagine, evoking an affective memory of sliding into the abyss of depersonalization—the edge of annihilation. For all such patients, any apparent failure of their dis-sociative mental structure to do its "proper" job makes their highest priority the restoration of stability, which in therapy means, "keep your hands off my ability to put things out of my mind." A patient chooses to see a therapist because of an implied promise that she may become more able to live her life with well-being, spontaneity, and creativity, but most patients for whom developmental trauma is a big issue have already settled for relative stability through believing that "the only safe hands to be in are my own, and you are not me," which is why the heart of therapy is about negotiation of otherness. The therapist's goal of helping them restore their right to exist as a whole person has to *earn* its place in the analytic relationship and, paradoxic-ally, it is earned *because* of the patient's misgivings, not in spite of them.

The patient/analyst relationship is enabled, through the enactment of self-state collisions, to become the most powerful doorway to a gen-uinely productive analytic process—a process that cocreates the condi-tions necessary for growth of the relational mind. The relationship is not a vehicle to get rid of the tsunami—as if the past were an illness—but a means to live together in its shadow, allowing it to shrink a little bit at a time, freeing the patient's natural capacity to feel trust and joy in "the nearness of you" and a stability that will endure.

The capacity to pleasurably experience "the nearness of you" is part of our endowment but it is not a gift that becomes usable just by being born. We are born. We are raised. We develop. During the process of development we are exposed to the impact of relational trauma. When the shadow of the tsunami reduces one's capacity to safely trust "the nearness of you," for some, dissociative mental structure is all-encompassing while for others less so—*but for all patients, healing*

*(unfreezing this structure) and personality growth are part of a single process
even though each element can be conceptualized individually.*

What do I mean by "the nearness of you?" And equally to the point,
why not just call it the capacity to have a good relationship? Researchers
in mother–infant interaction have been greatly illuminating here, and
I ask the reader to consider what Ed Tronick (2003) has to say about
the nearness of you when seen as "a dyadic state of consciousness" that,
when achieved, leads to "feeling larger than oneself" (p. 476):

> *When mutual regulation is particularly successful–*that is, when the
> age-appropriate forms of meaning (e.g., affects, relational inten-
> tions, representations) from one individual's state of conscious-
> ness are coordinated with the meanings of another's state of
> consciousness–*I have hypothesized that a dyadic state of conscious-
> ness emerges.* Though it shares characteristics with intersubjective
> states, a dyadic state of consciousness is not merely an intersub-
> jective experience. A dyadic state of consciousness has dynamic
> effects. It increases the coherence of the infant's state of con-
> sciousness and expands the infant's (and the partner's) state of
> consciousness. *Thus, dyadic states of consciousness are critical, perhaps
> even necessary for development.*
>
> *An experiential effect of the achievement of a dyadic state of conscious-
> ness is that it leads to feeling larger than oneself.* Thus, infants' experi-
> ence of the world and states of consciousness are determined not
> only by their own self-organizing processes, but also by dyadic
> regulatory processes that affect their state of consciousness.
>
> A fundamental principle … is that the form of the interaction
> and the meaning of the relational affects and intentions that regu-
> late the exchange emerge from a co-creative process. *Co-creative
> processes produce unique forms of being together, not only in the mother–
> infant relationship, but in all relationships.* Co-creation emphasizes
> dynamic and unpredictable changes of relationships that under-
> lie their uniqueness … . Co-creativity implies neither a set of
> steps nor an end state. Rather, it implies that when two indi-
> viduals mutually engage in a communicative exchange, how they
> will be together, their dynamics and direction are unknown and
> only emerge from their mutual regulation. Thus, while we can
> look at an exchange that has taken place and make a narrative
> account of it, we must realize that there was no narrative or blue-
> print structuring the exchange before or even as it was happen-
> ing. *Seeing this difference–that what has happened can be narrated, but*

what is happening cannot be narrated—and holding on to the distinction
has critical implications for understanding what goes on in relationships,
including the therapeutic relationship. (pp. 475–476, emphasis added)

With regard to the phrase, "feeling larger than oneself," I must here make mention of a topic that I have touched on in this book (most extensively in the final chapter) but have as yet been unable to *fully* write about in the needed state of mind that characterizes my work as a whole. Robert Frost calls this state of mind "aberrationist": It allows a writer to plunge in with "wildness pure … as of a hot afternoon in the life of a grasshopper"—surrendering to raw experience while allowing what he calls "the figure a poem makes" to *show* the writer how the poem "can have wildness and at the same time a subject that shall be fulfilled." The topic to which I am referring is the existence of people, perhaps for reasons of native endowment, perhaps for reasons unknown, who retain or develop the seemingly *uncanny* ability to make mutual contact with the "other" in ways that cannot be understood within what we call a rational frame of mind. At present, though I draw heavily from the work of Elizabeth Lloyd Mayer (1996, 2001, 2007) as my conceptual base for discussing this topic, many of my clinical vignettes do indeed illustrate that this "wild" phenomenon takes place with startling ubiquity in and around therapy and is intrinsic to what I term "the nearness of you."

But this is a preface to a book I *have* written, not one I don't know how to yet. Hopefully, there is enough "wildness" in this text to keep the reader going. Let me finish my preface with one last look at the dual achievements by way of saying goodbye to the reader, as I have been imagining him or her right along, and anxiously releasing this book to its fate before *real* readers. During the course of a psychoanalytic relationship, increased trust, confidence, and pleasure in human relatedness is generated through the openness of both partners to "the nearness of you"—cumulatively, nonlinearly, and little by little. As this takes place there develops, *simultaneously*, an increased capacity for relational affect regulation which "shrinks" the shadow of the tsunami—also nonlinearly, cumulatively, and little by little. Experientially, however, "shrinking the tsunami" and "the nearness of you," though nonlinear, concurrent processes, are separate *phenomena* and can be explored separately to great advantage, and opportunity for such exploration is offered in the present book. Hopefully, this exploration will allow the reader to accept and honor, as *paradox*, that the "growth of the relational mind" depends on the coexistence of two

PART I

AFFECT REGULATION AND CLINICAL PROCESS

1

Shrinking the Tsunami[1]

CR I begin with something personal—my mother's favorite story about me—a one-liner that took place when I was 4 years old. Even back then I was given to reverie states and while I was sitting next to her, silently lost in thought, I suddenly "woke up" and asked, "Mommy, when I was born how did you know my name was Philip?"

I'm still trying to figure it out. At 4, the concept of nonexistence had begun to interest me but I was still young enough to not worry about it. I simply knew I existed before I was born and I was trying to learn the details. There was no such thing as "nonbeing" much less the shadow of an abyss or a thing that grownups called "death." It was unthinkable; nonbeing had no personal meaning for me. Where was I before I was born? Wherever I was, Mommy must have been with me. There was no discontinuity in self-experience. For me, self-continuity had not yet been subjected to developmental trauma serious enough to tamper with it. Is that possible? Sure, but only to a degree, and only if we look at trauma not as a special situation but as a continuum that commands our attention only when it disrupts or threatens to disrupt the continuity of self-experience.

There are, however, certainly people for whom my little tale can have no meaning, people who in one way or another have had experiences, often terrifying experiences, of nonbeing. Even at the age of 4. Or earlier. For such people my question to my mother touches on a topic that is never to be touched on. Something inside them tells them

---

[1]An earlier version of this chapter, "Shrinking the Tsunami: Affect Regulation, Dissociation, and the Shadow of the Flood," was published in *Contemporary Psychoanalysis, 44,* 2008, 329–350.

that nonbeing is a real threat, that a powerful and terrible tsunami of chaotic and disintegrating affect lurks within.

If we accept that developmental trauma is a core phenomenon in the shaping of personality then we also accept that it exists for everyone and is always a matter of degree. If that is so, then the stability achieved by even secure attachment is also a matter of degree. That is to say, everyone is vulnerable to the experience of having to face something that is more than his mind can deal with, and the differences between people in how much is unbearable is what we work with in the large grey area we call "developmental trauma" or "relational trauma."

The "Giftie"

Robert Burns (1786), the Scottish poet, wrote, "Oh wad some Power the giftie gie us/To see oursels as ithers see us" (p. 44), but it is not all that easy to accept an image of yourself as seen through the eyes of an "ither," and it is especially hard when the other's image of you is based on what for you is a dissociated part of self–a "not-me." So whenever I hear that line of poetry, there is a part of me that feels like telling Burns to do you-know-what with his "giftie" and to be careful what he prays for.

Nevertheless, the giftie to which Burns refers is undeniably a developmental achievement even though using it involves a lifelong internal struggle, a struggle that includes those times you would like to return the giftie to the store for an exchange. But, irony aside, it may be the most valuable gift that any human being will ever receive–the gift of intersubjectivity.

When you are able to see yourself as others see you, while not dissociating from the experience of how you see yourself, you are relating intersubjectively. The problem is that a human being's ability to relate intersubjectively is variable, uneven, and sometimes requires what feels like having to stare at sunspots. For anyone, seeing oneself through another's eyes can become too stressful. Why? Because the other's view may feel too starkly discrepant with one's ongoing self-experience at the moment for both views to be held in mind simultaneously. When such is the case, the mind is geared to ease such stress by the defensive use of a normal brain process–dissociation. We are accustomed to thinking of dissociation as triggered by internal cues, but in fact the signal initiating the process typically comes from an "other," no matter whether the other is another person or another part of self. Regardless, overly disjunctive self-experiences are then adaptationally held in separate self-states that do not communicate with each other, at least for a while.

For some people, "for a while" means briefly; for others it means a very long while or even permanently. For people in the latter group, dissociation is not just a mental process to deal with the routine stress of a given moment but a structure that rules life itself by narrowing the range in which it can be lived. The mind/brain organizes its self-states as an anticipatory protective system that tries, proactively, to shut down experiential access to self-states that are disjunctive with the dissociatively limited range of the state that is experienced as "me" at a given moment. This rigid sequestering of self-states by means of dissociative mental structure is so central to the personality of some people that it shapes virtually all mental functioning, while for others its range is more limited. But regardless of degree or range, its evolutionary function is to assure survival of self-continuity by limiting reflective function to a minor role, if any. The mind/brain, by severely limiting the participation of reflective cognitive judgment, leaves the limbic system more or less free to use itself as a "dedicated line" that functions as what van der Kolk (1995) calls a "smoke detector." It is designed to "detect" potentially unanticipated events that could trigger affect dysregulation.

Because it is a proactive solution, the diminished capacity for cognitive self-reflection in favor of an automatized emphasis on safety comes with a price. It requires the person to, at best, "smuggle in" a life that is secondary to a process of constant vigilance–a vigilance that, ironically, mostly produces what information theory calls "false positives." It might seem that, if such is the case, the person would sooner or later figure out that there is a connection between something being wrong with his life and the fact that he spends most of it waiting for something bad to happen. The reason a person tends not to make that connection is that the dissociative structure is itself designed to operate out of cognitive awareness. Each state holds a relatively non-negotiable affective "truth" that is supported by its self-selected array of "evidence" designed to bolster its own insulated version of reality. If the person tries to reflect on the question, "Why am I living my life this way?" the potential for an internally destabilizing affective collision between incompatible versions of personal reality is triggered. Even to formulate such a question is a threat to the integrity of the dissociative mental structure that, to the mind/brain, is the only reliable safeguard against affective chaos. Nevertheless, the question is asked at least indirectly, often out of desperation. Sometimes it leads the person to seek out a therapist, albeit with certain parts of the self denouncing the idea so ferociously that, by the time he arrives at your office, he may not be able to tell you why he is there.

Once in treatment, the fact that he or she is "of more than one mind" about being there leads to the enacted emergence of another question—and the ongoing struggle over allowing it to be put into words might be said to shape the entire course of the therapy. Implicitly, this second question might be seen as: To what extent is the protection against potential trauma worth the price paid for it? Initially, the question is played out in the form of an internal dispute among a patient's panoply of self-states, some championing affective safety, others endorsing what is life-enhancing even if it involves risk. This self-state war pulls the therapist/patient relationship into it, thus giving them a chance to participate enactively in a here-and-now externalization of the patient's fraught relationship with his own internal objects.

Shrinking the Tsunami

Enactment is a shared dissociative event. It is an unconscious communication process that reflects those areas of the patient's self-experience where trauma (whether developmental or adult-onset) has to one degree or another compromised the capacity for affect regulation in a relational context and thus compromised self-development at the level of symbolic processing by thought and language.[2] Therefore, a core dimension of using enactment therapeutically is to increase competency in regulating affective states. Increasing competency requires that the analytic relationship become a place that supports

---

[2]My preference is to limit the term *enactment* to the patient/analyst relationship even though this dissociative communication channel is indeed a fundamental and omnipresent aspect of all human discourse. I refer the interested reader to an astute and illuminating discussion by Tony Bass (2003) about this dilemma, in which he proposes a temporary means of differentiating the respective uses of the term in published papers by identifying its *clinical* usage through capitalizing the first letter of the word, as [E]nactment. This suggestion, not unlike the effort to distinguish "massive trauma" from "developmental trauma" by writing the former as "Big T" [T]rauma, addresses a pragmatic need but, as we both recognize, leaves the deeper questions still haunting us.

risk and safety simultaneously—a relationship that allows the painful reliving of early trauma, without the reliving being just a blind repetition of the past. It is, optimally, a relationship that I have described as "safe but not too safe" (Bromberg, 2006a, pp. 153–202), by which I mean that the analyst is communicating both his ongoing concern for his patient's affective safety *and* his commitment to the value of the inevitably painful process of reliving.

Fine phrases, but I am not the patient. For a trauma survivor, "safe but not *too* safe" initially has no meaning because relative safety as an *experience* has no meaning as subjective reality. For the trauma survivor, the shadow of the tsunami looms. Indeed, when I speak of "safe but not too safe" I am aware of a part of me that holds an unspoken sense of apology that is not dissimilar to what I felt when I came up with the title "Shrinking the Tsunami." I am pretty sure that if I had personally experienced an actual tsunami, close up, I would not have been able to use that word figuratively in my title. It would have hit too close to home. For a trauma survivor, language holds the potential to trigger an affective reliving of dissociated traumatic experience. By contrast, I was as free to play with the word *tsunami* as I was to play with the word *shrink*. In therapy, the growing ability to play safely with something that has so far existed only as a dissociated shadow of past trauma is what I mean by "shrinking the tsunami" and is what the rest of this book is mainly about.

I shall describe how, through interactions that constitute "safe surprises" (Bromberg, 2003b), a patient's ability to emotionally distinguish nontraumatic spontaneity from potential trauma (the shadow of the flood) is increased. I shall address here the transformation in analytic treatment of unthinkable "not-me" self-states into enacted here-and-now events that, in the form of safe surprises, can be played with interpersonally, compared with the analyst's subjective experience of the same event, and become part of the patient's overarching configuration of "me."

I offer the view that the transformative process of shrinking the tsunami not only leads to a greater capacity for affect regulation, but also is fundamental to the core of the growth process in psychotherapy, which for me has never been better described than by Ronald Laing (1967) in his phrase, "an obstinate attempt of two people to recover the wholeness of being human through the relationship between them" (p. 53).

The foundation of this growth process is an analytic situation that permits collisions between subjectivities to be negotiated. The

negotiation takes place through the creation of a shared mental state–
a channel of implicit communication that supports what Buck (1994)
calls a conversation between limbic systems (cited in Schore, 2003a,
p. 276)–amounting to nothing less than the cocreation of a relational
unconscious that belongs to both persons but to neither alone. The
patient/analyst relationship becomes a therapeutic environment to the
extent that the boundary between self and other becomes increasingly
permeable.[3]

When I speak of the traumatic past of the patient being played
out, the concept of play, as I use it here, is similar to what Philip
Ringstrom (2001, 2007a) calls *improvisation*. It is a form of play in which
the mutual recognition of each other's subjectivity is, in Ringstrom's
terms, more implicitly played with than explicitly enunciated. His
point overlaps with my concept of collision and negotiation (Bromberg,
2006a, pp. 85–150) and with Schore's (2003a) concept of state-sharing
(pp. 94–97), but Ringstrom (2007b) underlines something additional
that is worth repeating: "Improvisation often entails playing with the
other as an *object* [because] when the two parties can play with one
another as objects they intrinsically reveal something about themselves as *subjects*." This is especially important because the collision
part of what I call the process of collision and negotiation is, indeed,
all about the developing capacity of patient and analyst to move from
experiencing the other as an object to control or be controlled by,
to being able to play with each other (although at first as objects).
I believe it is this meaning of *play* that makes possible the negotiation
that then leads to intersubjectivity–experiencing each other as subject.

For instance: I am committed to the value of the analyst's sharing
with his patient his subjective experience of the relationship itself–
including the details of his states of mind and his awareness of the
shifts in mind/body experience that take place during a session. In my
writing I have made a point of the importance of communicating to
the patient one's personal concern with the effect on her of what one
is doing, including the effect of the *sharing*, so that your patient knows
you are thinking about her affective safety while you are "doing your
job." Do I always remember to do that? No. Do I hear about it when
I don't? Frequently! Do I like hearing about it? Not especially. But the

---

[3]My perspective here (see also Bromberg, 2007) resonates with Jessica
Benjamin's (1988, 1995, 1998, 2007) formulation of "thirdness," which she
describes as the shared process that opens up "the coexistence of opposites."

more I can accept my patient's "giftie" of seeing myself through her eyes (especially those aspects of self I had been dissociating), the easier it becomes for my patient to negotiate the transition from experiencing me as an object to control or be controlled by, to experiencing me as a person who is committed to recognizing her subjectivity even though I am doing it badly at a given moment.

Alicia

Let me tell you about a session in which such a moment of transition was particularly vivid. Alicia was a woman who had achieved fame, financial success, and critical acclaim as a novelist but lived as a recluse. At the time she became my patient I had been a fan of Alicia's writing for many years and was also familiar with her well-known reputation for social isolation. What I was still to find out, however, was that her reclusiveness hid a shocking inability to engage in authentic discourse with another human being, a truly bewildering incapacity for authentic interpersonal communication. As an author, Alicia described social interactions with penetrating wit, sophistication, and a flair for the deliciously unexpected. The characters in her novels were clearly crafted by a mind that understood the complexity of human relationships, but, as I was to find out both from her and with her, in the few social interactions she could not escape (she of course refused book tours), it was an open secret that the very qualities that made reading her books such a delight, existed in face-to-face encounters only in their opposite form.

The early phase of our work was not easy for me. It was confusing and frustrating, and, because I had eagerly anticipated being with the stimulating person I knew through her writing, I also lived with a partly dissociated experience of disappointment—almost as if someone else had written Alicia's novels and I would never get to know her. In our relationship her personality was characterized by an unimaginative concreteness that informed everything she said, although she did not come across as unintelligent, nor did her literalness appear to stem from depression. The one-dimensional quality of her thinking and mode of relatedness was, as she herself put it, "just the way I am around people." It was not too difficult to recognize that her self-state as a writer was dramatically dissociated from her self-state "around people," though early on there was no clear route to addressing the discrepancy without both making her self-conscious and heightening her concreteness. Which is to say, early on there was no clear route to free ourselves from what was being enacted.

Over time, the *processing* of enactment began to play an increasingly greater role in our work, and slowly the dissociative gap between her disparate self-states lessened. It became easier to recognize the presence of the "writer" in the way Alicia talked about herself in sessions even though the qualities of wit and playfulness that were so evident in her writing remained minimal in our direct interactions. Nevertheless, I found the change that was taking place so heartening that I told myself that the increase in coherence across her self-states was more stable than it was—and I got lazy.

In the session I describe here—a "moment of transition"—Alicia and I were once again participating in our enactment. As I had often done in the past, I shared with her my experience that something was feeling affectively "off"—something felt discrepant with what was being spoken in words. But unlike similar moments in which I had been careful to inquire about the impact of sharing my state of mind, this time I did not attempt to find out from each of Alicia's separate self-states what effect my act of self-revelation had on each. Even in the moment, I was slightly aware that part of the reason for my laziness was that I had been yearning for a chance to have a stimulating conversation with one of my favorite authors, and I was hoping to create the occasion by unilaterally deciding that she no longer needed me to treat her as if she was "just" a patient. As I ended my self-disclosure and readied myself for the hoped-for pleasure of a creative negotiation of our respective experiences, she replied with just a single sentence—a "one-liner" that was more than I could ever have hoped for. Alicia looked at me with a twinkle in one eye and a glare in the other and said, "I think you are starting to have delusions of *candor*." I broke up in laughter and so did she. There it was—spontaneity, wit, and feisty playfulness—emerging in a way that belonged to neither of us alone. It belonged to the joint creation of a relational unconscious that became infused with a life of its own—a joint creation that allowed my concept of "standing in the spaces" to become embodied as a physical (see Ogden et al., 2006) and interpersonal reality, a conjunction that invited us to play together with what was in both of her eyes, her twinkling eye and her glaring eye.

There is little doubt that this transition out of enactment, or rather through it, facilitated a powerful shift in my patient's capacity for spontaneous creativity in a relational context—an achievement that I believe provides direct support for the treatment model I am advancing. But, if this is indeed such a great treatment model, why does such a shift take so long to appear? Why is the balance between safety and risk in working with enactments so difficult to achieve, and what makes the balance so unstable during the course of the analytic process? Although I cannot answer these questions with any great confidence, I think that the road is most brightly illuminated by understanding why such a patient's interpersonal capacity for creative spontaneity needed to be sacrificed in the first place and, once sacrificed, why the sacrifice needs to be preserved. This takes us back to the shadow of the tsunami and the threat to self-continuity.

Michael Cunningham (1998), in his brilliant novel about Virginia Woolf, *The Hours*, signals in two wickedly provocative lines that when the natural harmony between multiplicity and wholeness is disrupted, the safe boundary between creativity and madness must be protected: "Laura Brown is trying to *lose* herself. No, that's not it exactly—she is trying to *keep* herself by gaining entry into a parallel world" (p. 37, emphasis added).

In treatment, the dissociated horror of the past fills the present with affective meaning so powerful that no matter how "obviously" safe a given situation may be to others, a patient's own perceptual awareness that she is safe entails a risk that is felt as dangerous to her stability of selfhood. The risk is due to the fact that the safer she feels in the relationship the more hope she starts to feel, and the more hope she starts to feel the less will she automatically rely on her dissociative mental structure to assure hypervigilance as a "fail-safe" protection against affective dysregulation. Consequently, the parts of self that are dedicated to preserving affective safety will monitor and oppose any sign that the patient is starting to *trust* feeling safe but not too safe.

A dissociative mental structure is designed to prevent cognitive representation of what *may* be too much for the mind to bear, but it also has the effect of enabling dissociatively enacted communication of the unsymbolized affective experience. Through enactment, the dissociated affective experience is communicated from within a shared "not-me" cocoon (Bromberg, 1998a) until it is cognitively and linguistically symbolized through relational negotiation. In the early phase of an enactment, the shared dissociative cocoon supports implicit communication without mental representation. Within this cocoon, when the patient's self-state that is organizing the immediate relationship switches, the therapist's self-state also switches, equally dissociatively, to a state that over time can receive and react to the patient's dissociated state-switch.

Because mental representation is compromised by trauma, it is worth reflecting on Laub and Auerhahn's (1993) famous observation: "It is the nature of trauma to elude our knowledge because of both defense and deficit. ... [T]rauma also overwhelms and defeats our capacity to organize it" (p. 288). Traumatic experience may take the form of episodic memory, often inaccessible to the person except affectively, but it may also consist only of either somatic sensations or as visual images that can return as physical symptoms or as flashbacks without narrative meaning. Which is to say that the sensory imprints of the experience are held in affective memory and continue to remain isolated images and body sensations that feel cut off from the rest of self (P. Ogden, 2007). The dissociative processes that keep the affect unconscious have a life of their own, a relational life that is interpersonal as well as intrapsychic, a life that is played out between patient and analyst in the dyadic dissociative phenomenon that we term *enactment*.

The analyst's job is to use the enactment in a way that the patient's "not-me" experience can be given representational meaning as a shared phenomenon by enabling a perceptual link to be made in the patient's working memory between the dissociated experience and the here-and-now self as the agent or experiencer. The process begins by the "not-me" entering the here and now implicitly—through an affectively disjunctive event in the *analyst's* internal world occurring simultaneously as a reciprocal phenomenon linked to the patient's dissociated subjectivity.

What makes the process feel so unstable is that it is nonlinear. Enactments take place repeatedly, each time being processed a bit more. The reason for the seeming repetition is that a highly limited representation of trauma is the only kind of representation a traumatized person is likely to have at first, and each enactment can be considered an effort to symbolize further an episodic memory that slowly becomes cognitively representable in long-term memory (see Kihlstrom, 1987). The more intense the unsymbolized affect, the stronger the force that is attempting to prevent communication among the isolated islands of selfhood that among them hold separate realities vis-à-vis the past and how or whether to deal with it. For working memory to represent the unsymbolized aspect of the trauma during its dissociated reliving in an enactment, the analytic relationship must contain an interaction between two essential qualities—safety and growth. The patient's experience of the enactment must be one in which the shadow of the destabilizing affect is strong enough to be felt but not strong enough to *automatically* increase the use of dissociation (see also Bucci, 2002).

In distinguishing between traumatic affect and anxiety, Sullivan (1953) used the term *severe anxiety* rather than the word *trauma*, but what he had in mind are experiences that, in current terms, are understood as being so potentially destabilizing that they lead automatically to dissociation. The affect evoked by trauma is not merely unpleasant but is a disorganizing hyperarousal that threatens to overwhelm the mind's ability to think, reflect, and process experience cognitively. This is especially true of affective dysregulation that carries the person to the edge of depersonalization and sometimes self-annihilation. Continuity of selfhood is here most truly at risk, and it is here that shame most contributes its own terrible coloring.

Sudden shame, a threat equal to that of fear, signals that the self is or is about to be violated, and the mind-brain triggers dissociation in order to prevent a recurrence of the original affective tsunami. Shame that is linked to trauma is a horrifyingly unanticipated sense of exposure as no longer the self that one has been. Shame is not the affect associated with something bad that one has *done*. As Helen Lynd (1958) described it, "I am ashamed of what I *am*. Because of this over-all character, an experience of shame can be altered or transcended only in so far as there is some change in the whole self" (p. 50). When trauma is relived in the here and now of analytic treatment, a patient's attempt to communicate the relived experience in language is painfully difficult because of what Lynd (1958) called a "double shame":

> Because of the outwardly small occasion that has precipitated shame, the intense emotion seems inappropriate, incongruous, disproportionate to the incident that has aroused it. *Hence a double shame is involved;* we are ashamed because of the original episode and ashamed because we feel so deeply about something so slight that a sensible person would not pay any attention to it. (p. 42)

One of the hardest parts of an analyst's job is searching out the shame that is evoked by the therapeutic process itself so that it can be addressed in a relational context. I use the phrase *searching out* rather than *being attuned to* because the shame is embedded in a here-and-now "shame about the shame" that most often leads to the entire shame experience becoming dissociated. To the degree the patient's shame is indeed dissociated in the here and now, the analyst is highly unlikely to notice it, especially when he is attending mainly to the patient's words. Thus, when working in areas where the reliving of trauma is taking place, the manifest absence of shame is a cue to search for its whereabouts. Shame as part of the process cannot be avoided, and the essence of the analytic work is for the patient to know you are thinking about it. If he knows that you are, then, with you as a companion who is holding his dissociated here-and-now shame in your mind, he can make it back from the edge of the abyss because he has an "other" whose act of recognition can make possible the transition to self-reflection. To put it more succinctly, one might say that the goal in working with enactments is to help a patient recognize the difference between feeling *scared* and feeling *scarred.*

Clinically and neurobiologically, evidence is increasing that successful psychoanalytic treatment restores an impaired capacity for affect regulation through affective/cognitive communication between patient and therapist that facilitates the development of intersubjectivity. The importance of this to psychoanalytic "technique" becomes especially profound when we accept that repression as a psychodynamic resource cannot always be assumed to exist and that part of our work as analysts is to enable the restoration of links among sequestered aspects of self so that the necessary conditions for intrapsychic conflict and its resolution can indeed be present. That is to say, the effectiveness of conflict-interpretation is always tied to its dialectic relationship with affect dysregulation and dissociation.

Except for highly unusual occasions, the therapeutic reliving and cognitive processing of unsymbolized traumatic affect does not create an experience that is genuinely traumatic even though patient and analyst may both feel at times close to the brink (Bromberg, 2006a, pp. 92–95). What makes it not real trauma? The scenario is enacted over and over with the therapist as if the patient were back in the original trauma, which one part of the self is indeed re-experiencing. But this time there are other parts of the self "on call," watching to make sure that they know what is going on and no surprises occur, and ready to deal with the betrayal they are sure will happen. Through this enacted scenario the patient relives mini-versions of the original trauma with a hidden vigilance that protects him from having it hit without warning (the sine qua non of trauma). But for a seriously traumatized patient the experience is frequently one of being dangerously "on the edge."

Some of the most rewarding experiences in my own work are sessions when a patient becomes aware of his own dissociative processes and the function they serve. Such moments are almost inevitably unanticipated, and I believe this is because change always precedes insight. Here is an example of such a moment that may help clarify why I place such emphasis on recognizing the here-and-now nonlinearity of the psychoanalytic growth process.

Mario

Mario had been extremely dissociative to the point that he was virtually unable to be present in the here and now with another human being. He had no idea of what it meant to engage with another person intersubjectively—to know the other through how he is experiencing the person experiencing him, and vice versa. Mario used his extraordinary ability to "size-up" people from outside his relationship to them and then related to them through what he had observed. Otherwise he was basically "mind-blind."

In sessions when Mario felt himself beginning to feel hopeful about finding new ways to relate to people, he would enter a self-state in which he experienced himself as an ugly, forbidding presence, and in this state he would divert me with a mantra about how his grotesqueness placed him beyond the pale of what would be acceptable, say, to a dating partner, much less a marital partner. Over time we came in the sessions to look at this self-state and the mantra that came with it as the core of an enacted response to having his shame and fear be insufficiently recognized by me. In one way or another he could feel that I was not attending to the importance of his need to protect himself against taking risks in a world of people with minds of their own and the danger of his being overwhelmed with shame if he were to relax his vigilance and trust that spontaneous interchange could be safe.

The following vignette took place many years into Mario's treatment, at a point where he was relying only minimally on dissociation as an automatic response and had developed, simultaneously, a greater capacity for self-reflection, spontaneity, and intersubjective relating. In this session, as though it were no big deal to him, Mario recalled that the previous night as he was getting ready for bed he had an insight into his mantra. It is noteworthy that this recollection came as a response to my having just voiced a blatantly self-confident pronouncement that his current anxiety about a woman with whom he was developing a friendship showed that he no longer had the "same old" problem with women, but that he was relating to this woman in a way that was very different. I told him that the kind of difficulty he was now having is part of the normal angst that everyone feels when they are trying to negotiate a new relationship. I added that I could feel his

presence when he was with her to be very "related" and that, regardless of what ultimately happened with this woman, I could feel that
he had inside himself an ability to make dating a part of his life that
was not fraught with dread. A rather pompous celebratory speech like
that would typically have evoked Mario's self-state mantra of being so
grotesque and so ugly that no one would ever want him as part of a
couple, and I had the thought that I should probably curb my enthusiasm. But I was not *feeling* wary of triggering that self-state switch. It was
as if somehow we were sharing a new piece of affective turf that did
not yet have words—just a shared willingness to take a risk in what we
could say to each other that had not been possible before. Strangely,
although my words struck me as remote I was not feeling unrelated.

After a silence, Mario replied by telling me about the insight he had
had the night before. He had been thinking about this girl and whether
or not to call her. As he was about to get into bed, he found himself
starting to repeat his mantra and realized that he did not want to say
the mantra because it felt false. He recognized that he was anxious
about calling this girl and that the effect of his mantra was to put him
into a trance state that let him eliminate the anxiety, a necessity if he
was going to be able to fall asleep. Mario then realized that by means
of his mantra he made his self-image of grotesqueness more and more
horrible as he repeated it, until he dissociated in order to escape it.
Once he dissociated, he could then fall asleep because the anxiety
about a potential phone conversation in the real world would not keep
him up all night. For *me* this moment with Mario qualified as a safe
surprise; I had never before been made privy to how Mario used his
mantra when he was alone.

Mario's use of his mantra was equivalent to someone who stares
at a spot on the wall until his eyes glaze over and he goes into a "safe
place" inside himself. Rarely had I heard so clearly a formerly dissociative patient identify this particular type of self-abuse as being in
the service of self-soothing by triggering a dissociative trance state.
Although it has obvious similarities to binging and purging and self-
mutilation, I think it is sometimes difficult for a therapist to recognize
this form of trance-induction as a means of self-soothing because it is
so easy to look at its quality as simply self-destructive or as obsessive-
compulsive rumination.

The relationship between dissociation and right-brain to right-brain
state-sharing has such a powerful impact on the patient/therapist relationship that Schore (2003b) writes that "dissociation, the last resort
defensive strategy, may represent the greatest counterforce to effective

psychotherapeutic treatment of personality disorders" (p. 132). Mario was surely an example of this, but I want to emphasize that Schore simultaneously sees dissociation as a *communication process* whereby right-brain to right-brain state-sharing becomes the pathway to facilitating the very therapeutic process in which, as a defensive strategy, it represents a counterforce. He (personal communication, 2007) argues, as do I, that the sharing of mental states that are essentially private is what psychotherapy is all about, and I think that both Mario's and my own ability to take a risk at that moment is a really nice example of it.

Within a shared mental state, the frozen attachment patterns that help a patient adapt to early relational trauma become available to be experienced conjointly and processed cognitively and linguistically in a shared mental space. As this takes place, each reenactment permits a negotiated degree of intersubjectivity to develop, which is what makes the nonlinearity of reenactment not simply a process of repetition. As the nonlinear cycles of collision and negotiation continue, a patient's capacity for intersubjectivity slowly increases in those areas from which it had been foreclosed or compromised. The potential for the coexistence of selfhood and otherness becomes not only more possible, but also gradually begins to take place with greater spontaneity, with less shame, and without affective destabilization.

The complementarity between Schore's formulations and mine includes our mutual emphasis on the discontinuity between states, the nonlinearity of state changes, and the all-important fact that, as Schore (2003a) puts it, "discontinuous states are experienced as affective responses" (p. 96). Elaborating, he writes:

> Dynamically fluctuating moment-to-moment state-sharing represents an organized dialogue occurring within milliseconds, and acts as an interactive matrix in which both partners match states and then simultaneously adjust their social attention, stimulation, and accelerating arousal in response to their partner's signals.... [M]inor changes, occurring at the right moment, can be amplified in the system, thus launching it into a *qualitatively different state*. (p. 96, emphasis added)

The relationship between dissociation and state matching is especially notable in patients with a history of Disorganized/Disoriented (Type D) Attachment, a point originally made by Hesse and Main (1999) and expanded on by Schore (2007):

[T]he disorganization and disorientation of type "D" attachment associated with abuse and neglect phenotypically resembles dissociative states. ... During episodes of the intergenerational transmission of attachment trauma the infant is *matching the rhythmic structures of the mother's dysregulated arousal states.* (p. 758, emphasis added)

Matching the rhythmic structure of the other (synchrony) has long been a basic technique of hypnotic induction. I discovered this relation between synchrony and dissociation first hand while working with a patient, Gloria, who, incidentally, during the course of her long history of searching for the "right" therapist had studied with Milton Erickson.

Gloria

Gloria had for some time been one of my "favorite" patients–someone with whom I felt so wonderfully tranquil and at ease that I was not aware of anything amiss until one session when I was uncomfortably conscious that I did not feel like asking her about something I knew I should be addressing and that I knew she would not want to think about. At that point I began to emerge from the dissociative cocoon in which Gloria and I had jointly been held, and for the first time I became aware, *perceptually*, of something else–something right in front of my eyes: Whenever I changed my body posture, Gloria changed hers to mirror it.

Why did I not see this sooner? Gloria was someone whose way of life was characterized by doing things for other people and was so powerfully attuned to the other with seemingly total satisfaction that she appeared to be without self-interest. Her seemingly pleasurable adaptation to others came across as characterologically seamless. Indeed, I found it to be a hollow intellectual exercise whenever I tried to address with her the possibility of her attunement to others being at least in part self-protective and that another part of her might have more information about this.

In this session, however, it was the very pleasure I felt in her synchronizing her rhythmic structure to mine that began to feel oddly uncomfortable. This type of discomfort has been aptly described by Donnel Stern (2004) as an "emotional 'chafing' or tension, an unbidden 'hint' or 'sense' that something more than one has suspected is going on in the clinical interaction" (p. 208). Once an analyst starts feeling this, something new becomes *perceptually* noticeable that has been dissociated, and he finds himself thinking about the patient along certain lines that would have once felt forced but now feel authentic even though not well formulated. In Gloria's case, what finally came into focus for me was that more often than not she was unable to feel satisfied that she had done enough for the other and thus she could never quite appreciate her own generosity. What had seemed to me simply like dedication to the needs of others now began to include a compulsive element that spoke to a dissociated component. I began to look differently at the fact that the other person's needs dominated every interaction and were all that seemingly mattered to her. In time, so did she.

Saving Hamlet's Butt

I'm going to end this chapter with a clinical vignette–well, it's kind of clinical–that addresses the vicissitudes of shrinking the tsunami. It's a scene from Shakespeare's (1599–1601) *Hamlet* that also illustrates Schore's concept of state-matching as portrayed by the relationship between Hamlet and his friend Horatio. You shall see in a moment why I whimsically call this vignette "Saving Hamlet's Butt."

Hamlet, midway through the final act of the play (V, ii), reveals a secret. It is a secret that most of us who spend time at the gym would prefer remained so–that no matter how much you work out, eventually your butt is going to drop anyhow. Shakespeare, of course, puts it more poetically: "There's a divinity that shapes our ends, rough-hew them how we will."

In this scene, Hamlet has reached the end of his rope and is explaining to his friend Horatio that the reason he hasn't yet killed his uncle isn't his fault. What he says, in essence, is that we do not always succeed in following through on our plans because a higher power–a divinity–has a different agenda. At that moment, Hamlet becomes to me more recognizably human than at any point before or after. It does not have to do with whether I do or do not believe in a divinity the way Hamlet put it. It has to do with the great timing of his spiritual awakening, and with the old saw that there are no atheists in foxholes.

By the time Act V gets under way, Hamlet is a guy under a lot of stress. And why not? The play is almost over, he still hasn't taken action, and his ruminating about it is bringing him closer to the edge of madness. What to do? He has no prescription for Paxil, and everyone around him has personal axes to grind except for Horatio. Horatio takes him seriously but is so even-handed that it is not easy to see exactly what good Horatio is doing him. What to do is certainly not obvious, but even so, Horatio's role invites us to look at him the way a therapist without a treatment plan is looked at by a managed-care company. To take action, Hamlet needs to free himself from the obsessing that has robbed his desire of what he calls "resolve." Horatio has no treatment plan.

But Shakespeare finds Hamlet a nifty solution—an insight into God that comes to him just at the right time. It has been said that Harry Stack Sullivan (1953) used to call those kinds of user-friendly insights "happy thoughts" because they solve the most painful dilemmas with astounding ease. Hamlet can now suspend his self-recrimination long enough to act. He has an external explanation—a "not-me" explanation—for the disturbing fact that no matter how much we sweat, our ends seem to have a will of their own. Maybe the bottom line, argues Hamlet, is that it's God's will—it's surely not *mine*!

"Yeah," says Hamlet. "It's not *me* that's the problem. It's 'not-me.' *I* want to kill Claudius. It's not *me* that gets in the way." And here the divinity enters with a plan of its own. Now, freed by the divinity from the tormenting impossibility of trying to turn an affective tsunami into something "thinkable"—internal conflict—Hamlet feels a sense of personal resolve in his wish to kill Claudius, a resolve that has been lacking. His formerly pale desire is now felt in color. What he calls its "native hue of resolution" has returned and lends an unquestioned purity of purpose to his taking action.

If you think about it, Hamlet's tendency to find "not-me" solutions was there right from the beginning of the play. Whose idea was it to kill Claudius in the first place? Not Hamlet's. It came from the ghost of his father. And his subsequent misgivings about it are not really felt as his either—they are felt as nameless flaws in his character that he cannot control.

Talking about "me" and "not-me" helps to make dissociative processes understandable as part of the human condition. Faced with a shadow that holds the potential to become a flood, the mind recruits its self-states into a covert survival team. Its members are aware of one another only on a need-to-know basis and they exercise their skills through their insulation from each another. Each self-state has its own task and is dedicated to upholding its own version of truth. Each is a piece of a larger-than-life enterprise designed to sequester the part of self that already knows the horror of a tsunami and then to obscure the existence of the dissociation itself. A hypnoid brain process takes over whereby, in Laing's (1969) brilliantly convoluted language, we are unaware there is anything of which we needed to be unaware, and then unaware that we needed to be unaware of needing to be unaware.

Hamlet was no different in that regard. What was felt as "me" at one moment was "not-me" when a different self-state took over. To each "me" there were no opposing parts of self, so at any given moment he was haunted by the states that could not find a place in "me" for their own voices and desires. Hamlet had no place to hide. His torment had no resolution because his mother and his uncle were always in his face, and the disharmony of voices in his head would not leave him alone, even in bed at night. Shakespeare's choice of words in Hamlet's incredibly contemporary description of what trauma sufferers describe as "the war inside my head" echoes loudly for any therapist: "Sir, in my heart there was a kind of fighting that would not let me sleep" (V, ii, lines 5–6).

Notwithstanding all his self-reproach, Hamlet was unable to experience internal conflict about any of it, and in this regard his mental functioning is typical when self-state collisions are too much for the mind to bear and cannot be contained in a single state of mind. But I want to make it clear that I am not suggesting we are all just versions of Hamlet. Difficult self-state collisions are inherent to routine mental functioning and we are all vulnerable to affect dysregulation that has the potential to increase under certain circumstances. I see Hamlet's situation as an example of the power of early developmental trauma to make adult-onset trauma especially "massive" for some people and less so for others.

The murder of Hamlet's father was what we could reasonably call an adult-onset trauma that became affectively "massive" because it triggered earlier developmental trauma, doubtlessly involving his mother and father both. Hamlet's plan to kill Claudius was doomed to be no more than a temporary stop-gap because, like all one-sided dissociative solutions, there was another internal voice—another "not-me" that gave him no peace—and there was nothing to weaken the power of the dissociative gap between the voices.

So here's the point: Despite the fact that we are not simple versions of Hamlet, I do believe that the following is true for all of us. *It is impossible to permanently avoid an internal war between adversarial parts of the self simply by trying to increase the degree of power held by only one part.*

For everyone, there is a downside to dissociation when it is enlisted as an anticipatory defense. The person is able to more or less survive but is also more or less unable to live, and this is especially true for someone suffering the kind of emotional overload that Hamlet was facing while trying to keep intact the thin membrane separating developmental from adult-onset trauma.

Was Hamlet crazy? That is, psychotic? Opinions vary, and most of the play's main characters are pretty sure he was. My own view is that he was not, despite his enlisting a group of actors to create a "more real" reality for him. I would say that he was close to the edge but that Shakespeare "saved his butt" by giving him someone to talk to who listened—Horatio.

Although Horatio did not say anything like, "This must be awful for you," he was fully listening and was very responsive to Hamlet's state of mind. This is why Hamlet and Horatio are a good fit for Schore's concept of state-sharing as the foundation for therapeutically addressing affect dysregulation. When Hamlet was confronted by his father's ghost, Horatio did not say, "His *ghost?* I'm afraid I didn't see it. Perhaps we might look at what it might mean that you saw it." Nor did he suggest that Hamlet's sudden turn to religion might be worthy of comment. In fact, Horatio didn't talk a lot, and it is possible to view what he said when he did talk as no more than a caricature of, "That's interesting; tell me more about it!" From my reading of the dialogue between them, I would argue that it went far deeper. I suggest that Hamlet's relationship with Horatio was the main factor keeping the shadow of the tsunami from overwhelming Hamlet's mind even though he could not ultimately avoid death. Horatio's consistent ability to match Hamlet's state with a reciprocal state of his own calmed Hamlet enough to allow him to go forward.

Developmental trauma is a core relational phenomenon and invariably shapes personality in every human being. It contributes to every human being's potential for affect dysregulation, which is always a matter of degree even in those for whom secure attachment has led to relative stability and resilience. We all are vulnerable to the unanticipated experience of coming face to face with our own "otherness," which sometimes, albeit temporarily, feels more "not-me" than our minds can deal with. This is part of the human condition. The big difference between people is the extent to which the sudden affective hyperarousal touches an area of unprocessed developmental trauma and is not only unpleasant, but mentally *unbearable* and thus unavailable to cognition. The risk of this happening is a central aspect of working with enactments. I argue that *for all patients*, regardless of how minimal the scope or duration of the vulnerability, enduring personality growth in analytic treatment is interwoven with the ability of the patient/analyst relationship to increase a patient's threshold for affective hyperarousal. This use of the patient/analyst relationship takes place through the nonlinear joint processing of an enacted (dissociated) communication channel in which the patient's fear of affect dysregulation (the shadow of the tsunami) is "shrunk" by the broader ability to safely distinguish the likelihood of mental shock that could indeed be affectively overwhelming from the kind of excitingly "edgy" experiences that are always interwoven with the risk of spontaneity. The patient's fear of dysregulation, as it is relived in the enacted present, becomes increasingly containable as a cognitive event, thus enabling the mind/brain to diminish its automatic reliance on dissociation as an affective "smoke-detector."

I believe that the transformative process of shrinking the tsunami is fundamental to the depth of the analytic growth process itself, and that it derives its power from the coexistence in the analytic relationship of two essential qualities, safety and risk. Through the creation of a dyadic space that includes the subjectivities of both patient and analyst but is not the exclusive property of either, the patient/analyst relationship becomes a therapeutic environment by being "safe but not *too* safe." As long as the analyst's ongoing commitment to doing the "work" involves an effort to communicate his being simultaneously concerned about his patient's affective safety *while* working, the coexistence of safety and risk becomes the essential element of therapeutic action that makes the reliving part of a growth process rather than a blind repetition of the past.

PART II
UNCERTAINTY

2

"It Never Entered My Mind"[1]

Once you warned me that if you scorned me
I'd sing the maiden's prayer again
and wish that you where there again
to get into my hair again.
It never entered my mind.

–Rogers & Hart (1940)

CR This chapter is about "secrets," so let me begin by telling one of mine. I've always felt an oddly satisfying self-contradiction in my having become a psychoanalyst, given how much I hate change. I was the last kid on my block to have a new bike because I felt such loyalty to my old one, and I was also the last kid on my analytic block to buy a computer, because I couldn't bear to part with my yellow pads and my typewriter. Even after I capitulated, my friends who couldn't easily open my attachments or who stumbled over my formatting, talked about the outdated version of my word processing program as if they had just run into Norman Bates' mother–I wouldn't admit she died and I was refusing to bury her. I'm not arguing that this is a good way to be; it's just the way I am. The most flattering account of it I've heard is from a patient from whom I can't seem to hide anything: She has

---

[1]An earlier version of this chapter, "'It Never Entered my Mind': Some Reflections on Desire, Dissociation, and Disclosure," was published in J. Petrucelli (Ed.), *Longing: Psychoanalytic Musings on Desire* (London: Karnac, 2006, pp. 13–23). It was originally presented at a 2004 conference at Mount Sinai Medical Center in New York City, sponsored by the Eating Disorders, Compulsions and Addictions Service of the William Alanson White Institute.

referred to it as my "retro approach to modernity." Attachment to what I know, even with its limitations, is part of my comfortable familiarity with my ways of being in the world. From one vantage point I'm talking about "procedural memory" (Bromberg, 2003b); from another, I'm talking about fidelity to my different selves as I live them.

The same attitude can inform my work. I remember an initial consultation with a man who came to me only because he was in a state of total desperation. His marriage was falling apart, and he couldn't "get" why none of the things he did to improve it seemed to help. But even as he was saying this, I could feel the presence of another part of him that was being dragged unwillingly into my office, a part that felt it was being required to obliterate its existence for the sake of learning some "better" way of being—a way that it knew in advance would feel irrelevant. My heart went out to him and I found myself saying, "I want to share a secret. Even though I'm an analyst I hate change; so don't worry, you'll be the same when we end therapy." He didn't laugh, and I could see he didn't exactly know what I meant, but I could also see that his eyes were teary. I could see that a part of him could *feel* what I meant. He cried even though he had no conscious awareness of *why* he cried. That moment became a watershed that helped us during future moments when we were struggling to stand in the spaces between different self-states with different agendas. As the poet and scientist Diane Ackerman (2004), in *An Alchemy of Mind*, has put it, "consciousness is the great poem of matter." Conscious awareness, she writes, "isn't really a response to the world, it's more of an opinion about it" (p. 19).

> Life feels continuous, immediate, ever unfolding. In truth, we're always late to the party ... Part of that delay [is] so that the world will feel logical and not jar the senses.... All that happens offstage. It's too fussy, too confusing a task to impose on consciousness, which has other chores to do, other fish to fry.... Instead, we feel like solo masters of our fate, captains of our souls, the stuff of homily and poetry. (pp. 20–24)

What Ackerman is describing as the "stuff of homily and poetry" I have tried to capture in my concept of "staying the same while changing" (Bromberg, 1998b), a phrase that itself contains a secret. The secret is that "staying the same while changing" is logically impossible. It embodies two phenomena that can't coexist, even though they do. Somehow, the process of "change" allows a negotiation between different internal voices, each dedicated to *not* changing, that is, dedicated to "staying the same" in order to preserve self-continuity. This impossible coexistence of staying the same and simultaneously changing is why trying to track "change" in psychoanalysis (Bromberg, 1996a) calls to mind Gertrude Stein's (1937) comment that when you finally get there, "there's no there there" (p. 298). The direct experience of "self change" is indeed a secret that eludes conscious awareness. It seems to be gobbled up by the relatively seamless continuity of being oneself, which necessarily includes parts of the self that remain secret from what is "me" at any given moment.

Robert Frost (1942) wrote: "We dance round in a ring and suppose,/ But the Secret sits in the middle and knows" (p. 362). Every therapist knows the truth of this, particularly when developmental trauma has been a significant issue in a patient's early life. The therapist can feel the inadequacy of words as a means of reaching his patient, and often experiences a growing sense of futility about "really" knowing her. This feeling of futility is a small sample of the abysmal hopelessness felt by his patient at being unable to communicate in language from the place that Frost calls "the middle." Therapist and patient "dance round in a ring and suppose," but their dance of words does not unite them within the place of the secret because the secret that "sits in the middle and knows" is a subjective form of reality that is incommunicable through ordinary human discourse. It is organized by experience that Wilma Bucci (1997a, 2001, 2003, 2010) has termed *subsymbolic*, and is communicated through enactment.

Enactment is a dyadic dissociative process—a cocoon within which the subsymbolic communication taking place is temporarily inaccessible because it is deadened to reflective functioning. In a human relationship, no person's capacity for aliveness can be sustained without an alive "other," so if the other is a therapist, and is for too long listening to the "material" without being alive to his own internal experience of the relationship itself, a dissociative process often begins to develop in the therapist that may have started in the patient but quickly becomes a cocoon that envelops both patient and therapist. Typically, the sequence of events is more felt than cognized by a therapist because the therapist's self-state almost always switches dissociatively so soon after the patient's that the switch is usually not perceived by the therapist until it becomes noticeably uncomfortable to him, what Donnel Stern (2004) calls "chafing." Until then, a clinical process that may have been experienced by the therapist as alive at the outset of a session subtly diminishes in aliveness, typically without the therapist's cognitive awareness. This change in the therapist's state of mind eventually compromises his ability to retain his focus on the "material." Why? Because when one's affective need for an alive partner is being disconfirmed by another mind that is dead to it, a therapist is no different than anyone else. Through dissociation, he escapes from the futility of needing from an "other" what is not possible to express in words. What begins as "material" evolves into empty words.

Because therapist and patient are sharing an interpersonal field that belongs equally to both of them, any unsignalled withdrawal from that field by either person will disrupt the other's state of mind. The disruption, however, is usually not processed cognitively by either person, at least at first. It becomes increasingly difficult for the therapist to concentrate, and only when this experience reaches the threshold of perceptual awareness by becoming distressing will the therapist's struggle to concentrate become the pathway to perceptually experiencing the deadening power of what is taking place between them in the here-and-now. Invariably, the therapist's own response to this (some might say lack of response) contributes, interactively, to the construction of a communication process that both acknowledges the recapitulation of the patient's past experience and establishes the context for a new form of experience at the same time.

Just a Pebble in Her Shoe

The relationship between dissociation and enacted "secrets" is best grasped clinically, so I'm going to present a vignette from my work that shows me in the middle of an enactment as well as showing how I was thinking about it while in it.[2]

A bulimic patient, whose dissociated acts of purging were starting to become more emotionally recallable by her during therapy sessions, began to have flashbacks of abuse at the hands of her parents. At first,

---

[2]An abbreviated description of this enactment can be found in *Awakening the Dreamer* (Bromberg, 2006a, p. 89). My reason for returning to it in the present chapter isn't just that I can't bear to let go of my old bicycle. I've chosen it because I feel it highlights especially dramatically a number of key issues relevant to the present discussion that were insufficiently elaborated earlier. One of these is the way in which the relationship between longing and desire exemplifies the broader relationship between implicit and declarative forms of mental experience.

she couldn't let herself think clearly about these images, describing them as like "having a pebble in my shoe that I can't get rid of." But as she began to talk about what the pebble felt like, she recognized that the part of herself holding the memories of abuse was keeping them secret and that the pebble substituted for having to relive her actual emotions. Moreover, the experience during her sessions of feeling something so painful about her *vomiting* was making her past pain feel "real" rather than something she was never sure existed. Her pain was becoming increasingly complex and more intense the more she relived it with me. The more real the experience felt the more its existence threatened to betray those who had hurt her, and betray the parts of herself that identified with them. For all these reasons the possibility of ever talking about the abuse "never entered her mind." But the pebble, which was supposed to remain no more than a pebble, was starting to feel like a boulder.

The session I'm going to describe was in some ways the same as those that preceded it, but in other ways it was memorably different. "Why would I want to hurt the people I feel closest to just because I need someone to know?" she agonized. At that moment I began to feel some of her agony, and I also began to experience shame attached to my desire to help her reveal her secret. The shame was about inflicting what felt like needless pain upon a person to whom I felt close at that moment—I was hurting her just because I wanted to know. Until that moment I had been ignoring, *personally*, the extent to which she was vulnerable to dissociated pain inflicted upon her by another part of herself, for allowing "longing" (I *need* someone to know) to become "desire" (I *want* to tell you). The only part of her that had come to feel worthy of being loved existed by protecting the family secrets. By starting to remember and disclose them because she wanted to, she became vulnerable to internal attack by other parts of herself. I had not wanted to experience the degree to which she was being punished and denounced, internally, as evil. In this session, which followed a particularly violent night of purging, she screamed angrily at me, "You'll never get me to stop vomiting. I'll never spill the beans."

At that moment I became painfully in touch with my own dissociated feelings of shame about hurting her, and *I* decided to "spill the beans." I shared with her what I was in touch with, including my awareness and personal regret that I had been leaving her too alone with her pain because I was so enthusiastic about our "progress." I then asked if she might be aware of feelings of her own about what I had just said to her, including feelings about my having said it. After a pause, she allowed that she was feeling two ways at the same time, and that they were giving her a headache to think about: She could feel herself furious at me but at the same time she knew she loved me and didn't want to hurt me. I said that it was only when she got openly angry at me and said, "You'll never get me to stop vomiting, and I'll never spill the beans," that I woke up to what was there all along under her anger—her pain and shame in having to go through this so alone.

What I had been seeing as my therapeutic "success" in bringing about the reliving of her past had finally triggered within me an affective experience of her unmet longing for me to know, personally, what this was like for her, and to care. I had been dissociating the part of me that could feel it most personally. My "spilling the beans" and sharing the experience of how I awakened to her pain connected with her longing for me to know it personally. Her longing could not be put in words; it had not reached the level of cognitive awareness that would allow it to become conscious "desire." Yet, as longing, it remained operative; it remained true to that self-state. When dissociation is operating, each state of consciousness holds its own experientially encapsulated "truth," which is enacted over and over again. The secret that is being revealed through an enactment is that while your patient is telling you one thing in words, to which you are responding in some way, there is a second "conversation" going on between the two of you. Buck (1994, p. 266, cited in Schore, 2003b, p. 49) refers to this as "a conversation between limbic systems."

As my patient and I continued to put our dissociated states into words, her longing, a somatic affect that possessed her, began to be expressible as "hers," and evolved little by little from an affect into an emotion, an emotion we know as "desire." By sharing and comparing our respective experiences that took place during the enactment and finding words for them that had consensual meaning (Bromberg, 1980), she was able to move from *being* the secret to *knowing* the secret that had only been "supposed" by us until then. Until this moment we had, in Frost's words, been forced to "dance round in a ring and suppose." Now the doubly shameful secret was out and we could both "know."

Secrets and the Corruption of Desire

Secrets, such as my patient's, contain affective experience in the form of implicit memories of selves that became "not-me" because the subjective realities they held were "lost in translation." These self-states remain uncommunicable through words because they are denied symbolic meaning within the overarching canopy of a "me" that is allowed to exist in human relationships. My own clinical experience leads me to believe that these self-states most frequently become dissociated when the person is quite young, but that regardless of age they occur in a context where self-continuity is threatened. I'm speaking of experiences that have been invalidated as "real" by the mind of some significant other who used language not to share these experiences but to "translate" them out of existence. When the original "other" is a primary attachment figure, a parent or an other whose significance is interpersonally similar to a parent's, that person holds the power to destabilize the child's mental state by rupturing a relational connection that organizes the child's sense of self-continuity. In order to preserve the attachment connection and protect mental stability, the mind triggers a survival solution, dissociation, that allows the person to bypass the mentally disorganizing struggle to self-reflect without hope of relieving the pain and fear caused by the destabilization of selfhood. Dissociation narrows one's range of perception so as to set up nonconflictual categories of self-experience as different parts of the self.

Inevitably, desire becomes corrupted. The child's healthy desire to communicate her subjective experience to a needed other is infused with shame because the needed other cannot or will not acknowledge the child's experience as something legitimately "thinkable." The attachment bond that organizes self-stability for the child is now in jeopardy. She feels, not that she *did* something wrong, but that there is something wrong with her *self*, that is, something wrong with her as a person. To survive this destabilization of selfhood, she sequesters the now "illegitimate" part of her subjective experience by dissociating the part of herself that knows it to be legitimate. She has dissociated a part of her subjectivity that originally felt real and thus "legitimate," and because it is dissociated the child starts to doubt her own legitimacy as a person. She is thereafter in doubt both as to her own legitimacy as a person and the reality of her internal experience. As an adult, she is left with a sense of something bad having happened to her but that sense is not organized as a cognition; she is left not with a memory that is felt as belonging to "me" (a declarative memory), but with its affective ghost in the form of an uncommunicable state of longing that shrouds the implicit memory. The longing is a "not-me" ghost that haunts her (Bromberg, 2003a) because her own desire to communicate it to her therapist from her internal place of "illegitimacy" becomes a source of shame in itself. Thus, her sense of shame is compounded: The first source of shame comes from her belief that what she feels will not be real to the other. The second source of shame derives from her fear that she will lose the other's attachment (and thus her core sense of self) because she believes the therapist will not attribute validity to her desperation that he know what she is feeling. This fear of attachment loss makes her even more desperate for evidence that the other has not indeed withdrawn his attachment, and the more evidence she seeks the greater is the shame she feels for seeking solace that is somehow tinged as illegitimate.

A patient's "longing" to communicate dissociated self-experience must be recognized by the analyst, but what must simultaneously be recognized is that she cannot mentally experience this longing as legitimate without being shamed by other parts of herself, leaving her feeling undeserving of consolation or solace. When she tries to tell you her secret, she is *always* "at a loss for words" because the real secret can't be told, at least not in words. The affective truth with which the patient lives becomes suspect by her as a "lie" or at least an exaggeration, and she is never sure a secret really exists or if she is making it up.

There are no thoughts that bridge past and present so as to link her subjective world of pain with the subjective world of another person. The patient, in this respect, lives in tortured isolation, and this experience becomes the patient's essential truth, her "secret," and words and ideas become empty "lies." What could not originally be said without traumatic pain could not come to be thought, and what cannot now be thought cannot come to be said.

As Masud Khan (1979) wrote about his patient Caroline in his famous paper "Secret as Potential Space": "Caroline's secret encapsulated her own absent self" (p. 265). "The location of a secret of this type," states Khan, "is that it is neither inside nor outside a person. A person cannot say: 'I have a secret inside me'. They *are* the secret, yet their ongoing life does not partake of it. Such a secret creates a gap in the person's psyche which is reactively screened with all sorts of bizarre events–intrapsychic and interpersonal" (pp. 267–268).

Khan makes it clear that what was important for Caroline in their work was not his interpreting the symbolic meaning of her secret, but that in making such an interpretation, his mind needed to be alive to what he called her "absent self" (see also Chefetz & Bromberg, 2004, pp. 445–455). Thereby he was relating to the part of her that *was* the secret in a way that became an act of mutuality.

I believe that what Khan accomplished, relationally, in Caroline's treatment must take place with every patient to one degree or another as part of every analysis in order to free the patient's capacity for self-reflection. In other words, in every treatment the *development* of self-reflection is part of what is achieved by the analytic process; it is not something that the analyst requires a patient to already possess as a prerequisite called an "observing ego." Because each of the patient's dissociated self-states holds its own agenda about the patient's "secrets," each must become available in its own terms to the analyst's range of self-states. This requires that as part of the clinical process, the analyst increasingly recognizes his own dissociative contribution to the enactments and becomes more and more able to reflect upon and use this recognition, relationally, with each of the patient's selves or self-states. As this is taking place, the patient's dissociative subjectivity evolves, nonlinearly, into self-reflective subjectivity (and intersubjectivity). Through unfreezing the developmental process that Fonagy and his colleagues (2005) term *mentalization*, a patient becomes able, more freely and more safely, to experience another mind experiencing her mind experiencing their mind in those areas of mental functioning where dissociation had held intersubjectivity captive.

A final comment: As the reader may have deduced from my epigraph, the title of this chapter, "It Never Entered My Mind," is borrowed from a song by Rogers and Hart (1940) about the aching emptiness in a person's soul as he longs for an absent other he didn't think he would even miss. The song begins whimsically but ends poignantly. "It never entered my mind" isn't just a refrain. It is a low moan of anguish made all the more poignant because when, at last, the shock of loss does enter a person's mind it hits in a wave that floods the heart with pain. I'm sure that when Lorenz Hart wrote "You have what I lack myself" he didn't have attachment trauma in mind, but more than a few people have told me they get goose pimples every time they listen to it.

3

"Mentalize This!"[1]

CR Despite differences in emphasis, there is a shared sensibility among analysts interested in self-states and dissociation (e.g., Bromberg, 1998a, 2006a; Chefetz, 1997, 2000; Chefetz & Bromberg, 2004; Howell, 2005; Stern, 1997, 2009) and those whose contributions have focused on mentalization and reflective functioning (see Allen & Fonagy, 2006, for an informative bibliography). I am speaking of a sensibility that recognizes human relatedness as the essence of self-hood and as the key element in both normal development and therapeutic growth.

It is a feature of the new perspectives on mentalization that the capacity to relationally embrace one's own mind and the mind of the other as a coherent experience derives from the achievement of inter-subjectivity. In this chapter I am going to approach the topic of mentalization through an indirect route. First, I will consider anew what we have learned about dissociation as normal mental *process*–its evolutionary role in configuring and reconfiguring one's self-states in day-to-day life. Then I will turn to the topic of trauma–how dissociation is enlisted into a posttraumatic rigidification of self-state boundaries that transforms normal process into pathological *structure*. Only then will I attempt to link up with the context of psychotherapy and its potential to enhance a patient's ability to mentalize. To anticipate where I am going let me volunteer now that not only is the capacity to mentalize

---

[1]This chapter in an earlier version was presented at a 2005 conference at City University in New York City, "Reflecting on the Future of Psychoanalysis: Mentalization, Internalization and Representation," and published in L. Jurist, A. Slade, and S. Bergner (Eds.), *Mind to Mind: Infant Research, Neuroscience, and Psychoanalysis* (New York: Other Press, 2008, pp. 414–434).

compromised in the presence of trauma—this is widely accepted—but also that reclaiming it or, for some people, rescuing it from the ashes, is best facilitated through a therapeutic process that involves collision and negotiation.

Self-States and Dissociation

A human being's ability to live a life that allows both authenticity and self-reflection requires an ongoing dialectic between the separateness and unity of one's self-states; crucially, this dialectic must allow each self-state to function optimally without foreclosing communication and negotiation between them. When all goes well, a person is only dimly or momentarily aware of the individual self-states and their respective realities because each functions as part of a healthy illusion of coherent personal identity—an overarching experiential state that is felt as "I." Each self-state is part of a functional whole, informed by a process of internal negotiation with the realities, values, affects, and perspectives of the others. Each aspect of self has its own degree of access to the various domains of psychic functioning (e.g., capacity to feel and tolerate the pressure of one's needs and wishes, capacity to judge what is adaptive social behavior, capacity to love, capacity to act from a sense of one's values as well as from a sense of purpose, capacity to maintain object constancy in relationships, and capacity to mentally bear the experience of intrapsychic conflict). Despite collisions and even enmity between aspects of self, it is unusual for any one self-state to function totally outside of the experience of "me-ness," exiled from human relatedness and without the participation of the other parts of self.

In a relatively coherent personality, dissociation is a healthy, adaptive function of the human mind—a basic process that allows individual self-states to function optimally (not simply defensively) when full immersion in a single reality, a single strong affect, and a suspension of one's self-reflective capacity is exactly what is called for or wished for. I am referring to times requiring concentration, single-mindedness, task orientation, or full surrender to a pleasurable experience. "Under normal conditions, dissociation enhances the integrating functions of the ego by screening out excessive or irrelevant stimuli" (Young, 1988, pp. 35–36). In other words, the process of dissociation is basic to human mental functioning and is central to the stability and growth of personality. It is the intrinsic mental process that represents what is most human in the ongoing negotiation between what we subjectively experience as conscious and what we call *unconscious.*

Trauma and Defensive Dissociation

As part of its evolutionary function dissociation serves also as a defense, but a defense unlike any other. It is not just a different name for the process that Freud called repression. Repression as a defense is responsive to anxiety—a negative but regulatable affect that signals the potential emergence into consciousness of mental contents that may create unpleasant, but bearable, intrapsychic conflict. Dissociation as a defense is responsive to trauma—the chaotic, convulsive flooding by unregulatable affect that takes over the mind, threatening the stability of selfhood and sometimes sanity. Intrapsychic conflict becomes experientially unbearable, not just unpleasant. Why unbearable? Because the disjunction that takes place is not between inharmonious mental contents, but between alien aspects of self—between self-states that are so discrepant that they cannot coexist in a single state of consciousness without potential destabilization of self-continuity.

But the mind's need for the defense does not end when the trauma is "over." For the brain, it is *never* over. Trauma and anxiety differ not only in the "quantity" (the intensity) of the affect involved, but are also qualitatively different in the task required of the mind/brain. In other words, traumatic affect is not anxiety with its volume turned up. It is the *shock* of an affective flooding intense enough to disrupt thought because it is *inherently chaotic.* The primary source of the chaos is a mental apparatus that is attempting to function beyond its capacity because the different self-experiences the mind is being asked to contain and resolve as internal conflict are nonnegotiable for that person at that moment. The reason that trauma is never over for the brain is that it leaves a residue of unprocessed, dissociated affect that the brain was unable to regulate—"the shadow of the tsunami." *What the brain cannot regulate it tries to control.*

Posttraumatically, dissociation is enlisted by the mind to *proactively* assure that the destabilizing shock of the "tsunami" is never repeated: A dissociated mental structure now vigilantly anticipates the "shadow" before it can arrive unexpectedly, thus turning the mind into a smoke detector and life into an unlived waiting period. Dissociation is no longer a function of the mind; the mind becomes a function of dissociation. Why don't we just call it a stronger form of anxiety? To paraphrase Sullivan (1953), "anxiety permits gradual realization of the situation in which it occurs," but the effect of trauma (*severe anxiety* in Sullivan's terms), "reminds one in some ways of a blow on the head, in that it simply wipes out what is immediately proximal to its occurrence" (p. 152). Indeed, it is fairly clear that what is most responsible for wiping out here-and-now experience that is "immediately proximal" to the occurrence of trauma is the *automatic* triggering of dissociation as a defense.

When functioning as a mental structure, dissociation controls potentially traumatic experience by turning each domain of self into a discontinuous constellation of reality now kept apart from the others by the autohypnotic process that supports dissociation. Defensive dissociation shows its signature through disconnecting the mind from its capacity to perceive that which feels too much for selfhood to bear. It reduces what is in front of someone's eyes to a narrow band of perceptual reality that lacks emotionally personal relevance to the self that is experiencing it ("whatever is going on is not happening to *me*").

In the trauma arising from human relationships, what is drained of personal relevance are the here-and-now interactions that feel too disjunctive with self-continuity to allow cognitive processing. When self-coherence becomes a liability to self-stability it becomes no longer adaptive to "feel like one self while being many." The mind's ability to reflectively experience another person's subjectivity in a relational context—a here-and-now phenomenon—is compromised, which in turn impairs the capacity for intersubjectivity, thus highlighting a central link to the concept of mentalization. The individual is largely unable to see himself reflectively through the eyes of an "other" because self-states that formerly were able to coexist adaptively are now separated hypnoidally so that each can play its own protective role with its individual "truth" unimpeded by input from other self-states—or other people.

The gaps between dissociated aspects of self must be first linked by human relatedness in order for the experience of intrapsychic conflict to be possible. Conversely, it should be understood that the ability to experience intrapsychic conflict does not always exist. When patients are unable to contain an experience of intrapsychic conflict, the immediate goal is to use the therapeutic relationship to help them turn self-experience into something more than islands of "truth," to help them become able to "stand in the spaces" between self-states, so that reliance on the protection of dissociation is replaced by a capacity to feel internal conflict as bearable.

The overarching principle of clinical work is to enable a person to move from experiencing his patterns of behavior as who he is to experiencing them as something that he does. In classical language, at the start of treatment each self-state is ego-syntonic when it is dissociatively ascendant; the possibility of experiencing other self-states, *conflictually*, as ego-alien cannot be taken for granted. Nor can the existence of what has been called an "observing ego"–the agreed upon criterion for the therapeutic action of psychoanalytic treatment. From a postclassical perspective, what has been called the development of an observing ego I see as the patient's increasing ability to hold and process internal communication between disjunctive self-states without such communication being automatically foreclosed by proactive dissociation. I believe that regardless of a patient's personality style or diagnosis, every fruitful treatment process engages what is unsymbolized as well as symbolized in both the analyst's mind and the patient's as part of increasing a patient's capacity to process intrapsychic conflict. In this regard I also believe that every analyst might well consider the potential applicability to all of his patients of what Janet (1907) said about the manifestation of dissociation in hysteria–that if it is "a mental malady, it is not a mental malady like any other ... [but] a malady of the personal synthesis" (p. 332).

Dissociation and Mentalization

What Janet (1907) called "personal synthesis" I see best described as fluid self-state communication, which has led me to formulate my belief (Bromberg, 1993) that "health is the ability to stand in the spaces between realities without losing any of them" (p. 186). "Standing in the spaces" is my shorthand way of describing a person's relative capacity to make room at any given moment for subjective reality that is not readily containable by the self that he experiences as "me" at that moment. People who are able to reflect on someone else's subjective experience of them in the context of their own self-experience–people who can "stand in the spaces"–are relating intersubjectively, an extraordinary process which should impress and astonish us more than it does. It really is extraordinary that people can do this (the full reach of this capacity is touched on in chapter 8). Peter Fonagy, Mary Target, and their colleagues believe this process is mediated by a developmental achievement they have aptly termed the capacity for *mentalization*. This capacity allows a person to reflect on disjunctions between his own self-experience and the way he seems to exist in the mind of an other without having to automatically sequester the disjunctive views of himself in disconnected self-state islands of reality that are prevented from communicating. Or to put it another way, the capacity to mentalize makes it less likely that the mind will automatically enlist dissociation to protect its stability when confronted with "otherness."

Self-reflective recognition of another's subjectivity has become a topic of great interest to contemporary clinicians, researchers, and theorists representing different analytic schools of thought. A central focus has been on how best to facilitate the cognitive symbolization of unprocessed affective experience–experience of the kind that Wilma Bucci (1997a) calls *subsymbolic*, that Donnel Stern (1997, 2009) conceptualizes as *unformulated*, that I see as dissociated, and if you add the context of memory, includes terms like *nondeclarative* and *procedural*. My view is that this kind of experience first becomes noticeable to the analyst as a *perceptual* phenomenon. Most often what the analyst first notices is some change in himself, though of course he may also notice a change in the patient, but this awareness does not in itself immediately bring with it a concomitant awareness that something is taking place *between* them. The reason for this has to do with what dissociation does to otherness: The ordinary links between symbolic and subsymbolic communication have been broken–at least for a while.

The essence of dissociation is that it alters perceptual experience–and thereby drains the interpersonal context of personal meaning. By unlinking the mind from the reflective perception of dyadic affective experience, a person is isolated from the danger of directly experiencing an other's "otherness." As soon as dissociation creates self-states that are proactively serving this protective function, selfhood becomes a sequestered cocoon regardless of what self-state it embodies at a given moment. The crucial point is that when coherence across self-states is replaced by a dissociative cocoon, the person exists in a state of consciousness in which he has insufficient simultaneous access to his range of self-states to allow authentic interchange with the subjectivity of others. Without self-state coherence he is only partially alive; other people are simply actors in whichever mental representation of reality defines the self-state that exists at the moment. Whatever the individual's state of dissociated reality may be, the person to whom he is relating will be interpersonally "tailored" to fit the image of the internal object that is necessary to insure affective stability.

"Mentalize This!"

Now let me tell you why the title of this chapter ends with an exclamation point: "Mentalize This!" is intended to signify the inevitability of collisions between subjectivities as intrinsic to a therapist's effort to do his job. It's my view that negotiation between collisions and safety is at the heart of psychotherapeutic change, and that the core issue underlying the therapeutic action of psychoanalysis, which includes the fostering of mentalization, resides in the analyst's commitment to the joint processing of collisions between subjectivities. It is a commitment that requires the analyst to be as attuned as possible to a patient's shifting equilibrium between affective safety and affective overload (especially in the area of developmental trauma), and the remainder of this chapter is going to address the issue of that shifting balance.

When I chose the title I hoped that most readers would have either seen or at least have heard about the film *Analyze This!* I thought it was likely because it was a really popular movie among therapists; most everyone I know who saw it enjoyed it, including me. And since I never can leave well enough alone, I have tried to think about why therapists tended to like the movie. The tagline of the film is "New York's most powerful gangster is about to get in touch with his feelings. *You* try telling him his 50 minutes are up." The title of the movie was of course spoofing the tradition that the analyst holds the high cards because his role is always deferred to by the patient. The fact that Robert De Niro, as patient, was also a Mafia Don, gave new meaning to the term *resistance.* It gave him the power, at any given moment, to level the playing field—at gunpoint. To his reluctant therapist, played by Billy Crystal, De Niro was "other" and vice versa. The two men were about as "other" as anyone could imagine. Neither had any familiarity with what went on in the mind of someone like the other, but for very different reasons they each needed the relationship to "work," thus giving each a reason to fear the other's potential power. Intersubjectivity did not yet exist; it would have to be earned, indeed fought for. Each started off behaving dissociatively, as if the other was an object to be "managed," because there was no common ground for intersubjective negotiation. Because the interpersonal threat that each attributed to the other was perceptually blotted out before it could become traumatic, their mental processes did not allow reflective relatedness. Thus, an interpersonal/relational impasse was created initially in which the two people could not reach each other intersubjectively. The price paid for this temporary safety was emotional deadness and relational stagnation because spontaneity was preempted by a need for predictability.

Translated into language I've used in previous writing (Bromberg, 1995a), Crystal and De Niro started as two solitary people in a large, empty ballroom, each trying to move as if dancing with the other, apparently oblivious to the absence of shared "music." At those moments one hears mainly the presence of the absent music—the palpable absence of the ineffable vitality that Khan (1971) writes is "heard with the eyes," the mysteriously alive melody of authentic self-experience that stems from the relational wholeness that Winnicott (1949) called psyche-soma. When this melody is missing, both the "lyrics" and the interpersonal context in which they are "sung" feel off because each partner in his own way has become more of a visitor than an inhabitant of his own psychosomatic existence. If and when the melody is restored, it becomes the music of intersubjectivity and infuses the lyrics of a deadened relationship with life.

A positive therapeutic outcome seemed unlikely, but, unexpectedly, something took place *between* De Niro and Crystal that made otherness and selfhood become negotiable. Each found the other's mind interesting in a way he had not anticipated and began to get curious about it. Also, each had a sense of humor, which modulated the degree to which they experienced one another only as a source of potential harm. Yet, the sense of potential harm remained acute: In Crystal's case, there was his fear of being murdered if he pushed the wrong button in De Niro; and for De Niro, the potential trauma was being forced to get in touch with dissociated feelings about his relationship with his father, and being flooded with shame if Crystal recognized his vulnerability.

One thing that made the film so delicious to me was that it had the felt rightness of a real therapy relationship, and a good one at that. Its rightness was independent of whether the boundaries of their relationship were untraditional. Their personal encounters were stormy and potentially dangerous, but they were both able to persevere even though each wanted to throw in the towel many times. At first it was De Niro who made the "hanging-in" possible because when he didn't like what was going on he didn't hold back verbally, which then forced Crystal into the open because hiding would have made things worse for him. Unexpectedly, De Niro's openness became infectious, and as this happened, each of them began to experience the other as a real person to whom he could relate personally rather than as an entity who was just saying things. For each one, the other became a person who was open to hearing and thinking about what he himself was experiencing, even though the other might not like it. In the language of my title, each began to confront the other's subjectivity with his own, as if to say, "Mentalize *this!*"

Collision and Negotiation

For me, the key moment took place when Crystal, as a therapist, confronted De Niro about hiding his feelings, and challenged him to face them. De Niro finally broke down sobbing, after which he turned to Crystal with a look on his face that though it started as pure murderous rage, slowly became shadowed with genuine admiration. Out of this "impossible" mix of self-states, De Niro delivered what is deservedly the most quoted line in the film:

"You … You … You're good! You're *really* good."

Crystal, not knowing if he was about to be shot for being so "good," stood there, mumbling disclaimers about his expertise, and looking as though he didn't know what De Niro meant. But De Niro persisted, and in that moment, they joined one another in cocreating, between their subjectivities, a new and potentially therapeutic reality within which coherence across self-states–the ability to "stand in the spaces"–began to replace the dissociative cocoon. What made a transition from the cocoon to eventual intersubjective communication possible was when De Niro's state of mind shifted from fear camouflaged as trust to a genuine coexistence of formerly unbridgeable aspects of self. Though one state was organized by rage and the other by admiration, both states were expressed authentically. Despite the fact that the two self-states did not yet cohere in the form of conflict and ambivalence, they were simultaneously contained as a mind/body phenomenon that was indeed expressible in the here and now. De Niro's masterful delivery of the opposite meanings contained in "You … You … You're good! You're *really* good," although initially confusing to Crystal, was what initiated the coconstruction of shared mental space in which their respective subjectivities would begin to communicate.

What I believe permits intersubjectivity to develop out of enactment, even at a moment such as this, is when the edge of dysregulation–what LeDoux (1996) calls the "fear system"–is activated under safe but not *too* safe conditions. When those conditions are present, the analytic relationship repeats the failures of a patient's past but does something more than just repeat them. The "something more" is what

facilitates increased coherence across self-states and allows an enactment to become the context for therapeutic growth in which something
new emerges out of what patient and analyst do in an unanticipated
way. I've called these unanticipated relational events "safe surprises"
(Bromberg, 2006a, pp. 94–95, 198–199) because it is only through surprise that a new reality–a space between spontaneity and safety–is
coconstructed and infused with an energy of its own. Edmund Burke
(1757) labeled this phenomenon as "safe shock."

> If the pain and terror are so modified as not to be actually nox-
> ious; if the pain is not carried to violence, and the terror is not
> conversant about the present destruction of the person ... they are
> capable of producing delight; not pleasure, but a sort of delight-
> ful horror, a sort of tranquility tinged with terror.... Its highest
> degree I call *astonishment*; the subordinate degrees are awe, rever-
> ence, and respect ... distinguished from positive pleasure. (p. 165)

It is that thin but negotiable line between unanticipated, containable
shock, and the unanticipated, uncontainable shock of trauma that
separates what is perceived as potentially overwhelming from what is
perceived as a safe surprise. The therapeutic process requires patient
and analyst to "stand, together, in the spaces between realities and
move safely, but not completely safely, back and forth across the
line" (Bromberg, 1999, p. 64). Something transformational took place
between Crystal and De Niro, which, because it was a safe surprise
rather than a traumatic shock, allowed them to begin to communicate
intersubjectively. What was it?

De Niro's reaction contained different emotions and the shadows of
different self-states in one facial expression and one tone of voice, but
these were not synthesized into a unitary self-experience that could
be experienced as intrapsychic conflict or named. So too for Crystal. But because the disjunctive mental states could coexist, neither
state had to be denied as real, which allowed the formation of a joint
mental space in which dissociation was sufficiently surrendered to
permit each person to reflect on the other's mind experiencing his
own, and for that experience to become amenable to negotiation.
For each person, the other became more than an object to be managed. The dyadic impact of a safe surprise is what allows an enactment
to be more than a repetition of the past as well as a central ingredient in the therapeutic facilitation of mentalization, or so I would
argue.

The analyst's ability to provide a safe environment is not in itself the source of therapeutic action. While the analyst must indeed be trying not to go beyond the patient's capacity to feel safe in the room, it is an inevitable impossibility for him to succeed, and it is because of this impossibility that therapeutic change can take place. Collisions between the analyst's and the patient's subjectivities reflect external-ized self-state differences in what is experienced as "reality" within the internal worlds of the patient and analyst, and there is no way to avoid these clashes of subjectivity without stifling the emergence of dissoci-ated self-states that need to find a voice.

Mentalization depends on whether an individual is able to experi-ence the other as holding him in mind, whether lovingly, agreeably, disagreeably, hatefully, or bewilderingly, to name just a few possi-bilities. Ronald Laing (1962) points out that "confirmation" of one's identity does not depend on the other's approval of you, but on their "recognition" of you, that is, their accurate perception of you as you experience yourself. In "Help! I'm Going Out of Your Mind" (Brom-berg, 1998c, pp. 309–328) I had previously explored the question of what makes being held in mind so important. Part of my answer has to do with the importance of attachment in assuring self-continuity.

A person's core self–the self that is shaped by early attachment patterns–is defined by who the parental objects both perceive him to be and deny him to be. That is, through relating to their child as though he is "such and such" and ignoring other aspects of him as if they don't exist, the parents "disconfirm" the relational existence of those aspects of the child's self that they perceptually dissociate. This makes the disconfirmed aspects of the child's self relationally nonnegotiable because the subjective experiences that organize those self-states can't be shared and compared, communicatively, with how they appear to another mind. The main point is that "disconfirma-tion," because it is relationally nonnegotiable, is traumatic by defini-tion and I believe accounts for much of what we call developmental trauma, or as it's sometimes named, "relational trauma."

My interest in developmental trauma has always been more involv-ing than my interest in massive trauma–by which I mean the kind of gross invasion of mind and body associated with mental, physical, and sexual abuse or with the kind of sudden, unanticipated, and unspeak-able horror to which New Yorkers were subjected on September 11, 2001. I've worked with people who have been through each kind of trauma and have found that individuals who came to me because of having suffered massive trauma in adulthood, but who also had

a developmental history of pronounced disconfirmation, were typically more debilitated by the later event than were victims of adult-
onset trauma who did not have such a developmental history. I've also
observed that an individual who has a background of developmental
trauma is more likely, eventually, to become a "difficult patient" even
if he doesn't start out that way. No matter how successful that person
may be in certain areas of his life, and no matter how well put together
he may seem when first meeting him, you can be sure there is more
there than meets the eye.

Just a few more words about how I account for this. For every
human being, the preservation of self-continuity has the highest evolutionary priority. Everyone, to one extent or another, will continue
to preserve the procedurally learned early attachment patterns upon
which his core self rests in order to be recognizable as "himself" in all
circumstances and during all phases of life. Why? Because the way
any person is seen in the mind of an "other" must reflect the core self
that was "his parent's child." For most people the need to be their
parents' child evolves during the process of living, and is reshaped so
that the relational patterns defining the core self are built upon, modified, and integrated into a configuration of individuality that is largely
nondissociative.

However, if parts of the self were systematically disconfirmed early
in life, the task of continuing to exist in the mind of another person
(and thereby in his own eyes) as the same self that was "his parent's
child" is a much more complicated and difficult task because it includes
having to dissociate those self-states that are disjunctive with it. Those
parts tend to remain cognitively unsymbolized. They are organized as
islands of affective reality that cannot be modified by conflict resolution because they are sequestered. But they have a life of their own, a
life that shapes a person's destiny at least as much as, and often more
than, the "me" that can be thought about and put into words. The "not-
me" parts of self must become amenable to self-reflection by being
cognitively and linguistically symbolized in a relational context before
they can become part of what the person feels as "me."

Until that happens, the "not-me" parts continue to hang around
and enact dissociatively what cannot be thought or said, making
trouble both for the patient and for people in his life. Because they
are affect-driven voices from parts of the self that were disconfirmed relationally, their presence is communicated without a shared
cognitive context that could allow the affect to develop consensually
negotiated meaning.

Enactment is a process that takes place in what I think of as a "cocoon built for two," and it certainly is not unique to the analytic relationship. A patient has had plenty of experience with it before ever meeting his analyst, but it is in the analytic relationship that there is finally a chance to make use of it in a new way. Because it is dissociated, it pulls both patient and analyst into it like a pair of moths drawn to a flame. Each person is insulated from intersubjectivity, at least for a while. This leads almost inevitably to repetitive collisions between the patient's subjectivity and that of the analyst, but because the repetitions are nonlinear they hold a powerful therapeutic potential–the potential to generate a process of relational negotiation that becomes increasingly intersubjective in that there is room for newness.

A therapeutic posture that systematically tries to avoid collisions of subjectivities is eventually experienced by a patient as disconfirming. The patient feels that the analyst is not really holding him in mind. He comes to feel this because the analyst is not feeling *personally* the impact of the dissociated parts of the patient's self that are trying to find relational existence. Because the analyst is not reacting personally to them, the patient's dissociated self-states are robbed of a human context in which to be recognized and come alive. And it is by their coming alive that mentalization best occurs.

The De Niro/Crystal example brings this into high relief. At the most productive point in their relationship, each was communicating affectively, not just in words, that he was holding the other in mind; each was demonstrating by his personal reaction to the other that the other's state of mind was recognized. Although this created anxiety in both of them, it permitted them to process together what was taking place in the here and now. Yes, it was "edgy." It could have resulted in their breaking apart at any point, which for Crystal literally meant "termination." But it didn't. The fact that it didn't isn't my main point, however. My main point is that what did happen led to a stronger intersubjective connection that allowed the "danger of breaking apart" to become itself amenable to dialogue. It is equivalent to what we see as a patient's growing ability to "work in the transference."

The point of the De Niro/Crystal vignette is not that mentalization is all about confrontation, but rather that the therapeutic process of increasing a patient's capacity for mentalization invariably entails collisions between the patient's and analyst's subjectivities. The balance between affective safety and seeing ourselves as others see us is a constantly shifting one, and it is the analyst's attunement to these shifts, not the proper application of technique, confrontative or otherwise, that allows increased mentalization to take place. The best work is always done when collisions happen unexpectedly because the process of negotiation that increases mentalization is much more experience-near. Let me show you what I mean through some case material.

Roseanne

My patient, Roseanne, is a woman whose sense of self had been badly damaged in childhood by a disturbed, sadistic father who took pleasure in acting as if there was something wrong with her mind to think that someone as loving as he would ever want to hurt her. Those who remember the Charles Boyer/Ingrid Bergman film will know what I mean when I say she had been systematically "gaslighted." Attachment theorists would describe Roseanne as a prime example of the disorganized/disoriented type of attachment–extremely dissociative, with a vulnerability to annihilation anxiety that was apparent from day one.

The vignette that follows is about something that happened between us some 4 years into our work, at a point when I had become angry with her but did not recognize the extent of it, which is a central issue in the vignette. I knew consciously only about my growing "impatience" with Roseanne's state of hopelessness, particularly because it seemed to become most vocal at the very moments I felt real progress was being shown. At such times, her hopelessness felt almost spiteful– an insistence that she was exactly the same as she had always been, that what happened was nothing new, and that analysis had changed nothing. In the face of what I saw as ample evidence of her growth, I was feeling more and more helpless, and uncomfortable about it. I could sense another part of her trying to find a voice, but my efforts to enable it to speak were always greeted with both hopelessness and bewilderment about my crazy misunderstanding. I did not at that time see the ghost of "Daddy" hovering over me because I was experiencing her "hopeless self" *only* as getting in my way, and I was telling myself that the more hopeful part of Roseanne that was being masked at those moments would emerge if I did not bully it into silence. Put simply, I felt that if I did not respond to the hopeless part of her she would stop using it as what I preferred to believe was a mask to hide another part that I liked better and that supposedly was more authentic. Or so I felt. As you'll hear, my fantasy of "unmasking"

Roseanne was to apply equally to me, as we entered an intense new phase of our ongoing enactment.

The incident took place about 15 minutes into a session, after she had reported an encounter that, to me, showed a clear ability to trust people more than she acknowledged. Just as I was thinking about whether to say something about that, she began speaking in her predictably hopeless voice about the futility of ever trusting anyone to take care of her because eventually they would use her for their own deceitful purposes. At that moment I said something I'm sure I wouldn't have if I had been able to predict what was to follow.

I was feeling, once again, that I had been tantalized and then deprived. But knowing her history with her sadistic father, I was always concerned about triggering affective flooding if I addressed anything in our relationship that she could hear as an accusation. This time, as if by magic, a story popped into my mind–a story I had heard many years before but had never forgotten. Somehow it felt like the perfect metaphor to capture this moment with Roseanne, and I even told myself that because it was a metaphor she and I could "play" with it without risking what might happen if I spoke about the two of us directly. I didn't recognize how closely this "metaphor" literally overlapped her dissociated internal reality; nor did I come close to being suspicious about its sudden appearance in my mind. So, with great equanimity, I delivered it.

The story was so penetratingly identical to the reality of some dreaded "not-me" parts of her that she had no time to protect herself when it emerged so suddenly from my mouth. At one level the story is about sadism, and my telling it at all, much less so unexpectedly, certainly contained sadism on my part. However, it also pulled me more deeply into the already longstanding enactment between us, only this time I was not able to avoid getting dirty as a player in Roseanne's internal drama. Unlike her real father, I was to know first-hand what being abusive felt like. I *became* that object. I didn't just "understand" her sense of futility about ever trusting anyone to take care of her because eventually they would use her for their own deceitful purposes; I recognized from her point of view the function it served because I could feel personally the value to Roseanne of always being vigilant. I had been experiencing her "hopeless self" as *only* a spoiler because it had become noxious to me, but now I also knew its "user-value." Now to the "story."

I said to Roseanne that there was something about her image of hopelessness in being "taken care of" by another person that made me think of a story I once heard about a little girl who was told by her father that she was going to receive something very special on her next birthday, 10 months from then, but she was not to know what it was and mustn't ask. Being a very good girl, she kept herself from looking in the closet and most certainly did not ask Daddy any questions. But 10 months was such a long time. Nevertheless, the day did arrive and the little girl was filled with great excitement. She could hardly sit still. Sure enough, Daddy entered the room holding a very large box that was wrapped in gold paper and tied with a bright red ribbon and bow. It was so beautiful! "Daddy! Daddy! Can I open it now?"

"No," replied Daddy.

"But why? I've been so good!"

"I told you that you are not to know what it is and that you mustn't ask. That hasn't changed. Some day, when the time is right, you will be allowed to open the box. Meanwhile, we will put it in the closet just as it is, and you can look at the box anytime you want to." The good little girl was disappointed beyond words, but she knew better than to protest.

Four years went by. (Yes, I was unaware it was the exact length of time that Roseanne and I had been working together.) Several times a week she went to the closet and gazed hopefully at the box as if somehow it might open itself if she wished hard enough. Then one day, she did something she never thought possible; she went to the closet and took the box down from the shelf. Closing her eyes and holding her breath because the excitement was so great, she tore off the red bow, ripped off the beautiful gold paper, and opened the box. It was empty!

Roseanne's face contorted into a mask of horror. Her body seemed to shrink until it was almost lost in the chair in which she sat, and her clothes looked like a masquerade outfit—a costume of adult sophistication covering a bewildered and terrified child. I experienced her as recoiling from my "story" as if it were an instrument of torture. Her voice became a plaintive whimper. Her entire being had changed; to say that she became frightened is to deny the full impact of the experience. It was more than simply a shift in affect. She *was* the child of her sadistic father; and I, at that moment, *was* the father of that child.

I heard myself as if I was a character in a play mouthing a line that went, "I'm sorry I scared you, and I can see my story wasn't a good idea, and blah, blah, blah," but I knew I had lost all feeling of relatedness and was just trying to do "the right thing" by finding the right words. But just at the point when the "right words" were starting to fail me, the terrified child was gone as suddenly as she had appeared, leaving me in a state of consternation.

What came over me at that moment I don't have language for, but something reconnected me with my human feelings. Perhaps it was similar to what Ronald Laing (1962, pp. 95–96) described when a woman he was treating perceived his emotional withdrawal and said in a very small voice, "Oh, please don't go so far away from me." Laing wrote that each of the "right" therapeutic responses he could think of felt distant and inhuman, and that the only thing he could say to his patient was "I am sorry."

Well, that's what I said at that moment, but this time I said it because I meant it. I wanted the part of her that was technically no longer there, but whom I felt had to be still listening, to hear me as well. I told her I saw a very little girl come out, with horror on her face, and that even though she went back inside, I did see her come out. I said that if she was listening I wanted her to know that I was sorry I scared her. I said that I could understand her being scared because it was so different from anything I usually say to her, and that I had said it so suddenly that of course it shocked her, which was not a good thing for me to do. She had been holding her breath while I was talking, and when I paused, she exhaled, nodded to me that she had heard what I said, and the session ended on that note.

Roseanne appeared for her next session with a distinctly malicious gleam in her eye. "Admit it," she needled. "You didn't know what happened last time, and you didn't know what to do, and you were trying to hide it. But you couldn't and it's killing you. I want it to kill you! I want to rip you open so you can't hide anything. I want to live inside you. I want to feel your heart beat so I can feel mine beat. I know you're thinking right now! Stop thinking! I *hate* your mind."

"I'm not feeling too good about it myself, right now," I replied. I told her that I could see now how I was taking care of her as a patient in the same way her father took care of her as a child.

"Yeah," she replied, much to my relief, "That's how my father always took care of me. Nothing felt real, and I thought that was normal. I'm always forgiving him, but your story was too close. Everything he gave me I had to suffer for, and in the end it was only an empty box. When you told me the story, part of me got the point right away and appreciated what you were trying to do; but if I showed you that, it would be like admitting you were right, that I could see how I was treated, and worse, I could see that maybe it's how I treat you. And then I wouldn't be able to stay in a safe place anymore. I don't know if I'm really less stuck now, but I know you want it to be true so you *act* like it's true.

You act like it's me who feels it, when it's really you. It makes me crazy … well, maybe not crazy anymore, just confused."

I mumbled something like, "Just because someone who matters thinks he knows what's right for you doesn't make it true; but that's a new thought and you don't trust it, so it's even more scary to have it."

Over the next months we continued processing this event together, and the increase in my own range of consciousness allowed me to access and to speak with her about an aspect of my experience that I was becoming more and more aware of. I told her I had been think-ing about what might have been going on with me that allowed me to tell her that story without thinking at all about what it would be like for her to hear it. I told her that I've begun to realize I was releasing myself from something I hadn't even been aware I felt trapped by. I told her that in recent months, it had become more and more difficult for me to squash my own excitement about what I could see taking place in our work. I felt her growth, and felt more and more entitled to have it openly acknowledged so that I didn't have to always keep my good feelings about it pushed down inside me. I said that I also realize now, that in the last months before that session, I had begun to question whether my total commitment to taking care of her safety was keeping me from … here I paused. I was going to say "keeping me from being myself" but what came out was, "keeping me from having a birthday party, and getting a present that I'm allowed to open. *You* know what present I mean."

"Sure I do. The present was for me to tell you that I was getting bet-ter. Do you blame *me* that you didn't get the present?" I said that I *had* blamed her, but I didn't realize it because I didn't want to see myself as so needy. I told her I was remembering that for months before that ses-sion I had been making a lot of seemingly innocent comments about her growth and her new potential that probably were hints about the present I felt I should get. She said she knew that, but had "forgot-ten" it because she hated me when I did that and wanted to hurt me. I replied that maybe the way she tried to hurt me was to make me feel helpless like her parents did to her, and that I did often feel foolish about my excitement when she told me I was being "crazy."

In the following months we began to look together at not only my contribution, but also at hers, and the more we spoke the more our minds constructed cognitive meaning that was made real by being linked to affective meaning. She could at last begin to think and feel her personal history into the here and now, rather than just feel it somati-cally in her body. She began to reflect on her past and comprehend what she had needed to do to her mind and her ability to feel alive in order to cope with what had been too much to bear.

She spoke about her fear that if she acknowledged any change, I would try to take it over. I offered the possibility that as I felt more and more constrained, I became, without realizing it, little Roseanne– needing to break free of *my* "good girl" self and she became more and more her controlling father. I was finally able to say to her that my bursting out at that moment was not only coming from needing to "be myself" but from actually hating a part of her that behaved as if I was her father wearing his "nice guy" mask. "Well, the truth is," I said, "I did want to feel like a nice person. It was a shock to realize that what led me to scare you was hatefulness that had been eating away at me little by little, and I hadn't even known it was there."

"Good!" she retorted. "Remember when I told you I hated your mind? That I needed you to feel and stop thinking? That I wanted to rip you open and live inside you? Remember? So why wouldn't you feel eaten away little by little?" And then she added with a wicked giggle, "If I ate you all at once there wouldn't be anyone left to love."

Coda

I've found the concept of mentalization so compatible with my own perspective that I want to end by drawing from the first of the two seminal "Playing with Reality" papers published by Fonagy and Target in 1996. There the authors remind us of how easy it is

> to overlook the fact that the child may only be able to reflect on thoughts and feelings about real-life events during play if an adult is there to provide a necessary frame, and insulate him or her from the compelling character of external reality. The very young child's understanding of minds may be developmentally advanced in play, because of the segregation of this from external reality, and the avoidance of the sense of encroachment that they otherwise experience between thought and reality. (pp. 220–221)

Fonagy and Target also discuss the developmental need of the child to make a gradual transition from separating the "psychic equivalent mode" and the "pretend mode" of reality to synthesizing them. Dangers lurk. For the young child, Fonagy and Target write, "the difference between the equivalent and pretend mode has to be clearly marked.... If this is not ensured, it quickly becomes clear just how threatening the isomorphism of internal and external realities can become for the child" (p. 220). This last point touches directly on why, for Roseanne, the separate existence of my mind became too terrifying for her at that moment, and accounts for her felt wish to "cannibalize" my mind and know it from the inside. She could not, to use Fonagy and Target's words, "play with reality." This also helps clarify why my "empty box" story led to triggering her terror, which, for the moment, increased her dissociated reliance on the hypervigilant, "mistrustful" self to protect the various "child" parts.

To illustrate their view of how threatening the overlap of internal and external realities can become for a child, Fonagy and Target (1996) provide a lovely vignette from normal development, with which I will end the chapter:

> A 4-year-old boy was read a ghost story by his mother. Although the story was not expected to be particularly frightening, he was visibly shaken by it. The mother quickly offered a reassurance: "Don't worry, Simon, it didn't really happen." The child, clearly feeling misunderstood, protested in reply: "*But when you read it, it did really happen to me!*" (p. 220)

4

Minding the Dissociative Gap[1]

CR The gap between interpersonal/relational and classical schools of thought does not separate the clinicians in each community into separate groups, with each group holding a homogenously distinct version of the respective theory in which it was trained. Good clinicians are good clinicians no matter what their family of origin. But attachment bonds do influence how far a clinician can freely depart from the concepts and language of the theory–the "grown-up words" (see chapter 7) that originally shaped those bonds. What I want to write about is not the gap between different schools of thought but what I as an interpersonal/relational analyst believe to be the element that most needs to be addressed currently by all analysts. This element is the "dissociative gap" that is an inherent part of the treatment process. My own conviction, it will be noted, is that this element is addressed most felicitously from an interpersonal/relational perspective. Am I biased? Sure! But that's part of the reason for this chapter and the subsequent chapters that interface with it. There is no true dialogue that does not emerge from some collision between subjectivities, so let me begin.

The school of "relational" psychoanalysis was not born of a single seminal theorist or homogeneous group of theorists from which tributaries then evolved, diverged, or remained loyal, and its theories are

---

[1]This chapter materially expands and revises an earlier version published in *Contemporary Psychoanalysis*, *44*, 2010, 329–350. My thanks to the Program Committee of the New York Psychoanalytic Society and Institute for sponsoring the February 28, 2009 conference, "Minding the Gap," at which the original version was presented. My special thanks to Lois Oppenheim for her vision, dedication, and skill in making the conference possible.

thereby not subject to evaluation by their degree of deviation from orthodoxy. Freud, Klein, Ferenczi, Fairbairn, Winnicott, Sullivan, and Kohut are all important parental figures but none carries parental authority. The range of theory, moreover, is extremely diverse because the value accorded a given concept or system of concepts derived from any given figure is more clinically than theoretically determined.

The term *relational* was originally coined by Greenberg and Mitchell (1983) in their groundbreaking book, *Object Relations in Psychoanalytic Theory*. The exact term *relational psychoanalysis* then emerged by consensus at a meeting of a small group of analysts led by Stephen Mitchell, at which I was present. The name was selected for two reasons: It clearly and concisely represented the core viewpoint that united us, namely that the human mind, its normal development, its pathology, and the process of its therapeutic growth are relationally configured; at the same time, the term was not so conceptually specific that it would convey adherence to one given set of ideas. The further designation *interpersonal/relational* that I and many of my colleagues have since come to use to delineate the contours of our analytic identity explicitly honors the contributions of both Harry Stack Sullivan and object-relational thinking. It also makes plain that the concept of relational is not equivalent to *object-relational* nor are the two terms interchangeable. Interpersonal/relational is in its own way a tribute to the capacities of both the relational school and the interpersonal school to welcome the distinct identities of their individual members.

The gap between the classical and interpersonal/relational communities, as I see it, is currently held in place largely because classical conflict theory, even in its contemporary version (Brenner, 1976), constrains classically trained analysts from bilateral *participation* in the clinical relationship. This limitation, in turn, minimizes their opportunity for encountering, perceptually, what I hold as intrinsic to the nature of mental functioning—the self-state structure of the mind and the dissociative processes that are always in a dialectical relationship with the presence and absence of intrapsychic conflict. This is not an "anti-Freudian" position. I, too, believe that facilitating a patient's capacity to experience and resolve internal conflict is enhanced as part of the therapeutic action of psychoanalysis. My brief is with perpetuating a theory of mind that explains the analyst's role as though conflict were *always* organizing mental functioning even when the patient cannot experience it, and that a patient's defenses against recognizing its existence will inevitably give way to interpretation—if the patient is analyzable.

I believe that until Freudian theory foundationally includes the centrality of self-states and dissociation, classically trained analysts (including the most skilled clinicians) will continue to spend too much of their time trying to "make their point the hard way." Every craps shooter knows that expression, but for those who haven't been lucky enough to lead a misspent youth, in simplified terms it means one is betting that when the shooter's point is an even number, he will make it by the two dice showing identical values—so, betting on a "hard 6," for example, is betting that the dice will come up 3 and 3. It is called the "hard" way for the obvious reason that the probability of making the point that way is lower. When you win, you beat the odds and get a bigger payoff, and you of course feel it was a good bet. But you do lose more times than you care to remember. I'm pretty sure the reader knows by now where I'm going with this: An *analyst* is making his point "the hard way" when he bets that, if he continues to refine his interpretations, his patient will finally "get" what he is saying as emotional insight, not just as intellectual insight, and that the two dice—his interpretation and his patient's new understanding—will finally match.

That said, a summary of my view of mental functioning will provide the context for discussing how I think and work clinically. In previous writing (Bromberg, 1998, 2006a), I have presented a view of the mind as organized by an ever-shifting, dissociative relationship between self-state configurations that are more or less able to participate in the mental experience of internal conflict when called forth. I believe this to be the normal process of mental functioning, but it is anything but smooth. I am speaking not just of the dramatically visible use of dissociation we find in people who as children suffered "big-T" trauma such as sexual abuse or violence. I am speaking of the more subtly protective dissociation caused by developmental trauma—the trauma of nonrecognition that is an inevitable part of everyone's early life to one degree or another. In response to the trauma of nonrecognition, dissociative process becomes dissociative structure, at least in certain areas of mental functioning. The normal hypnoid gap between self-states becomes rigidified into a brain/mind early-warning system designed to protect against the potential for *future* affective destabilization. Self-states move from being separate but collaborative to being inhospitable and even adversarial, sequestered from one another as islands of "truth," each functioning as an insulated version of reality that protectively defines what is "me" at a given moment and forcing other self-states that are inharmonious with its truth to become "not-me" and unavailable to participate in the complex negotiation we call internal conflict.

In any analytic relationship, not-me self-states are dissociated by both patient and analyst and are enacted between them without cognitive representation. Each partner, through his or her way of being with the other (no matter what that way is), is affectively reacting to some part of what is taking place between them that lacks symbolic representation as an interpersonal event. When the work is going well, the individual affective reactions of each partner are jointly subsumed within a process of *mutual* knowing or "state-sharing" (Schore, 2003b) that not only is therapeutic in its own right but deepens and enriches the opportunity for symbolic processing, *cognitively and linguistically*, of each partner's "not-me" experience–thus allowing the greatest potential for new self-meaning to emerge and endure.

This image of therapeutic action is based on a view of mental functioning different from one based on an assumption that the patient's unconscious mental content, when it becomes sufficiently inferable by the analyst to be offered as an interpretation, will be available to insight if the patient's ego defenses against the insight are themselves properly interpreted. The focus of ongoing attention in my own listening stance is on the shifting states of mind that organize the content at any given moment, not on content per se. Active involvement with self-state shifts–one's own and the other person's–increasingly permits each partner's here-and-now self-experience to engage in a perceptual encounter with his or her not-me states, a process that could be called "minding the dissociative gap." But what about interpretation? I believe that the optimal utilization of interpreted meaning rests on a patient's "me" and "not-me" states' first becoming more at home with each other through the negotiation of enacted otherness during collisions of subjectivity between patient and analyst. This is what allows the inch-by-inch surrender of a self-cure that is worse than the illness–the automatic triggering of a dissociative mental structure that bypasses self-reflection.

As I see it, the therapeutic action entailed in the dissolution of this mental structure addresses the very mind/brain phenomenon that originated it and holds it in place. Reducing the mind's fear of otherness simultaneously reduces fear of affect dysregulation in the brain's neural networks (see next chapter). Through this shared minding of the dissociative gap, the automatic neurosynaptic warning signal that triggers immediate dissociation as a protection against potentially destabilizing hyperarousal becomes more selective at the *brain* level and, through a feedback loop, allows the patient's *mind* to support increased development of intersubjectivity. Little by little, the patient's potential to bear internal conflict is increased by easing the mental struggle to hold it cognitively. For a classical psychoanalyst, taking this perspective seriously does not lead to abandoning Freud, but it does lead to a different listening stance. It requires listening to clinical process not only dyadically, but also as an inherently confusing experiential event to be explored together, rather than as material to be "figured out," that is, organized by the analyst into something he deems coherent and then made available for potential interpretation. When the analyst's experience and the patient's experience don't "add up," this becomes a feature of the data rather than a feature of the patient.

Mayer (2007) has explored a domain of what she terms "anomalous experiences." These involve perceptions that are veridical but occur in a context that make them seemingly inexplicable within what we deem reality. Mayer makes the intellectually exciting case, however, that what makes these experiences "anomalous" is the frame of understanding that we bring to them. This brings her to consider the paradox that we may need different modes of thought to understand different kinds of experience. I see the same paradox as operative in the office as the analyst attempts to hold, as versions of a single reality, his patient's experience and his own, particularly when they are too disjunctive to accommodate both of them simultaneously. Mayer describes "anomalous" experience as the essence of paradox. In her words:

> *The perceptions that characterize potentially anomalous experience appear to emerge from a state of mind that is, in the moment of perception, radically incompatible with the state of mind in which perceptions characterizing rational thought are possible.* The mode of perception ... is a mode that depends on access to a state of mind in which ordinary linear thought is momentarily impossible, literally suspended. (p. 137, emphasis in original)

By my lights, this leap beyond linear thought exemplifies the key distinction between working with paradox and interpreting conflict resistance. When both experiences, the patient's and the analyst's, cannot be rational for the same mind at the same time, the analyst's acceptance of his own lack of clarity becomes an inherent source of therapeutic action by allowing the partners to participate in creatively accepting the contradictory realities within a paradoxical analytic field without the analyst's imposing his own need for clarity by invoking the concept of resistance to conflict. Through this joint process in which rational thought is temporarily suspended, the gradual creation of a "relational unconscious" becomes possible, empathy has its deepest meaning, and interpretation can then ultimately find a useful place. A relational unconscious belongs to both persons but to neither alone, and writing about it is no easy task. Adrienne Harris (2004, 2009) is one of the rare psychoanalytic authors to capture its essence as a concept by making it descriptively vivid as a clinical phenomenon—one that is inherently timeless, inherently dyadic, and inherently psychodynamic. She writes:

> The past, its representations, internal and interpersonal, is not a museum but a living program for action and being with self and others. ... An experience of presentness ... is being built out of both our experiences of limit. ... [T]ime moves in manifold directions, unspooling the past in order to create particular imagined futures. ... Clinical momentum is possible when a space/time matrix opens in the analyst and when the tumble into the abyss is genuinely possible. [T]he idea that death and mobility are so intimately connected seems very much *the essential working paradox and the engine of psychoanalytic work.* (2009, p. 19, emphasis added)

I hope it is relatively easy to see the self/other sensibility that links Mayer's image of *paradoxical suspension of rational thought* and Harris's argument that the engine of psychoanalytic work is an *essential working paradox that death and mobility are intimately connected by facing the abyss together.* In what follows I try to delineate some of the central clinical phenomena that become observable through this frame of reference and why they must be observed perceptually and not inferentially. Some schematic examples illustrate this dyadic process as it takes place in my analytic work.

Clinical Issues

Sudden Changes in "Topic"

If an analyst is listening carefully he will often be aware that a sudden change in "topic" is accompanied by a change in self-presentation, including affect but by no means limited to it. From my frame of reference, what is taking place is defined neither by the change in topic nor the change in affect but a switch in self-states and in the respective realities that organize them. One's clinical ear hears the voice of another part of self and has the opportunity to invite it into relationship by accepting it in its own terms rather than talking about it as though the part that has just emerged is simply a change in mood. For those who are not yet totally at home with how the concept of self-state is different from a shift in affect or mood, let me offer a one-sentence clarification: Self-states are highly individualized modules of being, each configured by its own organization of cognitions, beliefs, dominant affect and mood, access to memory, skills, behaviors, values, actions, and regulatory physiology.

When all has gone well developmentally, each self-state is compatible enough with the modes of being that are held by other self-states to allow overarching coherence across self-states, which in turn creates the capacity for sustaining the experience of internal conflict. In treatment, however, when proactively protective dissociation is operating, self-state shifts are most likely to reach the analyst's perceptual awareness if he is able to freely engage his patient from the stance of participant-observer. Or so I contend. Why should this be the case? Because the shifts may be discerned initially not as something in the patient, but as a destabilization of the analyst's own mental processes, an awareness of discomfort that he does not immediately recognize is a discomfort that is linking him to his patient through a dissociative enactment that is taking place *while* they are participating at a verbal level.

Misleading Use of Conflict Language

A patient may misleadingly appear to be conflicted when she is actually dissociated because she will use conflict language to maintain her attachment bond with the analyst. She may say, for example, that she is trying hard to feel one thing *instead of* another thing but can't seem to get it right. The phrase "instead of" is conflict language and, when dissociation is defining mental processes at a given moment, one part of the patient is attempting to secure her bond with the analyst by speaking as if her task were to obliterate another part of herself as sick and replace it with a "healthy" part, the part that she feels the analyst is currently encouraging to emerge. As part of my own way of working I might address this by saying something like the following:

There is something in the way you put this that made me have
a thought I want to share with you. I'm feeling the presence of
another part of you behind the scenes that doesn't like what
I just said and that you are trying to keep our relationship safe
by staying away from those unruly feelings. [Pt: "?"] I guess what
I was most in touch with when you spoke was that you seemed
somewhat afraid and were apologizing for not being the patient
I needed you to be. [Pt: "?"] Sometimes, without realizing it,
I am showing preference for one part of you over another and I
think I just did. Actually, I do want to hear from *both* parts of you,
especially because they don't get along with each other. [Pt: "?"]
Well, when you said you were trying hard to feel free *instead of*
afraid but can't seem to get it right, I felt you were experiencing
the noisy disagreement between the two parts of yourself as too
much for you right then and wanted be sure that I knew you were
trying to be freer even though you were scared. [Pt: "?"] Great
question! The best I can describe how I see the parts is to say that
the part of you who is talking to me right now wants to respond
to life freely and wholeheartedly, but another part of you is concerned *only* with trying to keep you emotionally safe. The other
part feels that you are leading yourself into danger because it is
convinced that you will forget to protect yourself from what it is
sure is the inevitable moment of the rug being pulled out from
under you when you don't expect it. That part makes you feel
you are being stupid when you begin to trust feeling safe, which
is why when you do feel yourself getting stronger and more hopeful it is so hard to let the feeling continue. The reason that you
feel that you can't seem to get it right is that the different parts
have different agendas about what is good for you, and each part
is absolutely sure that it knows the whole truth and the other is
wrong. [Pt: "!!"] *Sure* it gives you a headache to think about. We
did a lot today and there is plenty of time to come back to it when
your mind feels more relaxed." [Pt: "?"] Oh, you have another
question before we stop for today. Okay. [Pt: "?"] The part that
wants you to feel afraid when you start to feel spontaneous is not
just trying to ruin your life but is trying to keep you from feeling
emotionally overwhelmed if you let yourself trust someone and
then without warning you find that you made a horrible mistake
and it is too late. That part isn't an enemy. It is trying to protect you from something that happened a long time ago which
it believes will always happen. Each part is actually contributing

something you need, but because right now each wants to ignore the other, they can't collaborate. In fact, neither part can ever obliterate the other because both are you. Our job is to get them to work together. Little by little we will help you feel both parts *at the same time* so they can talk to each other without making noise in your head. Do you know what I mean? [Pt: "?!"] Well, do you *sort-of* know what I mean?

This is one possible example of "minding the dissociative gap." The analyst shares his experience of what he feels is going on, not because he knows what it portends, but because he doesn't, which means he continuously needs the patient's input.

Resistance?

Another situation frequently encountered is one in which a patient, after a productive session that seemingly was satisfying to both parties, returns the next session in an oppositional state–angry, accusatory, remote, despairing, or even ready to quit treatment. Analysts are often taken aback emotionally even if they are conceptually sophisticated enough to accommodate it within their own theoretical frame of reference. The fallback position for most classical analysts is to see this phenomenon as a form of transference resistance, and to attempt an interpretation within the framework of defense analysis, that is, as a defense against unconscious conflict. Most often this tack gets nowhere and usually makes things worse. Why?

My answer is that the patient's self that is *now* a participant was present as a dissociated not-me self-state during the previous "good" session and did not exist in it relationally. The not-me part of self that existed dissociatively was ignored in the prior session but is now here in vivid color. To this self, the seeming success of the analyst's interpretations during the previous session was anything but useful. Now, no longer not-me, this part of the patient is a participant and is attacking *because* the other part implied by its self-reflective behavior that the analyst was trustworthy enough to instill some hope–hope that the patient wouldn't be stuck forever in a life of fear, mistrust, and perpetual vigilance. In other words, both the analyst and the part of the patient that the analyst personally likes best are being attacked as having participated in a terrible session–a session in which the part of the patient being named a "defense" felt dismissed and of no value to the therapist, thus making it want to boycott the treatment. But what is the big crime that the analyst and the patient's "good" self have committed? It is the "crime" of having compromised the seamlessness, and perhaps even the integrity, of the patient's dissociative mental structure. When the fail-safe protective system is softened by a moment of genuine self-reflectiveness, the parts of the self that are the guardians of affective stability become outraged, and the part that holds the unprocessed affect of developmental trauma caused by attachment failure becomes fearful, depressed, or both, causing distress to all parts—for which the therapist's idea of "success" is then blamed.

From the vantage point of conflict theory, it is often at that moment that some analysts do something seemingly reasonable that is intended to set the stage for what they hope will be the most potentially powerful transference interpretation they can offer but that more frequently makes things worse. The analyst commences what Kernberg calls "interpreting the splitting" (see Caligor et al., 2009)—an intervention Kernberg sees as particularly apt for "borderline" personality disorders. Whether or not an analyst, consciously or unconsciously, evaluates or reevaluates his patient as borderline is not the point. He acts as if she were and challenges the patient with avoiding conflict. The analyst uses as evidence the patient's inconsistency from session to session and interprets the presumed dynamic. The implication is that the patient is "speaking out of both sides of her mouth." For the patient, however, "inconsistency" has no frame of reference as long as dissociation is operating. Only *one* "side of the patient's mouth" can exist experientially at any given time, turning the analyst's well-meaning use of conflict language into a suddenly bewildering attack on her affective stability that threatens her highly vulnerable, attachment-organized core sense of self. The patient's struggle to contain hyperaroused affect in the here-and-now relational experience increases her use of dissociation at that point so as to prevent a complete rupture of attachment, and her capacity to think clearly is often compromised.

Even worse, some patients may act as if they were seeing the light and finally "get it." From my perspective, because the patient's hippocampus and frontal cortex (see Bromberg, 2006b, pp. 181–189) are not processing as conflict what is taking place between patient and analyst, the analyst's use of conflict language widens the dissociative gap both interpersonally and within the self-state organization of the patient. Transference interpretations (including "interpretations of splitting") that continue to be offered in the face of a strong dissociative process are unresponsive to the patient's shame-ridden need for affective safety in the immediate relational experience. It is simply too much for the patient to hold the shame experience and represent it cognitively, so, when a patient responds to interpretation with a bewildered stare and a comment like, "I lost you," the reply is very understandable (not to mention its being a deliciously accurate attachment metaphor).

Concreteness of Thinking

A slightly different sort of indicator that a patient's thought processes are dissociatively "off-line" is a sudden increase in the concreteness of his or her thinking. This is most often observed by a rigid focus on the *content* of the analyst's interpretation, accompanied by complete obliviousness to the patient's experience of the *person* who offered it. In other words, the patient's here-and-now experience of the interaction with the one who made the interpretation is drained of *personal* meaning because the patient has "checked out" relationally even though the analyst's *words* were "understood."

State Dependent Memory

The issue of memory is possibly more pertinent than any other in demonstrating that mental functioning is inherently a dialectic between dissociation and conflict and cannot justifiably be seen as based on conflict alone. When dissociation is operating, memory is organized by the way something is known more than whether it is or is not remembered per se. For instance, a patient frequently will come in for a session and say, "I forgot what we talked about yesterday. I think it was something about ..." The previous session was not literally forgotten. The patient remembers *about* it, but does not remember *it.* He or she does not remember *it* because memory is state dependent, particularly when intense affective arousal has made a previous session threatening to a part of the self whose experience was not recognized or processed during that session. In other words, the patient does not remember the session "personally," because the self who is here now was not participating in it. At best, the self who is here now was only present in the previous session as what Ernest Hilgard (1977), in his groundbreaking research on hypnosis, called a "hidden observer." To remember the session "personally," the patient must be able to access the self-state that participated in it *and* the self-state that observed it. Otherwise, the patient's dissociative mental structure will allow the experience only to be "sort-of" remembered. An analyst working from a conflict-theory perspective will tend to see such moments as examples of particularly stubborn forms of resistance and will make an effort to get the patient to see both parts of her "conflict" at the same time, underlining the part that is believed to be repressed yet accessible to a well-timed and accurately formulated interpretation. Patients will respond in various ways, none of them therapeutically facilitating. One common response is for the patient to "agree" conceptually, by talking about the analyst's idea, while remaining experientially unaware of what she has agreed to. That is, the patient can talk about the analyst's idea without any access to the full ensemble of self-states that, together, know what they are talking about.

Perceptual Reliving and Affective Safety

I often find it useful in a situation such as I have just described to express the desire to speak with the part of the patient that had the strongest feelings during the previous session. My hope is that the patient might feel safe enough to access that self-state or at least to show signs of cognitive confusion brought about by my question—confusion that I might then openly address as an internal struggle by different parts of the patient that disagreed about whether to take the risk of reliving the dissociated experience with me in the here and now. Assuming that at that moment I was not too embedded in an enactment and was less dissociated than the patient, I might start by saying, "Let yourself see if you can go back to last session and reenter it as if you were in it right now." If the patient does indeed try, I might then ask, "What is it like?"—a seemingly simple enough question, the goal of which is to allow the patient to relive, with me, the actual experience, rather than my continuing to participate with another part in talking ideationally *about* it.

Iain McGilchrist (2009), in his extraordinary treatise, *The Master and his Emissary: The Divided Brain and the Making of the Western World,* elucidates why the wording of the phrase "what is it like" is so powerful. McGilchrist writes:

> If, as Thomas Nagel (1979, p. 166) famously put it, consciousness is that which exists "when there is something it is like to *be* that organism," this identifies that the experience of consciousness

is not a "whatness" but a "howness"—a "what is it like"—a way of being which distinguishes living things, and is bound to be at least as much a characteristic of the right hemisphere (which is excluded from the process of understanding to the very degree that we are focused on the issue and bent on analysis) as it is of the left (the hemisphere that does the focusing and analyzing. (p. 221)

Making this point even clearer, McGilchrist quotes Nagel (1979, p. 170, n. 6) as adding, "[T]he analogical form of the English expression 'what is it like?' is misleading. It does not mean 'what (in our experience) it *resembles*,' but rather 'how it is for the subject himself'" (p. 495, emphasis in original).

However, asking "What is it like?" requires that the patient do something very difficult and potentially disorganizing. In the act of being interpersonally reflective about what "it is like" to *be* herself at that moment in the relationship with me, the security of the patient's attachment-organized core identity is placed at risk because her need for my caring responsiveness to her fear of the reliving collides affectively with her intense shame, which I am evoking, and with my own shame that I am causing pain to someone I care about. *Then why do it?*

According to Kihlstrom (1987; quoted from LeDoux, 1989):

> In order for unprocessed subjective experience to become symbolized in conscious awareness, a link must be made between the mental representation of the event and a mental representation of the self as the agent or experiencer. These episodic representations ... reside in short-term or working memory. (p. 281)

The more intense the unsymbolized affect, the more powerful the dissociative forces that prevent isolated islands of selfhood from becoming linked within working memory. High levels of stimulation from the amygdala interfere with hippocampal functioning. When this occurs in treatment, and it occurs inevitably, the sensory imprints of experience that are stored in affective memory continue to remain isolated images and body sensations that feel cut off from the rest of the self. The dissociative process that keeps the affect unconscious is above all else a process that has a life of its own—a relational life that is interpersonal as well as intrapsychic, and is played out between patient and analyst in the dyadic dissociative phenomenon that we term *enactment.*

Wilma Bucci (2002) similarly believe that enduring personality growth pivots around whether a link is made between unprocessed

subjective experience *and a here-and-now* mental representation of the
self as the agent or experiencer. She postulates that the therapeutic
action takes place in what she terms emotion schemas–specific types
of memory schemas dominated by subsymbolic sensory and somatic
representations–and presents an argument much like my own:

> Emotion schemas can be changed only to the extent that *experi-*
> *ences in the present and memories of the past are held in working memory*
> *simultaneously with the pulses of core consciousness that depend on acti-*
> *vation of the bodily components of the schema.* ... The activation of the
> dissociated painful experience in the session itself is central to the
> therapeutic process. (p. 787, emphasis added)

Thus, part of the answer to "Why do it?" is "Because it is necessary."
The other part of the answer is that despite its instability and "messi-
ness," patient and analyst are typically able to "hang in" during an
enactment and make therapeutic progress as long as the analyst's own
dissociated shame does not lead, unreflectively, to an indefinitely long
period in which his patient's distress is experienced as though it were
a wish for him to give up his efforts rather than as an expression of her
need for him to recognize her pain and to *care* about it. Enactments
are always dyadic, which is why the analyst's ability to experience his
own dissociation and his own shame are as intrinsic to the work as
the patient's dissociated experience. During the reliving, a patient is
scared not just because of what was frightening in the past, but because
its enactment in the present *with the therapist* is itself frightening. Consequently, the coconstruction of new self-meaning always involves
some self-destabilization, and it is thus of paramount importance that
the analyst communicate his ongoing attention to the patient's safety
while doing the "work."

Living Through the Mess

I depict the process of working with enactments as involving a collision of subjectivities that I call "living through the mess"–a mess that
can be affectively felt as such by the analyst and through which he
hangs in relationally, rather than seeing the collision as either a failure of proper technique or the emergence of heretofore undiscovered
pathology in the patient. More often than not, when one of these latter
options is selected, it is in the interest of the analyst's own need for
restabilization. This point has been well made by Gerald Stechler

(2003), who writes that "the possibility of the emergence of new states and new organizations arising during times of dysregulation and apparent disorganization or chaos has become one of the hallmark principles of contemporary theories of self-organizing systems" (p. 716). In analysis, Stechler continues, "the work often consists of a renegotiation of old patterns, facilitating the creation of new organizations and new states" (p. 718).

> Whether that new state is a richer, more complex, and more appropriate foundation for further development, or is the less advantageous choice in the sense of narrowing through toxic adaptation, may depend on whether the partner in this self-organizing system biases it in one direction or the other. ... That is, if the therapist's ... primary aim is to reduce his own destabilization and its accompanying anxiety as if it were toxic and intolerable, the partner's aim and choice will be biased in the same direction. If the therapist can stay connected with his own and with the patient's destabilization and can bias his own subsequent state choice toward openness and affective authenticity, then the patient's will be similarly biased. On the other hand, if the patient feels the freezing or the pretense of the therapist at these critical moments, the work of the therapy cannot proceed well. (p. 723)

Martha

A clinical illustration may help the reader position Stechler's wisdom within my concept of "living through the mess" so that both become experientially alive. My patient, Martha, entered treatment with an eating disorder and monitored her weight with dieting and exercise to the point of obsession. For much of Martha's youth she had been a compulsive binge eater and, according to her, had been overweight to the point of obesity. Long before I entered her life, however, she had discovered compulsive dieting, and the only incarnation of "Martha" that was visible to me looked somewhat underweight. She was not technically anorectic because her weight wasn't that low, but her preoccupation with control over what she saw as her "ugly body" was equal in intensity to that of an anorectic whose body weight indexes the disorder. As with most trauma survivors, Martha's symptoms served to ward off affective hyperarousal and its potential to destroy mental functioning. The dread of plunging into an "abyss" of nonbeing had long been her constant companion, and the control of her body as an object substituted for the absent capacity for affect regulation in a human relationship. She believed that *experiencing* her lack of relational affect control would lead her to madness. Thus, a constant vigilance over her body weight replaced and foreclosed the possibility of spontaneity and aliveness in living.

A nice description. But it was not arrived at *mutually*, as a shared understanding of her internal experience. It was a conceptualization arrived at by *me* that, regardless of its possible theoretical accuracy, was consistently ignored by Martha by means of what I increasingly experienced simply as "distractions" designed to deflect us from "the business at hand."

Martha was now in her thirties. In my view she had clearly suffered a terrifying depersonalization experience at about age 8, but had found a way to hold herself together through a compulsive regime of rituals that warded off unanticipated feelings that might plunge her, once again, into madness. My picture of Martha's history was assembled over the course of the first 2 years of treatment through the disjointed versions of her past that she provided, and I didn't hesitate to volunteer its outlines when I felt it to be appropriate. But the accuracy of my portrayal was never acknowledged, denied, or elaborated upon by her even in response to my follow-up questions. Thus, the question of accuracy always remained a shadowy issue in the background until a session about two years into our work—a session in which she blurted out that she lived, and had lived, in fear of being driven mad by her unstable, unreflective, and perpetually enraged mother.

But even though Martha had implicitly acknowledged that my picture of her was at least in the "right ballpark," we could not pursue the investigation further because of Martha's fear that any differences in our versions would create conflict between us that would lead to unbearable affective flooding. This too was at the time just one more surmise on my part. What was not a surmise was that Martha was largely unable to stay present in a moment of potential conflict with someone upon whom she depended, and this of course included me. Essentially, the part of her that held the experience of disagreement became "not-me," and, as I mentioned, she supported this dissociation by her "distractions"—behaviors that drew attention away from our "work" and toward something else either humorous, interesting, or relevant and important in another context. If all this failed, she would become disorganized and just plain confusing.

She did not seem to notice my growing impatience with these behaviors, which was not surprising because she would rarely notice anything that could lead to potential attachment rupture. In general, anger was never directly expressed–by either of us. Even mild irritation led to a dissociative state-switch so immediate that her preceding state, to the degree that a hint of negative affect might have appeared for a brief instant, seemed almost a product of my imagination.

Her mother's anger had been the most annihilating force in her early development, and her fear of it was probably the factor most responsible for her minimal capacity for intersubjectivity. As you will see from my report of the enactment in the vignette that follows, it is in this regard that Fonagy and Target's (1995) observation about the impact of parental malevolence is particularly relevant: A caretaker who is openly hostile toward the child will severely undermine the child's capacity for mentalization because the child no longer feels safe to think about her object's thoughts about her.

After about three years Martha and I had developed a relationship that had tested and retested my reliability to help repair breaks in our connection. Trust was a word that had no meaning when she began treatment, and was still viewed with scorn by some parts of her. The work at this point was all about whether the ongoing disjunctions between our subjectivities could be revealed by her without causing her to feel that we were breaking apart and that this time the descent into annihilation would be unstoppable. Martha's need to control how I experienced her increased in intensity, and its oppressiveness became for me (as it had with most of her previous therapists) the primary source of tension between us.

In the enactment I will describe, Martha said something to me that was so interpersonally irrational that from a different frame of reference it could be heard not just as confusing but as psychotic. It was said with dead seriousness, with no humor, and with no sign of self-reflectiveness. It occurred during an interchange in which I was asking her for more information about why she had missed her last session. She had already said she "forgot" about it and remembered it only when it was too late to come. As she now began to report the details of the event, her self-state shifted and she began laughing while talking, as though she was telling a very funny story that she "knew" I would find equally funny:

I just had a really great run in Central Park and was walking home and feeling fantastic about the workout I had, *you* know, and saying to myself how great it felt to be able to do this on a Wednesday afternoon because normally I can't. Then suddenly it was like *you* came into my mind and I said, "Oh gee, I was supposed to be at Dr. Bromberg's office ... Oh, that's so funny. Wait till I tell him." It was so *great*, Dr. Bromberg. I wasn't upset at all, and I had a terrific workout. *Why aren't you smiling?*

I replied, "Because I'm not finding it *funny*," followed by, "What do you imagine I *am* feeling?" As soon as the question left my mouth I wished I could take it back although I didn't yet know why. I could only sense that it was a bad question to ask at that moment—especially in the way I asked it. To make things worse, I was not consciously aware of being irritated with her. What I was aware of in my "no-nonsense" attitude reflected primarily the limited range of what I could accept in myself at that moment—my curiosity and my wish to explore this event with her in a "serious" way. I was unaware that I was over-using "seriousness" to mask something else. Nevertheless, there was enough displeasure in my voice about what I perceived as her effort to distract us from our "task" to trigger *her* early warning system.

Martha's self-state switched. Not only had her laughter disappeared, but everything about her that went with it seemed gone also. Her entire physical being had become that of a scared, unhappy, little girl, whose clothes, uncannily, now seemed too tight on a suddenly flaccid body. Without missing a beat, she replied—"*I'm too ugly to answer that question!*"

Because I was accustomed to state-change phenomena, her physical transformation did not shock me, but I was nonetheless stunned by the irrationality of her reply and the seriousness with which it was said. My shock, however, became contained for me not by the concept of "thought disorder," but through the perspective of self-state structure. I felt the presence of a dissociated part of Martha's self, a part that I had been told about but had never seen, a part of her that was now here, *unannounced*, trying to find its own voice in our relationship—and in so doing had verbally combined two domains of reality that made her a "walking non sequitor"[2] without concern for my expectation of consensual logic (which is what I meant when I earlier used the expression "*interpersonally* irrational").

---

[2]I am grateful to my colleague Susan Robertson, the creator of this phrase, both for her spontaneous wit and her generosity in sharing it with me.

"What do you mean?" said I. Martha began to squirm, and repeated her last statement about being too ugly to reply. I was now a bit recovered from my shock, and I'm sure that my tone of voice reflected the tenderness I was feeling as I responded, "I think my question about what you imagined I was feeling was very upsetting. Was it?"

She replied, "Can I have a piece of candy?" referring to the cough drops I kept on my desk.

I nodded and said, while reaching for the box of cough drops, "Maybe you want me to understand how upsetting my question was, and that eating is the surest way you know to feel less upset?"

She smiled and replied, "Yeah." I then asked if the one that went running in the park dislikes her. She said, "Yeah, she *hates* me because I'm always causing her trouble and she won't talk to me except to yell at me."

I said that I understood, and "would like to try to help find a way that they might talk to each other better. If I could speak to big Martha to find out whether she was listening to our conversation, it might be a good start. Would that be okay?"

In a voice very much that of the Martha I knew best, but in a manner that was considerably more related though much less deferential, she replied, "Yes, I heard the whole thing and didn't like it." I asked why she didn't like it, and Martha said that the "ugly one" was a "stupid baby" because she was "always scared of everything." I then asked if the "little one" got scared by my question about what I might have been feeling when she was talking about her really great workout. I used the term *little one* rather than her term *ugly one* in what I hoped might be a step toward potential peacemaking between the two parts. I had already referred to *her* as "Big Martha" and I now I wanted to see what would happen if I didn't side with her disparagement of the other part. In the moment, Martha accepted my rephrasing without comment–which should have cued me that more was going on than met the eye. She replied, "Yeah, she started to get real scared and that's why I sent her out to see what you would do when you met her."

I said, "And? How did I do?"

She said, "Well, *she* liked you"–the word *she* was dripping with disdain–"But I don't know how *I* feel about that."

Ignoring the disdain, I then took a risk I might not have taken before I knew that the "little one" liked me. I asked, "If you had been less worried about upsetting her when I asked my question, do you think that the answer might have been not, 'I'm too *ugly* to answer' but 'It's too *scary* to answer?'"

An angry look appeared on her face—angrier than I had ever seen her. But this time it did not feel like a switch to a dissociated aspect of self; rather it seemed more like a change in *mood*. She spoke:

> I don't understand this, and I don't like being confused. So what if I was ugly and fat and strange when I was growing up. Suppose I *was* really weird; what difference should that make now? I was the object of hate all around me, everywhere; it was threatening and violent. What possible good can come from feeling this all over again?

Well, she finally was angry at me! But I wasn't feeling it as a therapeutic breakthrough. I was feeling more than a bit defensive at this point, and also hurt, because I thought that my last intervention was just so brilliant. I felt unappreciated. I believed I was taking *all* of her parts into account and that she was just being mean.

I suddenly noticed that she was looking at me unusually thoughtfully and I felt that she could see what I was feeling. As she eyed me she began to speak:

> I'm not even sure what I'm talking about. How's *that* for confusing? I don't know the answers, and I don't want to talk about whatever it is you're getting at. I can hear another voice in my head telling me that there is nothing to hide—that I'm really healthy. I'm afraid of that voice. I feel like I'm just drawing attention to myself by allowing you or anyone else to think there is something healthy in me to be discovered.

Martha said all of this in a way that was so unguarded, so related, and so genuine that I could feel its honesty as a physical experience, and I became aware that I was no longer feeling defensive and hurt. I was feeling something I had been successfully dissociating: my own shame—my shame that I had shamed *her*. I was conscious both of my shame and of the fact that it was not hidden from her—even though I had not, yet, said anything explicit about it to her. We each "knew" the other person without questioning how we knew what we knew— and part of what was known was that we both could accept having our vulnerability exposed. It was implicit, mutual, and powerful, and in turn brought us nearer to one another without sacrificing our respective individualities.

I feel it is reasonable to hypothesize that our state-sharing contributed centrally to Martha's shame being diminished enough for her to not only experience, but to *reveal*, the existence of her "other voice." I further suggest that the affective reach of this *personal* connection enabled what we then explored together, in cocreated verbal language, to synthesize affect and cognition as inseparable elements in the continuing evolution of our professional relationship.

A new domain of shared space had been created between us and, simultaneously, between each of our own different parts. We were both "awake" to this space and could now express in *language* the personal feelings that before could be only enacted. The fact that the cognitive processing was confusing didn't get in our way. The confusion felt more like a natural part of where we were together. It was part of what was allowing her to be with me, and me with her. It allowed me to feel personally the part of her that I had been immune to—immune because I had been dissociating the part of myself that could most relate to it affectively. I said to her that I had been unable to experience her new joy that she felt free enough to miss a session in order to have fun, and that she had wanted me to know about it but I behaved like a stuffed shirt—as though her laughter was nothing more than another effort to distract us from the seriousness of helping her "get better." I added that I couldn't recognize the way in which she was *already* getting better and was trying to let me know about how good it felt but also how scary it felt.

She seemed to be feeling a little nervous at this point (as was I), and I said that I thought we were *each* nervous about drawing attention to something in us that would make us vulnerable by exposing it, and that for me, it was my anxiety about showing hurt feelings when I thought she was not taking me seriously. It kept me from being able to recognize the part of her that was taking me seriously by being genuinely playful. "But," I added, "I also knew I had done something hurtful. I felt sorry, and you saw it in my face and reached out to me by telling me about the *other* voice you could hear." She smiled again, and I could feel our connection deepening. But the reason wasn't just because of her smile. This time, added to Martha's smile was her emerging ability to risk conflict by putting her thoughts into words and comparing them with mine—including the *differences* in our experience. More and more, the shared thoughts of the other person, even thoughts that weren't completely welcome, enlivened the spontaneous sharing of our own—and we were no longer delivering monologues to each other. There was a feeling in the air that "getting better" was something happening in the here and now rather than a fantasy about the future.

As the work continued, other of Martha's self-states became part of the therapy process, including the part of her that was trying to make sure she wouldn't be stupid enough to trust an "other." It was in fact this "distrustful" protector that got Martha to "forget" our session when she went for her run so that when she shared her new sense of freedom with me I would react in a predictably self-serving way, just like her parents, showing the more innocent and trusting parts that it was hopeless to believe that anything could ever be different.

In the kind of clinical process I have just described–a process I have metaphorically termed "awakening the dreamer" (see Bromberg, 2006a)–what I call "the dreamer" is a self-state that is most familiar during sleep when it inhabits the dissociative mental space we call "dreams," but that's only one manifestation of it. One's dreamer is present in all of life, and when permitted, a patient's dreamer will participate in the treatment process and make its presence felt most beneficially through enactments, especially when the analyst finds his own "dreamer" awakening in synchrony with his patient's. In this vignette a "dreamer" of Martha's was awakening. And as it awakened, it entered into relationship with a reciprocal dreamer of my own that also began to awaken. I could then feel personally how liberating it was for Martha to feel free to just have fun and how liberating it was for me to share the experience. I had, until then, been dissociating the part of me that could pleasurably connect with that part of her, because, like Martha, I was afraid of exposing my own capacity to hurt and be hurt should I compromise the part of myself that I relied upon to protect me from exposure, the safe anchorage of being a serious, that is to say "well regulated," analyst.

PART III

STUMBLING ALONG
AND HANGING IN

5

Truth and Human Relatedness[1]

> So often has my judgment deceived me ... that I always suspect it, right or wrong.... For all this, I reverence truth as much as any body; and when it has slipped us, if a man will but take me by the hand, and ... search for it, as for a thing we have both lost, and can neither of us do well without–I'll go to the world's end with him.
>
> –Laurence Sterne, *The Life and Opinions of Tristram Shandy, Gentleman* (1762)

☙ A lawyer is obliged to accept the legitimacy of an oath that what is about to be said will be "the truth, the whole truth, and nothing but the truth." For a psychoanalyst, however, the concept of truth is like an itch that is not relieved by scratching and I sometimes wonder if the reason we continue to itch is because we are supposed to keep scratching.

Many years ago, while trying to please my first analytic supervisor with a story about a "compliant" patient who had openly disagreed with something I had said about her, I described the moment as an important event in her treatment because it also made me aware that what I had said to her was not true.

"What do you mean by true?" said he.

Taken aback, and a bit irritated, I restated it a bit more loudly, "Um, you know–it wasn't true!"

---

[1]This chapter materially expands and revises an earlier version, "Truth, Human Relatedness, and the Analytic Process: An Interpersonal/Relational Perspective," published in the *International Journal of Psychoanalysis, 90*, 2009, 347–361.

"It sounds more like it wasn't *accurate*," he countered.

"What do you mean by 'accurate'?" I asked, somewhat defiantly. One thing led to another, and even though I didn't appreciate his smugness, as the supervision went on I did come to appreciate the fact that whatever took place between us could always be talked about. But what I came to value even more was the power of his distinction between truth and accuracy. Truth, as a subjective phenomenon, continues to have an important place in my clinical work, but only as it emerges in the context of an ongoing dialectic with the intersubjective phenomenon of accuracy. My supervisor's openness to jointly processing our somewhat contentious "moment of truth," and his similar openness throughout the supervision, helped me also to experience the distinction between doing psychoanalysis and *being* a psychoanalyst. And it is the intrinsic tension between doing and being that lies at the heart of the clinical sensibility I will try to convey in this chapter.

My highest priority is determining whether a compelling clinical framework exists for expanding and enriching the texture of a patient's experience–whether it is a useful way of representing the patient's experience to himself. Stephen Mitchell (1993) made pointedly clear that this sensibility is far from being "atheoretical":

> Abandoning the belief in a single, objective, analytic Truth (or multiple analytic truths that approach a singular, objective reality) *does not lead to a valueless relativism*. There are an infinite number of ways to paint a vase with flowers–that does not mean they are all equally moving, that they have equal claims to capture and transform experience. (p. 65)

Mitchell was addressing, evocatively, the essence of our shared conceptual perspective: The process of expanding a patient's self-experience is based not in discovering enduring truths, whether singular or multiple, but in the actuality of two human beings cocreating what they do together with an increasing capacity for spontaneity. Truth as an *objective reality* is not deemed to exist in the mind of one or the other alone, which is of course the point of the epigraph from *Tristram Shandy* that introduces this chapter: Truth is "a thing we have both lost, and can neither of us do well without." To search for it we must take the other "by the hand" and be prepared to "go to the world's end with him." Psychoanalysis, when seen in this light, is another name for the interpersonal/relational crucible in which opposing subjective truths can come to coexist. This perspective, it may be noted, is not

incompatible with the sensibility that looks upon the patient's progress in developmental terms. Lawrence Friedman (1988) eloquently
portrays how the two sensibilities coexist in the analytic relationship.
At one level, the analyst is the holder of the patient's developmental
potential:

> [O]ne sort of childhood need which is not only sought in analy-
> sis, but is also fulfilled by analysis, is the need to identify with
> one's own growth potential as seen in the eyes of a parent. Being
> reacted to like that not only provides hope in general but struc-
> tures reality in a relevant and promising fashion. (p. 27)

But, says Friedman, there is a necessary paradox at work. Hope is what
makes a patient engage in treatment and is what enables him to surrender old ways of being, but "hope can only be a present hope, in the
shape given it by the patient's present psychological configuration."

> In other words, the analyst must accept the patient on his own
> terms, and at the same time not settle for them. If he does not
> accept the patient on his own terms, it is as though he is asking
> him to be someone else, *the patient will not have cause for hope*, and
> he will not recognize the analyst's vision. If the analyst settles for
> the patient's terms, he is ignoring the concealed part of the per-
> sonality and betraying the patient's wish for a greater fulfillment.
> (p. 34, emphasis added)

To this I would add but one thing: I believe that the "hope" of which
Friedman writes comes not from just being "accepted" as you are but
from being *needed* as you are–from the recognition that, in some genuine way, being with you as you are brings your analyst *pleasure* despite
your "problems." Call it "love" if you will, or at least the fountain from
which love flows. But regardless of the name we choose, it is this, I
submit, that most nourishes the soil of therapeutic (as well as early
developmental) growth–a patient's capacity to change while remaining the same–the foundation of development because it is the foundation of hope.

   Its *absence*, especially in early development, quite likely interferes
with, and sometimes shuts down, the acquisition of later capacity for
state-sharing, intersubjectivity, and the resilience to withstand failures
in adaptation that might not be traumatic for other children. I would
even argue that this aspect of the trauma of nonrecognition–the child's

or patient's self-experience being shaped around being valueless as a source of pleasure to a needed other—may be what makes some patients especially vulnerable to their "not-me" self-states remaining filled with darkness, unreality, and fear because self/other boundary permeability remains too unsafe to allow the development of a relational unconscious.

I have come to view the analyst's dual responsibility, described so well by Friedman, as greatly facilitated by surrendering the notion that there is a "real you." What do I mean? People often come into treatment hoping to find out who they "really" are. An important goal of treatment, I would argue, is to help them recognize that the person they hope, or worry, that they really are no more reflects a truth about them than the part the world sees, a part they may think of as a "cover-up" masking a hidden but "truer" part. The negotiations between these various parts can become quite a tangle—and the search for a "true" self may become tortuous indeed. This point is implicit in the old saying that "a hysteric is someone who goes through life pretending to be who she really is." I suspect that hysterics have been singled out because their particularly rapid self-state switching makes others, and often themselves, doubt the authenticity of their self-presentation. "I don't know if it is true." "I somehow feel it is true but I also think I may be lying." Such vacillation is a function not of inauthenticity, but of the presence of dissociated ("not-me") self-states that hold affective realities unable to be resolved conflictually because they have no narrative context for relational self-expression.

Dogmentative

In frustration with me a patient blurted out, "*You're so dogmentative.*" Sputtering, half in laughter, half in consternation, I replied, "You have no right to make up a new word; it's not fair." I had no idea what I meant by that. I only knew that she had somehow "won" the battle of words because there was no way I could, as succinctly as she had, use language to neutralize her description of the way I was being. Was what she said about me "true?" If the word *dogmentative* did not exist then how could it be true? More importantly, was it *accurate*? The answer to the latter question, which we arrived at only after sharing our individual experiences of our encounter, was a mutual "Oh yes!" But here's the point: We were able to recognize that her neologism represented different parts of herself, including one that feared her perception of me would be felt as *too* accurate if heard seriously and could potentially destabilize the procedural attachment pattern that organized her core identity—unless she came across as a little "ditsy."

What do I mean by different parts of herself? In my writing (Bromberg, 1998a, 2006a) I have consistently presented a view of the normal mind as a multiplicity of self-states that we inhabit every day of our lives. I have argued that a flexible relationship among self-states through the use of normal dissociation is what allows a human being to engage the ever-shifting requirements of life's complexities with creativity and spontaneity. From this vantage point, normal dissociation, a mind/brain mechanism that is intrinsic to everyday mental functioning, attempts to select a self-state configuration that is most immediately adaptive within the constraints of self-coherence. This flexibility is what gives a person the remarkable capacity to negotiate character stability and change simultaneously—to stay the same while changing.

An inherent part of every analytic process involves working with constellations of a patient's dissociated experience that are internally organized by the mind/brain into "not-me" self-states (see Chefetz & Bromberg, 2004). To be noted, these parts of the self are cognitively unsymbolized in a relational context, and in Donnel Stern's (1997, 2009) terms exist as "unformulated" experience. Optimal mental functioning consists in a person's being able to access multiple self-states conflictually, and psychoanalytic treatment must provide a favorable context for facilitating internal communication between disjunctive states that are kept sequestered from each other dissociatively. In treatment, through the joint symbolic processing of enactments played out between patient and analyst, a patient's sequestered self-states come alive as a "remembered present" (Edelman, 1989). This *nonlinear* process is cumulative. It allows the patient, affectively and cognitively, to use the remembered present in constructing with the analyst an authentically remembered past. Because the ability to experience internal conflict safely is also increased, the potential for resolution of conflict is in turn facilitated for all patients.

Truth and the Discontinuity of Consciousness

Though consciousness is discontinuous (see Osborne & Baldwin, 1982, and Hermans et al., 1992, for detailed discussions), in day-to-day life we are not subject to the potentially disruptive awareness of discontinuity because of a necessary illusion that masks it. The illusion of ongoing self-unity is generated by the mind's evolutionary ability to ground consciousness in whatever self-state configuration is most adaptive at a given moment. Mitchell (1991) formulated these different configurations of subjective truth as "versions of the person [that] embody active patterns of experience and behavior, organized around a particular point of view, a sense of self, a way of being, which underlie the ordinary phenomenological sense we have of ourselves as integral" (pp. 127–128). And he noted that "the result is a plural or manifold organization of self, patterned around different self and object images or representations, derived from different relational contexts. *We are all composites of overlapping, multiple organizations and perspectives, and our experience is smoothed out by an illusory sense of continuity*" (p. 139, emphasis added). Mitchell concludes by asserting, as do I, that the self is simultaneously multiple and integral. That is, the sense of unitary selfhood is an experiential imperative that stabilizes the self-state structure of mental functioning by making the mind's network of states feel seamless—and the transitions between states feel natural and easy. Each state, "true" to its self, is able to feel relatively self-contained in its own right while simultaneously feeling continuous with an overarching experience of "me."

Truth, I would thus argue, is a phenomenon that serves to support the subjective need of each state to feel legitimate in itself without being destabilized by otherness. In other words, *one's truth is state-dependent and subjective.* It lacks consensual validity (cf. Sullivan, 1953), but this does not create problems in living unless the truth held by a particular state is so insulated that negotiation *between* self-states (and with other people) is compromised. In treatment, interpersonal engagement allows increased self-state negotiation to become possible, which in turn allows the state-dependent experience of any given truth to give up some of its sovereignty to a more flexible self–other experience. As this takes place, truth becomes opinion, belief, or even conviction, but is no longer absolute certainty. The link between truth and the discontinuity of consciousness as it applies to the psychoanalytic process has been articulated well by Mitchell (1993) as follows:

> At any given point, the patient can only report a particular construction of his experience, which may overlook or obliterate many other important constructions of his experience (which the analyst might be more in touch with). At any given point, the analyst can offer only his own construction of some aspects of a

patient's experience, a construction of a construction. The "only" in the preceding sentence should not be taken as a minimization of the importance of interpersonal understanding. Our constructions of each other's constructions make possible mutual growth and the reciprocally facilitating use of imagination. (p. 60)

From this perspective, reality and truth cannot be distinguished from fantasy and uncertainty in absolute terms because the ability of different parts of the self to recognize other parts as *me* is always relative. Consequently, reality and truth for the part of the self that is "me" can be fantasy and speculation to the parts that are "not-me." What we call reality, and in turn what we call "truth," will depend on which part of self has access to consciousness at that moment.

Bringing "reality" into the picture does not change my stance. Marcia Cavell (2000), in a published exchange concerning our respective views on the topic of reality, stated that although "points of view are multiple ... reality is one and the same for all of us" (p. 525). My reply (Bromberg, 2000b) was that although I felt this to be a useful point when made by a philosopher (see also Cavell, 1998) it was highly problematic if offered by a clinician because a clinician is always working within a complex field where such a distinction more often than not inhibits rather than facilitates personality growth. My perspective on the nature of reality and truth is derived from a self-state view of the mind wherein reality is shaped by the self-organizing configuration of each self-state. The reality experienced by one self-state will be consistent or inconsistent with the realities of other self-states to the degree that dissociative protection against affect dysregulation is present as a mental structure.

A patient's therapeutic growth depends on facilitating the negotiated coconstruction of a transitional space within which the question of objective versus subjective, and "true" versus "false," loses its meaning. As Winnicott (1951) put it, in discussing whether transitional phenomena were "true," "no decision on this point is expected. The question is not to be formulated" (p. 240). In this transitional space, reality is a *shared* mental state—a channel of implicit communication that supports what Buck (1994) calls a conversation between limbic systems (cited by Schore, 2003a, p. 276). It is by allowing the boundary between self and other to become increasingly permeable that the patient/analyst relationship permits the development of a relational unconscious—a shared therapeutic space in which old truths can be reorganized into new patterns of self/other meaning.

Neural Networks and Self-State Networks

The source of therapeutic action is a mind/brain phenomenon. One reason that therapeutic growth takes as long as it does is that the mind's self-state organization is linked to the brain's organization of neural networks—groups of neurons that have fired and wired together to form a community of neurosynaptic connections. As long as the same groups of neurons in a neurosynaptic community continue to fire together in a relatively unchanged manner, the more difficult it is for new groups of neurons to wire into that community and bring new information to the network. Both the brain and the mind, in other words, have their versions of "truth." Edelman's (1989, 2004) theory of neural Darwinism speaks to the neurobiology of the brain as "a pattern of constancy and variation leading to highly individualized networks" (2004, p. 29), a description that parallels my portrayal of the self-state structure of the mind. I could easily choose to use Edelman's language of neural networks to talk about self-state networks as patterns of constancy and variation leading to highly individualized modules of being—each configured by its own organization of cognitions, beliefs, dominant affect and mood, access to memory, skills, behaviors, values, actions, regulatory physiology and, when all has gone well developmentally, each compatible enough with the truths held by other states to allow overarching coherence across self-states. But Edelman's key phrase is "*constancy* and variation." Though part of the brain's Darwinian adaptation depends on allowing the neural networks to expand through the use of new information, there is always a struggle between constancy and variation. Stability (survival through constancy) has an evolutionary priority equal to and often higher than that of growth (survival through variation), requiring that neural-network "truth" and self-state truth work hand in hand to prevent new information from challenging the *stability* of mind/brain functioning.

The brain uses the process of normal dissociation to routinely inhibit simultaneous consciousness of maladaptively discrepant self-states (overly disjunctive truths). But life is never that simple. In emotionally heightened, unanticipated situations, the conditions are ripe for self-states to become *traumatically* discrepant, triggering defensive dissociation when an attempt is made to hold them simultaneously in consciousness, especially when the attempted negotiation of self-state truth is attachment-related (cf. Main & Morgan, 1996). While pervasive dissociation is almost always evident in patients who have suffered massive trauma (either single-episode or a pattern of overt abuse), it is most inherently and ubiquitously a response to developmental trauma. Developmental trauma (sometimes termed *relational trauma*) is always part of what shapes early attachment patterns (including "secure attachment"), which in turn establish what Bowlby (1969, 1973, 1980) calls "internal working models." The internal working models include procedural memories which organize the core self and its relative degree of vulnerability to destabilization. Developmental trauma is thus an inevitable aspect of early life to varying degrees, and is of significance in all analytic work. That is, attachment-related trauma is part of everyone's past and a factor in every treatment experience, but for some patients it has led to a dissociative mental structure that virtually takes over personality functioning and mental life and thereby dictates the "Truth" about the present and the future.

One could even suggest that the impact of trauma leads to the most rigid dissociative mental structure when one of the resulting disjunctive states is highly organized by *the attachment-related core-self,* and the trauma threatens its violation. In such instances, the threat of affective destabilization carries with it a potential identity crisis. In attachment language, the mind is overwhelmed by sudden "strangeness" that begins to make one a stranger to one's self and triggers actual or incipient madness—the horror of what we call "depersonalization." I offer the view that the source of this experiential assault to the mind/ brain is the following: Notwithstanding differences in attachment style (see Ainsworth et al., 1978), the core-self is configured by early established behavior patterns (procedural memory) rather than reflective thought (narrative memory) and cannot be held as a cognitive element of internal conflict. There is thus no possibility of resolution, and the *futile struggle to think* only makes it worse because it escalates the felt absence of mental control that is created by the experienced rupture of attachment. A patient may try to obsess, may try to engage in rituals, may seek to institute self-soothing procedures, but whether a patient is in the office or alone at home he feels unable to arrest the panic and control his own thoughts.

In situations like this, dissociation comes to the rescue, often in its most rigid form. To protect the mind from struggling indefinitely with a strange and emotionally threatening situation that is inherently inaccessible to thought, neural Darwinism readjusts the brain's evolutionary function before the struggle to think becomes itself an uncontrollable source of dysregulation and potential depersonalization. The priority of balancing constancy and variation is reduced as the brain turns directly toward survival. Dissociation is triggered automatically and proactively, accomplishing what Frank Putnam (1992) calls "the escape when there is no escape" (p. 104).

Porges (1997) has described this in neurobiological terms as "the sudden and rapid transition from an unsuccessful strategy of struggling requiring massive sympathetic activation to the metabolically conservative immobilized state associated with the dorsal vagal complex" (p. 75). Allan Schore (2007) suggests that this sudden switch accounts for "what Bromberg calls dissociative 'gaps in subjective reality'; 'spaces' that surround self-states and thereby disrupt coherence among highly affectively charged states" (p. 758).

Obviously, Edelman's theory of neural Darwinism must account not only for the stability of selfhood but for the process of creative self-change as well—a process that requires a certain amount of self-destabilization. The ability of the mind to function creatively is dependent on the brain's neuroplasticity—the brain's adaptive ability to *modify* its synaptic wiring by learning new information that makes its neurons fire in new patterns and combinations. Insight, the centerpiece of Freud's clinical contribution, has been shown to require (Bowden & Jung-Beeman, 1998, 2003; Kounios et al., 2006, 2008) that the brain's synaptic networks, especially those of the right hemisphere, be "transformed by accidental, serendipitous connections" (Lehrer, 2008, p. 43). Current work in the neurobiology of interpersonal experience (e.g., Schore, 1994, 2003a, 2003b; Siegel, 1999) demonstrates that such serendipitous connections are facilitated by *conscious and nonconscious interactions with other minds in new ways*—such as in an analytic relationship— whereby new combinations of neurons increasingly wire together, allowing self-state evolution to modulate the rigidity of self-state truth.

Increasing self-state negotiation therapeutically increases affect tolerance and lowers the fear of dysregulation (the shadow of the tsunami), strengthening the capacity of each neural network to accept new information and simultaneously strengthening the mind's capacity to hold and resolve internal conflict. But the restoration of coherence across self-states is possible only when the multiple self-states of each partner can surrender some of their individual truths and recognize otherness as more than "not-me."

Conflict, Repression, Resistance

Dissociation as a normal mental function ordinarily works in a comfortable dialectic with internal conflict. It is designed to assure that the version of truth held by a given self-state is respected, while assuring that each state can flexibly access other states holding discrepant versions and thus allow an individual to experience internal conflict and engage in its potential resolution. But because dissociation can also be a means of proactively assuring the stability of the self by preventing the mind from experiencing chaotic traumatic affect, it is not simply a different term for the concept of repression. Repression defines a process that is designed to avoid disavowed mental content that may lead to unpleasant intrapsychic conflict. But conflict can be *unbearable* to the mind, not simply unpleasant. When such is the case, dissociation is not functioning in a dialectic with conflict, but showing its signature through the patient's alienation from aspects of *self* that are inconsistent with his experience of "me" at a given moment.

In certain areas of every individual's personality the experience of intrapsychic conflict is difficult to bear much less resolve, and for some people this incapacity goes back to early childhood because the mind's ability to access and safely tolerate two or more disjunctive self-states at the same time was virtually foreclosed at that time. But for any patient, in those areas where the natural dialectic between conflict and dissociation is either compromised or shut down, conflict interpretations are useless or even worse.

I am not arguing against the concept of conflict. I am arguing that conflict theory needs to make room to accommodate the phenomenon of dissociation without trying to explain it as another form of conflict, and I am by no means without allies from other schools of analytic thought. Jorge Canestri (2005), for example, in a direct challenge to those who conceptualize dissociation as a form of conflict that can be assimilated into contemporary conflict theory, writes that my hypothesis of a shift from dissociation to conflict "is very similar, from the point of view of logical presuppositions, to those of Winnicott (1965, 1971), Gaddini (1992), Greenacre (1969), and others who predict the existence of a primary conflictual phase, with a *subsequent* shift that leads to the constitution of the structure and ultimately of the conflict" (p. 308, emphasis added). Which is to say that when dissociation is in full flower, the capacity to structure conflict is not yet present. Canestri thus takes strong issue with the view that dissociation, when it appears in clinical work, is a compromise formation and can be analyzed as such (by interpretation). His main point, like mine, is that dissociation is *inherently* nonconflictual, and that the effort to account for the dissociative gap between self-states as though it were a stubborn version of conflict is "an ad hoc hypothesis intended to salvage the theory of conflict as an organizing principle omnipresent in the mind" (p. 308). If his critique is worth taking seriously, one must ask how it is possible for anything new ever to take place in treatment. Why doesn't each self-state "island of truth" maintain an analytic status quo indefinitely? If an analyst does not believe that therapeutic action is predicated on the successful discovery of Truth, then what principle replaces it?

I find it interesting that two different authors have approached this question by reexamining the time-honored conceptualization of "resistance," each arguing that it is overly content-bound (cf. Bromberg, 1995b). Lee Rather (2001), writing from a contemporary Kleinian perspective, puts it that:

> resistance occurs not only to the specific contents of the unconscious, but also to the very existence of the "other" from which unconscious phenomena are felt to emanate. The aim of psychoanalysis may be ... [in one way] conceptualized as the formation of a collaborative internal relation with an aspect of the psyche I have termed the "unconscious other." (p. 529)

To be noted, Rather's "unconscious other" specifically refers to another part of the patient—the patient's "dreaming self" (see Bromberg, 2006a), not an internalized object. What Rather calls the "unconscious other" I call "not-me" self-states—dissociated constellations of affective reality that, by engaging their "otherness" through unplanned here-and-now interaction, can make internal conflict become safer and thus more possible. Terminology aside, I agree with Rather's broad implication that by expanding the concept of resistance beyond its tie to unconscious content, the fundamental *source* of unconscious phenomena—the internal world of self/other configurations—will be freer to participate more directly and spontaneously in the clinical process.

Adam Phillips (1993) similarly argues that the concept of resistance, traditionally conceptualized as a repetition of the past in different terms, is more usefully understood as resistance to surprise or novelty. He, too, offers the view that there has been such a pronounced focus on unconscious content that a conflation of theory and observation obscures the analyst's clinical experience that "what is repressed in advance is the novelty of experience" (p. 87). With that phrase, Phillips is setting the stage for what I and many other postclassical analysts would support: A new organizing frame of reference to replace "analytic truth" and its powerful pull toward unilateral clinical judgment. I am speaking of the replacement of a focus on content with a focus on process. When the focus is on content, contends Phillips, "the relationship to truth becomes a sadomasochistic one, truth being that which it is better for us to submit to" (p. 5). Extrapolating from the arguments presented by Rather and by Phillips, I would add that the focus on content creates a collusion between patient and analyst that leads to searching for what seems to *be hidden within the patient* and masks what is *absent between them* in the here and now. The inferential search for what is hidden in the patient deflects the attention of both analyst and patient from their potential perceptual awareness of something taking place, affectively, between their "not-me" self-states that both partners have dissociatively bled of personal meaning. Thus, at points of "resistance," the novelty of a new experience is not available to be addressed because the mind/brain, *in advance*, "drains experience of the feeling and the potential for narrative vigor" (Stern, 1996, p. 259).

Safety and Risk

Each patient/analyst couple must strike its own balance between safety and risk, but for any patient, confrontation with the analyst as a separate center of subjectivity will be most enlivening and safe if the analyst is not trying to figure things out on his own and then using his own truth about his patient as a *means* to a good therapeutic outcome. The more an analyst's communication is based on sharing his subjective experience because *he wants it known*, as opposed to wanting it to have a preconceived impact on his patient's mind, the more it will be felt by the patient as "affectively honest" (cf. Levenkron, 2006) and the more likely the patient will respond in a similar way. Honoring this principle allows many seemingly fragile patients to hang in while facing an analyst's intrusions because the patient is not putting his own subjectivity at risk by having to trade it off for the "truth" being offered by another.

I do not believe that hidden truth or unconscious fantasy is ever "uncovered" (see chapter 7) regardless of how flexibly, thoughtfully, or even plausibly an analyst offers his formulation of it. I argue that the source of therapeutic action in psychoanalysis is the synthesis of affectively alive interpersonal engagement with the shifting self-states that organize the internal object worlds of both patient and analyst—a "coconstructed royal road" (Bromberg, 2000a, pp. 86–87) that begins to allow previously unformulated self-state truths to be cognitively and linguistically symbolized in the involved minds of both partners. I further argue that this takes place most powerfully during spontaneous and unbidden interpersonal interaction—the feature of clinical process that Russell Meares (2001) terms "what happens next." Interpersonal novelty is what allows the self to grow because it is unanticipated by both persons, it is organized by what takes place between two minds, and it belongs to neither person alone. The reciprocal process of active involvement with the states of mind of the other person allows a patient's here-and-now perception of self to share consciousness with the experiences of incompatible self-narratives that were formerly dissociated. This process leads to what could be called the therapeutic "internalization" of otherness. As long as interpersonal experiences are safe but not *too* safe, the permeability of the self/other boundary is increased, externally and internally, and psychoanalysis becomes a powerful transformational process. It is through the novelty and surprise of this reciprocal process that the therapeutic action of psychoanalysis takes shape and it may well be what accounts for the enhanced spontaneity and flexibility of a patient's personality structure that results from a successful analysis.

In an interpersonal/relational clinical process, the nature of the analytic relationship differs epistemologically from that of classical treatment because the primary source of therapeutic action *is* the relationship, not something created *through* it. As the joint processing of dissociated self-state communication progresses, a patient gradually becomes more able to sort out, interpersonally and between self-states, what feels like too much, without shutting down spontaneous here-and-now interactions that include "safe surprises." A feedback loop is thus created between greater spontaneity and reduced fear of dysregulation, which allows a patient's dissociated areas of developmental trauma to be relived in the moment as part of a caring but humanly imperfect relationship that frees his internal object world from captivity. Again, the source of therapeutic action is a mind/brain phenomenon: The brain reduces its automatic triggering of dissociation and the mind supports the increasing development of intersubjectivity, thus facilitating a patient's potential to bear and resolve internal conflict.

Do I believe that psychoanalytic growth is all about increased affect tolerance and nothing more? Not at all. In my view, what I have just described does lead to greater capacity for affect regulation, but is better understood as what Ronald Laing (1967) called "an obstinate attempt of two people to recover the wholeness of being human through the relationship between them" (p. 53). How does the recovery of wholeness become possible? How does the development of intersubjectivity become possible in the face of two opposing and equally obstinate affective truths, each of which feels misunderstood by the other?

Enactments, to the degree they relive aspects of attachment-related developmental trauma in a patient's past, can activate the brain's "fear system" (LeDoux, 1996), but a good analytic relationship also provides what the past lacked—a self-reflective, involved, and caring other who will not indefinitely protect his own truth by holding it to be self evident. It is this paradoxical combination that allows something new to emerge that impacts both mind and brain. Self-states that embody insularly entrenched truths become more able to communicate with other states because their own truths are not at risk. At the brain level, new groups of neurons fire and wire together within old communities allowing new information to become part of a neurosynaptic network that had been relatively unable to evolve previously. Safe surprises are able to foster the development of an intersubjective channel of communication that restores what Laing terms "the wholeness of being human" *during* the cocreation of new self–other meanings through shared events that are infused with an energy of their own because spontaneity and safety can coexist.

Rarely has Laing's concept of psychoanalysis as "an obstinate attempt of two people to recover the wholeness of being human through the relationship between them" been stated more eloquently or profoundly than by Jean-Max Gaudillière in a 2010 online colloquium on psychoanalysis and the trauma(s) of history:

> Maybe it could be time to cease our speaking of trauma as a nosological symptom. ... Traumas functions as a history-catcher, like the dream-catcher in certain Indian cultures. Even the word *disclosure* is not relevant, a propos the psychoanalyst who is able to talk to patients from his/her own trials at certain moments: We are not the owners of "our" traumas, we are bearers of a half, or a third, or a minimal part of the truth. And we have to adapt the technique and theory of our psychoanalytical practice, in order to try to be at the level of that historical stake.... *We are not performing like actors, or singers, but we are summoned to create something new, at the place where traumas stayed as dead letters, continuing the infinite production of ghosts and murders.* (emphasis added)

I believe that the most far-reaching therapeutic impact of Gaudillière's wisdom, that "we are bearers of a half, or a third, or a minimal part of the truth," is brought about by the interpersonal negotiation of dissociatively enacted collisions between the subjectivities of patient and analyst. It is the *interpersonal* foundation of safe surprises that allows the synthesis of old and new meanings through the paradoxical co-existence of safety and otherness. If, as Gaudillière suggests, trauma is indeed a history catcher rather than a nosological symptom, and analysts are summoned to participate in the cocreation of something new rather than performing a cure, his statement that we have "to adapt the technique and theory of our psychoanalytical practice" barely needs explanation. I would argue that a central aspect of this adaptation is the analyst's understanding that during the process of collision and negotiation, because the patient's experience of affective safety is constantly shifting, the analyst's overarching attunement to the moment-to-moment shifts must be openly communicated as part of the process. A patient's safety in the relationship is shaped by the willingness of each partner to struggle with the other's experience of him at any given moment, and it is through the authentic mutuality of these encounters that patient and analyst are able to make therapeutic use of their affective collisions of personal "truth." A therapeutic posture that systematically tries to avoid collisions between the patient's and analyst's subjectivities eventually is experienced by a patient as disconfirming the vitality of the patient's dissociated self-states that are trying to find relational existence. If the analyst is not responding affectively and personally to these parts, they are robbed of a human context in which to be recognized and come alive.

Genuine mutuality brings noisiness. What do I mean by "noisi-ness?" Any experience of disjunction between subjectivities that raises the level of affective disharmony. The therapist cannot prevent interpersonal "noise" from sometimes being too loud no matter how nonintrusive he tries to be. What matters here is the therapist's affective honesty. What matters is whether his patients can feel in an ongoing way his effort to *be* with them—his effort to keep their dissociated fear and shame in mind while he is doing the "work." It is the felt continuity of *being*, especially under adverse conditions, that provides the safety, not a hypothetical capacity to do the analysis in some right way. Affective honesty is rarely communicated through content or through language per se. It is primarily communicated through a relational bond that Schore (2003a, 2003b, 2007) and others including myself (see chapter 1) believe is mediated neurobiologically by right-brain to right-brain state sharing. It entails the feeling of self/other unity that occurs when otherness becomes part of self—a special quality of human relatedness that I believe accounts for why a therapy that is "safe but not *too* safe" entails a risk that a patient is willing to take.

The Genie in the Bottle

Winnicott (1958) describes the developmental process that leads to "the capacity to be alone" in very much these terms, famously postulating that another person is required: "The basis of the capacity to be alone is the experience of being alone in the presence of someone." As to how to conceptualize the relationship with this necessary other, Winnicott suggested that "ego-relatedness might be a good term for temporary use." But he went on to note pointedly that the state of ego-relatedness was not devoid of input from the id. To the contrary: "In a frame of ego-relatedness, id-relationships occur and strengthen rather than disrupt the immature ego." As this strengthening continues to happen, development goes forward: "Gradually, the ego-supportive environment is introjected and built into the individual's personality, so that there comes about a capacity to actually be alone" (p. 36).

Winnicott is saying that through the internalization of the relational bond he calls "ego-relatedness," a capacity to *actually* be alone because the inner world has become relationally nourishing can develop out of what had earlier depended on the external presence of the other. And, most important, he is implying that the internalization of the relational bond is strengthened rather than disrupted by having to deal with an absence of perfect harmony, provided the disharmony is reparable (see also Tronick & Weinberg, 1997). Reparability requires the participation of both partners, which is why, as Winnicott so astutely noted, the affective noisiness emerges not from the Freudian id per se, but within "id *relationships*." (emphasis added) It is just this eruption within id relationships that I see as an aspect of enactments that I call self–other collisions. It seems plausible to me that Winnicottian development of the capacity to be alone is thus interwoven with the mature development of the capacity for relational regulation of dysregulated affect. I might even go as far as to wonder if an authentic capacity to be alone and an authentic capacity to relate to an other each depend on the relative success of this combined developmental achievement.

Let me expand on this from a clinical perspective. If analytic therapy is indeed a process through which rigidified self-state structures are reorganized again and again into increasingly flexible and complex patterns, then each reorganization changes the analytic relationship itself and, in turn, makes new and different demands on the analyst's clinical judgment. What makes this fact worth mentioning in the present context is that insofar as the patient's "internalization" of the relational bond is making her feel more and more secure within her own skin, an unusual kind of enactment often takes place—one that almost always catches the analyst off guard: One's patient seems suddenly to have changed the "ground rules" of the relationship. Typical is the instance of Martha, who we met in the previous chapter, forgetting a session in order to run in Central Park, and thinking to herself what fun it would be to share that with me. Sometimes it can feel almost as if the relationship has been hijacked while the analyst wasn't looking, and in a certain sense this is accurate. Why so? Because, like a hijacking it takes place unilaterally and without warning—a phenomenon that intrinsically lacks a shared transitional bridge. Why hasn't it been gradually accessible to the patient/analyst relationship? Not an easy question to answer but I am willing to speculate.

The hypothesis I would offer is that the patient's newly discovered capacity to be what Winnicott calls "actually alone" is allowing her to utilize this experience in a way that embraces two components, both of which further her continuing growth, but in different ways. Because the first component is unshared the second component seems to come out of nowhere.

Try to imagine what it is like for a patient, perhaps for the first time in her life, to feel safe and whole inside her own skin and to *know* it is not an illusion that will disappear—to realize that it will not go away when some real person is no longer keeping her in mind. The "therapeutic" aspect of this experience is sharable, if not directly then at least implicitly. The gratitude, the security, the hope, the relief—things that have to do with growth and feeling healed. But there is something more; something that is not part of feeling healed but of feeling *whole*—an experience of pleasure that often approaches pure joy. In the past, joy did not exist except perhaps for brief moments because it interfered with hypervigilance. Joy was unsafe. Now, suddenly, she experiences herself as feeling safe without worrying how soon it will be taken away, and along with it she is allowing herself to luxuriate in her joy that this is so. She is able to fully embrace her joy, to bathe in it as long as she chooses, and to keep it as a special treasure that will be shared if and when she is ready. This is done not with some external goal in mind nor to clutch it as a secret "truth" that might be taken from her if she shares it. It is done because the *capacity* to experience her inner world as a source of joy in its own right is suddenly part of who she now is. In joyfully savoring her new self-experience she is not withholding something she should be sharing. Rather, she is further utilizing her new capacity to be *actually* alone—and by so doing is strengthening her inner world as a private space in which she can choose to be comfortably alone rather than a place in which, as Winnicott (1963) has written, "it is a joy to be hidden but a disaster not to be found" (p. 186). In these circumstances, a patient arrives at a new form of "truth," a truth that is true, in part, precisely because it is not shared, but also is new because she does not *need* to share it. She no longer needs to give over part of herself in order to diminish internal isolation through what Winnicott called "a sophisticated game of hide-and-seek."

At a certain point, however, her private pleasure in using her inner world will make her ready to test out with the analyst her new sense of relational empowerment—her experience of personal agency that isn't compromised by the shadow of the tsunami. And now we get to what I formulate as the second of the two components that further her continuing growth—the one that (as with Martha in the previous chapter) seems to come out of nowhere because the first has been unshared. What is it that comes as such a shock to the analyst? Try to see it as a version of the Arabian Nights legend of the fisherman who frees a supplicating little genie from a bottle in which he was imprisoned for a thousand years only to find, to his consternation, that he is facing a seemingly new genie who, now freed, is not only ungrateful but is big, bad, confrontational, and totally unlike his earlier hapless self. My hope is that with this image in mind, it may be easier for the reader to visualize the newly freed patient who is no longer imprisoned in an inner world populated with "not-me" self-states that shame her into being well behaved.Privately, she has felt liberated for longer than the analyst is aware and is now ready for a public journey of the private self, filled with vitalized enthusiasm for flexing the muscles of personal empowerment.

All fine, except for one thing: As with the fisherman, the analyst has no transitional context that he can use to comprehend the person he is now seeing. The patient could not have announced herself in advance because her new self-experience is not yet relationally defined. Here the Arabian Nights legend becomes no longer applicable: First, the analyst is not a cunning fellow. Second, more importantly, the analyst is faced with a problem of greater complexity. Unlike the fisherman, the analyst doesn't want his patient to return to her "bottle," but without an interpersonal context that feels recognizable, and without the ability to make sense of what happened, he feels temporarily resourceless. For the analyst, a dissociative escape from the here-and-now is pretty much inevitable—as is the subsequent cocreation of an enactment, most often ushered in by an unanticipated return of collisions between subjectivities that, affectively, will generate noise in the relationship.

Here is where Winnicott's wisdom is especially evident: In this phase of the work, self–other "noise" is strengthening the patient's internalization of the relational bond in a way that supports but also adds something new to its prior contribution. Using her newfound sense of affective sturdiness, the patient is able to risk something that had never before been possible: Not only is she herself authorizing noise in their relationship, but she is doing so more or less knowingly–because it is pleasurable. The patient is engaged, intrapsychically, in the process of cognitive self-resymbolization, a pleasurable reconnection of mind to "psyche-soma" (Winnicott, 1949), and is relating to the analyst as more than simply a nonimpinging object. She is relating to the analyst *from* a more coherent experience of selfhood and less as a means of achieving it. *It is here that what Winnicott terms "internalization" of the capacity to be alone is most noticeably linked to an increased relational capacity for processing and regulating potentially traumatic affect.*

I have indeed been making a case for the therapeutic action of what I call the analyst's "stumbling along and hanging in." For a period of time he loses his bearings and is not able to think clearly about what he is experiencing. He cannot even find what appears to be a useful way of engaging with his patient in the here and now because his patient's mind is feeling so unfamiliar. He then dissociates, which leads to his disconnecting affectively from his patient and turning inward to the library of his mind where he can at least rummage around for some almost new ideas that might even be true. Is this bad therapy? Only if the analyst is content to be relationally unawake for too long. If he can *feel* his own disconnection, then this messy clinical process becomes fertile ground for collision between subjective "truths." And as I have argued, it is from the relational negotiation of such collisions that the most authentic and far-reaching growth takes place. In other words, what is most pertinent is that the process through which the analyst "wakes up" and can begin to think about the ongoing experience depends on his gradually developing ability to realize that an enactment is indeed taking place and that they either find a way to process it together or they will remain stuck in a shared dissociative cocoon. An example from my work may be useful at this point.

Claudia

Claudia was almost 40 years old when she began treatment with me. She had been sexually abused at age 5 by her psychologically impaired older brother, but unlike the perhaps more frequently observed after-math, Claudia still retained a clear visual memory of the scene. It was in fact the first thing she mentioned when she began therapy–but not because she thought it was a problem. To the contrary, she said that she feared I might make a big deal out of it and she wanted to get it out of the way before that could happen. "I don't want to waste time with something unimportant," she said. She also volunteered, casually, that her mother knew about the event but that she had no idea how her mother found out. When I commented that it was interesting how clearly she could visualize the scene, almost as if she were watching a movie, and yet seemed to have no recall of any emotional impact of it, on either herself or her mother, her reply was that this made it even more evident how unimportant it was–so unimportant that it never needed to be talked about, *and still didn't.*

As we began to work together it became clear early on, at least to me, that Claudia's childhood involved a large element of personal invalidation in many ways other than the early abuse–so many that her wariness of looking into her past for one "obvious" cause of her current problems made perfect sense in that context alone. My per-spective on Claudia's childhood was more or less the following: Her normal developmental need for an interested mother who wished to help and support her in coping with the *routine* challenges of growing up had been declared invalid, and in effect, she was told again and again by her mother that her desire for such attention was a sign of self-ishness because, unlike her handicapped older brother, Claudia was not "defective." Only if there was a serious crisis that she was unable to handle could she put forth a claim for help, but this could never happen without great shame. Such "crises" were thereby rendered "nonexistent" ahead of time. As a burdened but proudly "nondefec-tive" child, the cumulative trauma of neglect and disconfirmation led to an expectation that each next thing to come along–always some-thing she was determined to handle alone–would be too much for her. But it was this very determination to carry the burden without complaining to her mother that became the key ingredient in the pro-cedural attachment pattern that shaped her core sense of self. Claudia lived, most visibly, in a self-state of "good little soldier," kept in line by an internal voice denouncing the "not-me" part of her that yearned to communicate her inner despair.

From the time she was 5 years old she escaped from this inner tor-ment by using her capacity to dissociate. "Spaced out" was what she called it. Sometimes it was "taking naps" that she knew were not really naps. But the full rigidity of her dissociative mental structure didn't develop until adolescence, at which time she began to experience its social cost.

Claudia eventually married, had a child, and functioned fairly well at a job that entailed considerable responsibility but, as you might expect, she was always putting out brush fires and felt constantly on the edge of everything falling to pieces in her relationships with others. Despite the developmental trauma of her childhood, Claudia was actually a pretty good parent in most ways, but for years had been terrified that if she relaxed her maternal vigilance for even a moment she would be placing her daughter, Alice, in great danger (including, of course, from other parts of Claudia herself). Alice, who was getting older, was increasingly demanding more freedom, and this was not easy for Claudia. The issue of her hypervigilance in "'protecting" Alice was in fact something that Claudia and Alice were dealing with together with some interpersonal success, but when Claudia talked to *me* about their relationship this progress was never acknowledged. The internal collision between Claudia's dissociated self-state truths was enacted in our relationship, and I was unaware of the degree to which I experienced her as more embedded than she actually was in the single truth of "I must protect my child or disaster will strike." I thus experienced her as more in need of my input to help her sort things out than she actually was, and was so busy trying not to relate to her as her mother did—as the "nondefective child" who didn't need help— that I failed to recognize I was relating to her in the way she related to Alice, making sure that I protected *my* child lest disaster should strike.

But Claudia, as it turned out, was doing something more complex than "holding out on me." She had already grown profoundly and was discovering the joy of using her mind as a "private space," a development about which I knew nothing. I was, however, at least somewhat aware of a shift that seemed to be taking place in her mental functioning: Periodically, the concreteness of her thinking seemed to diminish, allowing the shadowy presence of something almost like humor to briefly appear. But because this came and went without any apparent linearity, the power of our ongoing enactment was strong enough to keep me from looking at it as something to take seriously, and in the following vignette, as the reader will observe, I am seeing Claudia through a glass darkly, not only with regard to her capacity for mothering but also with regard to her capacity for sophisticated thinking—and I am being set straight by her on both counts.

The Session

The session was preceded by a voicemail message from Claudia that she had left for me earlier in the day. In it, she stated only that since she had not gotten me on the phone and she would be seeing me for a session in the afternoon anyway, she would wait till then to tell me the reason for the call and that it wasn't important for me to call her back.

I did not retrieve the message until just 2 hours before she was due to arrive for her appointment, and experienced an uncomfortable sense that, despite what she said in words, she indeed wanted me to call her back. Notice that I used the word "wanted." It would be more accurate to admit that I felt she "needed" me to return her call, a difference so important that I am underlining the distinction. Why did I not want to feel her need? Because I didn't *want* to return her call. I was busy and didn't feel like interrupting what I was doing. Moreover, I didn't want to deal with the fact that not only was I failing to "protect my child lest disaster should strike," I also was feeling distressingly like her mother. So I told myself that she was being "mature" and that I should heed the explicit *content* of her message, as opposed to its implicit *affective* message, and not return her call. Like most examples of unilateral clinical judgment, my decision was based on a "truth" that was at least partially self-serving, and it is this aspect that is most frequently dissociated.

When Claudia arrived for her session she began by casually mentioning that she had left me a voicemail message earlier in the day. In a calm voice she then stated that she had had a "strange and disturbing experience" the night before, which was why she called me. Then, without elaborating on her feelings about the phone call itself she began to tell me about the "unimportant" reason she had called. She said that she was feeling overwhelmed by everything caving in on her all at once—work, marriage, and motherhood—and that it was all more than her mind could handle.

With her typically high level of efficiency, she had just dealt with a day in which she had seen a new apartment that she and her husband, ignoring serious marital discord, were considering buying; a day in which her boss, with whom she was having personal conflicts that she believed threatened her job, *had left her a message to call her back without saying what it was about*; a day in which she was anticipating her next day's appointment with her daughter's therapist to discuss her "insufficiencies" in being a mother; and finally, an appointment with me to continue working on her arguably improved ability to stay present in the here and now in the face of interpersonal experiences that she believed would overwhelm her mind.

An inhuman agenda! Inhuman even for Claudia's attachment-organized determination to deal with everything that came along all by herself. For Claudia to mentally hold this overload as a state of conflict was not possible for her that night, so her brain turned to a solution she hadn't used in a long time: She went into a trance "sleep"–an altered state of awakeness. She awoke with a terrible migraine headache, a dream she could not recall, *and a total loss of vision in her right eye.* She then started to panic, not about the visual loss itself but about the possibility that she wouldn't be able to see her daughter clearly enough to take care of her. I was not as shocked by the symptom as I might have been because I already knew that her right eye was the eye in which, as an adolescent, the pupil would suddenly dilate to a much larger size than the left eye.[2]

Keeping the above in mind, now hear the voice of Emily Dickinson (Poem 599, 1862)–a poet whose imagery and language so intimately embody traumatic affect that her verse has been known to evoke it in some readers:

> There is a pain—so utter—
> It swallows substance up—
> Then covers the Abyss with Trance—
> So Memory can step
> Around—across—upon it –
> As one within a Swoon—
> Goes safely—where an open eye—
> Would drop Him—Bone by Bone.

Earlier on, Claudia would have felt very recognized by Dickinson. This time, however, Claudia did not completely give herself over to the old dissociative solution. Even though her brain automatically reacted as if her possessing two "open eyes" would risk her dropping into the abyss bone by bone, her mind was in fact already capable of dealing with a level of cognitive complexity that transcended the

---

[2]This phenomenon has in fact been reported in a laboratory study of neurological manifestations in patients with severe dissociative disorders (Ischlondsky, 1955), and has been anecdotally reported to me by colleagues in regard to less dissociative patients who are under intense emotional distress.

brain's need for automatic protection at any cost. Claudia's use of her cognition was now robust enough to master the difference between being scared and being scarred. Her experience of the "shadow of the tsunami," the omnipresent signal that affective flooding is lurking around the corner and bringing with it, in Dickinson's imagery, a pain so utter that it swallows substance up, had lost its traumatic hallmark– the capacity to take her over completely. Indeed, Claudia was frightened and affectively dysregulated, but unlike what would have been characteristic of her in the past, when she "awoke" she telephoned me and left her message. One could say that although her physiological eye condition had returned as a dissociative response, it no longer was a bodily substitute for a psychological "I" condition. That is, she no longer faced the affective destabilization of self continuity.

Sounds hopeful, *right*? Indeed it was, but as part of the ongoing enactment my hopefulness was enlisted as a means of securing my own dissociation–in effect being used to blind one of my own eyes. I told myself how wonderful it was that despite Claudia's immense psychological overload she was able to be here in a self-state that, notwithstanding her dissociative symptom, she could be "fully" present– or so I chose to believe. My preferred definition of "fully" present was at that moment shaped by my relief that she came ready to work on her problems and didn't seem to be bothered that I had not called her back.

It was when she began talking about how much worse her relationship with Alice was becoming and how awful she felt about having to talk to Alice's therapist about her bad mothering that the following exchange took place–an exchange that left me breathless.

PB: You may need to give Alice more room to breathe. Your worry that something bad will happen to her if you leave her by herself for even a minute still makes you feel that you would be neglecting her.

CLAUDIA: [*primed for confrontation*] Are you saying that I'm an overprotective mother?

PB: [*nondefensively, because that was in fact what I was saying*] I suppose I am.

CLAUDIA: [*emphatically*] Well, you got it wrong! I'm not an overprotective mother to my child. I'm just a normal grandmother.

PB: [*bewildered*] Grandmother? What do you mean by grandmother?

CLAUDIA: Grandmothers were mothers once already. So with
             their grandchild it's the second time around being a
             mother. They know what to look for before it happens
             because they've been there before.
PB: [*totally bewildered*] What does that have to do with you?
             You are not a grandmother.
CLAUDIA: *Neglect* is what it has to do with me. I had to mother
             myself when I was a child so this is my second time
             around. I know what to look for before it happens so
             I'm just a normal grandmother.

Claudia was clearly enjoying her ability to play with my innocence.
But beyond that, Claudia was also enjoying her own mind. She was in
dangerous territory but her attachment was not threatened—certainly
not enough for her brain to trigger automatic dissociation. A new
capacity for ironic wit suddenly showed itself through an interpersonal
directness that I had not known existed—a directness that was both an
unmistakable challenge to my narrow perception of her, and also a
clear source of pleasure to Claudia. Even though she could see I was
bewildered by this change in her, she knew me well enough to know
that I was also enjoying this delightfully clever person even if I wasn't
sure "who she was." Our bond was still very much in place, and was
on the threshold of becoming even stronger.

It was then that she said it: *"I needed you to call me back. You should
have known that and you should have called—even though I said it wasn't
necessary."*

I could feel my head spinning. Everything that came to mind I dis-
carded because I could feel my defensiveness and I wanted to hide it
from myself as well as from her. Was what she said true? How could it
be? How was I supposed to know what she "really" wanted? Almost
as if I had asked that question aloud, Claudia continued, "Sure—you're
telling yourself you were in a no-win situation, but maybe what I am
blaming you most for is that you didn't think about what I was feeling
when I left that weird message."

To use my own language, Claudia had given *me* a "safe surprise." She was implicitly inviting me to join her in creating a shared
space in which we might explore together what she might indeed
have been feeling when she left the phone message—an invitation that simultaneously would lead to exploration of what *I* might
have been feeling that made me want to put that question out of my
mind.

Neither of us felt optimistic about what we were getting ourselves into, but we were nevertheless each ready to do our best. Claudia's first foray led her, dutifully, to her mother's perfunctory attitude toward her and to her feeling that mother was never "really" happy for her in a wholehearted way. My initial response to this was equally mechanical and flatfooted, centering around her mother's lack of interest in Claudia's experience when her brother abused her being the thing that had led to her wanting me to return her call and thus show her that I was different from her mother. I had offered this formulation many times before, and in many different contexts, and it felt as empty and experience-distant as always. It was, appropriately, greeted with sullen silence. My immediate reaction to her sullenness was disappointment. I had hoped we were out of the "mess" and here we were, seemingly worse off than when we started the session. I needed something to help me recover, so I reached again into my inner world for some formulaic but plausible "truth" to hold on to and found one: Her sullenness, I told myself, was her disguised anger that my formulation, mechanical though it was, had actually hit pay-dirt: That is, she was suddenly forced to recognize that even though she could still recall the visual details of the early abuse, her *emotional experience* of it and the fact that she was unable to share it with her mother was not only important, but was so *very* important that she could no longer render it insignificant and thus called me. Fortunately another part of me knew better than to say this aloud even though I believed that the general outline of it was right. Because I was aware of how distant I was feeling from her I was equally aware that my formulation, whether or not I believed it might be true in the abstract, would feel as experientially inauthentic and empty to Claudia as it felt to me.

What to do! It was clear that my cupboard was bare. There was nothing left in it that would "work" any better. The problem was with me, not my ideas. So I stopped searching. Strangely, it didn't feel so bad to give up. And even more strangely, it was at that moment that I could feel an option that I had not felt earlier—I could share my experience of what was going on in my mind. I could share it just because I wanted her to know it, not because it was supposed to lead somewhere. And that's what I did; I shared my formulation, and I also shared my feelings *about* my formulation—that I had turned to this formulation because I was upset about how disconnected I was feeling and was looking for some credible concept that I could offer her because I couldn't find a way of just being with her. I told her that even though my formulation did seem plausible to me I had no reason to believe that understanding its logic would be in any way useful to her. She listened attentively, obviously thinking about what I just said, and then tried restating the formulation on her own, after which she declared, quite thoughtfully, that she agreed it wasn't useful but that it was at least useful that *both* of us now knew it wasn't useful.

The humor in this moment didn't escape me. I had given up searching for understanding because I had run out of ideas and the result was that we ended up agreeing that my ideas weren't useful anyway. Though it wasn't exactly a gold-medal performance, there was something about what we just did that brought us together experientially in a way that hadn't been possible until that moment. For some reason, I was no longer feeling disconnected from her despite the fact that the only thing we agreed on was the lameness of my ideas. I was feeling not only close to her, but along with the closeness I could feel a sense of freedom that was, dare I say it, joyful. The pressure to solve the mystery of the "weird" phone message was gone. And in its place, we suddenly found ourselves sharing our experience of what our relationship felt like to each of us, and we were doing it as naturally as if it had been waiting to happen. Though it saddens me to formalize something this personal by the concept of "processing an enactment," from a clinical standpoint that is indeed what we were doing.

One of the things that became clearer as we processed our respective experiences of what was being enacted in our relationship was the overarching implicit meaning contained in her "grandmother" story—a meaning that was there to see when we were both ready to put words to it. Through her metaphor, "I'm just a normal grandmother," Claudia was telling me, both procedurally and linguistically, that her array of self-states was less organized dissociatively and more as a coherent experience of self that could verbalize its own existence and do so through the use of analogy. She had constructed a delightfully impish metaphor in which the complex interrelationship among daughter, mother, and grandmother became a form of self-representation. In sharing this with me, Claudia was proudly stating that, unlike the manner in which her self-states manifested themselves in the phone message, they had attained a structural coherence that transcended the times they had become and might yet again become "not-me" to one another. Mother, daughter and grandmother were more than separate entities. They were interrelated. In playing with metaphor while playing with me, Claudia was simultaneously telling me and showing me that she had attained wholeness. And she was having fun doing it. She didn't mind that her pleasure, which was being expressed just because she was feeling it, was not compatible with my state of mind.

By the time the session ended, the phone message no longer seemed weird and Claudia no longer seemed alien to me. The Claudia that I experienced as having hijacked our relationship was no longer an unknown "other." The boundary between selfhood and otherness had become newly permeable for both of us.

Over time, we became more and more aware of the complexity surrounding the issue of whether returning her call did or did not have merit. She got in touch with her part that indeed felt it didn't make sense to call back, and she then recognized she had not been able to make that explicit because she was protecting another part that felt very differently about it. This was why the message that she left, although it was supposed to be "sort of" a compromise, was also a quasi-dissociative solution. Because there was no self-reflective negotiation with the part that did need to speak with me imme-diately, the message lacked the hallmark of clarity that comes with conflict resolution. The needs of each part were at that moment too incompatible to be held as conflict, so they were enacted dissocia-tively, each through its own channel of communication. And as with any enactment, there are always reciprocal self-states of the analyst that are likewise enacting their dissociated presence, and so it was with me.

Most parts of Claudia were now communicating with one another and the reciprocal parts of me were likewise in dialogue. What took place in this session happened because we stopped trying to figure out the psychoanalytic truth. We freed ourselves from our dissocia-tive cocoon when Claudia could *feel* what she wanted from me, and I could *feel* my reciprocal desire for the same thing. And it was not about whether I should have returned her call. It was about each of us needing something from each other—something that transcended concrete behavior. Claudia needed me to experience the urgency of her need as legitimate—regardless of whether or not I returned her call and regardless of whether I *wanted* to do so. That is, the issue with which we were struggling was not one of "truth," but our difficulty in "feeling into" one another (state-sharing) *while* feeling legitimate in also having minds of our own—each mind holding and expressing its own reality without experiencing as "anomalous" the reality of the other (see Mayer, 2007, pp. 133–143). Let it be clear, however, that the cocreated relational space that we now shared was not, nor could ever be, identical for each partner because individual self-state truths continue to contribute to self-experience. The difference was that the other's subjectivity was no longer alien to our own.

I hope I have been at least somewhat able to convey the strength of my conviction that in psychoanalytic treatment the restoration of joy in simply being "me" is a goal in itself. Claudia's private joy in being herself was a needed aspect of what enabled her to share that self-experience in her relationships with others, but for her to undertake a "public journey of the private self" Claudia and I had to discover *together* the unspoken part of her phone message. What we discovered was that the message only *indirectly* had to do with the dissociated affective experiences of her brother's abuse and her mother's indifference. Although as time passed, both of those experiences became more and more consciously vivid and consciously discussible, the unspoken "message" that most directly mattered was not to her mother but to me. Why so? Because the processing of early trauma is, at its heart, relational: It does not free a patient from what was done to her in the past, but from what she has had to do to herself and to others in order to *live* with what was done to her in the past. This is why I argue that the therapeutically indispensable message was addressed to me and only indirectly to her mother, and why the affective recollection of her childhood trauma was a useful aftermath to processing our own enactment of it, but not a "prerequisite."

Ultimately, the most salient unspoken "message" was what Claudia was able to communicate to me implicitly, little by little: "You have the right to not always give me what I need. I have the right to have all parts of me *recognized*. I now can claim that right without feeling flooded with dread."

A Final Word on Human Relatedness

The development of a mature capacity for affect regulation rests on a utilization of the natural dialectic, always operative, between auto-regulation and relational regulation. Schore (2003a, 2003b) makes it clear that the degree to which early relational bonds are internalized as stable and secure actually determines significant aspects of the brain's structure, especially in the right hemisphere. This in turn determines whether later in life an individual can utilize interactive regulation, such as in a psychotherapeutic relationship, when his own auto-regulatory mechanisms are not available. Schore (2003b) also stresses the dual role of the analyst as psychobiological regulator and co-participant, and that this duality is especially vital during heightened affective moments. In other words, the analyst's role is therapeutic because his regulating function is not independent of his coparticipation, an emphasis that resonates with Winnicott's point that id relationships strengthen rather than disrupt a state of ego relatedness. Thus each formulation supports in a different way my own view that the process of collision and negotiation is therapeutic because it allows encounters with otherness to become not just less frightening but pleasurable. Why should "pleasurable" even matter? John Klauber (1980) has clarified this question by offering a fresh understanding of Freud's (1933) long-term goal of psychoanalysis—where id was there ego shall be. Klauber declares that for this goal to be reached:

> The ego must acquire an increased tolerance for crude impulse so that it can express it more easily both in direct and indirect form, thus increasing the number of satisfactions which can become available. ... Be that as it may, some internalization of the analytic process, perhaps in modified form, accompanied by an increased capacity for instinctual satisfaction, provide practical and logical criteria of analytic success. *Such an outcome implies that the patient has enjoyed the analytic process* (which I will not here further try to define). (p. 195, emphasis added)

I am suggesting that in order for what Klauber calls "internalization of the analytic process" to take place, the analytic relationship has to be affectively alive to all parts of the self, and in this regard I think that Klauber's revised understanding of the long term aim of psychoanalysis—where id was, there *id and ego* shall be—is a not unreasonable standard of successful analytic work. If Freud were alive he might argue that Klauber's rendering of his maxim is not "true," but I wonder if over time they might together arrive at something they felt was accurate.

My closing statement, therefore, is this: During my years of saying things to patients, nothing I ever offered has been the truth. I can say that truthfully, regardless of whether a patient agreed or disagreed with what I said. But neither have I lied, and I can say that equally truthfully. My use of irony here is not facetiousness but a final effort to engage the reader in the destabilizing experience of what it is like for me to swim with a patient in more or less raw clinical process and to swim as long as I am able without clutching the concepts of truth or objective reality as permanent anchoring points to relieve the fear of drowning. Without such anchoring points there needs to be some other source of security that allows an analyst to be with a patient in a way that makes both persons willing to tamper with the familiarity of their hard-won character structures in order to achieve gains that may or may not be realized. I believe that the source of this security is human relatedness.

6

If This Be Technique, Make the Most of It!¹

CR Historians of the American Revolution remain uncertain if Patrick Henry actually uttered the final five words of "If this be treason, make the most of it," but they do affirm that he later apologized for the intensity of the feelings he expressed in his famous speech that challenged the supremacy of British rule. What follows here is a chapter about analytic "technique" offering what I hope is a plausible case for severing or, at the very least, further loosening our historical tie to that classical concept. So, let me explain my "treason."

Obviously, certain tasks, including many that involve an interaction with another person, require both individual mastery of some technical skill and that this skill be incorporated within relational spontaneity. This fact has, paradoxically, provided psychoanalytic support for the classical concept of technique because it has been long understood that technique alone is not enough and that the human relationship matters equally. Here I offer a view that the process of self-growth is inherently and distinctly relational: It is not brought about *through* the relationship between patient and analyst. To the contrary, the source of therapeutic action *is* the relationship. Between them, patient and analyst jointly create a relational unconscious, and what emerges belongs to neither one of them as individuals alone. In this treatment context the analyst's professional role is subsumed within a shared personal field. From here it is but a short step to my treason: I submit

---

¹An earlier version of this chapter, "Stumbling Along and Hanging In: If This Be Technique, Make the Most of It," was published in *Psychoanalytic Inquiry, 31(6)*, 2011.

that to continue labeling what we do as "technique" slows the natural evolution of psychoanalysis, both clinically and as a body of theory.

My understanding of therapeutic process can perhaps be usefully compared with how I experience the process of writing. The state of mind in which I write is not topic-organized, and I am often pleasantly surprised to find that the assigned topic is somewhere in it. After 30 years of psychoanalytic writing I have come to realize that as I am working on each new manuscript I have very little idea of what I am writing about until I have lots of pages of "something," and can begin a dialogue with those pages to discover how, or even if, the predetermined topic fits in. But during the process of writing, each next thought, or to borrow Russell Meares' (2001) felicitous phrase, "what happens next," is being created by relationally organized shifts in my self-state experience—spontaneous shifts that are determined in part by the impact of what is already on the page and now has an identity of its own. In other words, it is my internal dialogue with the developing voice of what is being constructed that decides the de facto topic. The pre-chosen conceptual topic does not evaporate from my memory, but it is not what engages me. What matters is whether something emerges in an experientially alive way that makes that topic, or any topic, worth talking about. I offer this comment about writing because it could as easily be a description of my experience while being an analyst: Central to my functioning is my relationship to an "other," no matter whether the other is a patient, a paper, or one of my own self-states with a mind of its own.

How does the concept of "technique" fit into this? For any analyst, the usefulness of a given theoretical concept depends on its degree of consistency with other concepts that give coherence to what he believes takes place during a psychoanalysis. Does the particular concept in question feel important to the overarching context that defines what he believes happens between himself and his patient that leads to growth? This criterion applies as much to the concept of "technique" as to any other.

During an analyst's day-to-day work with patients, the context that determines his opinion about the value of technique is more experiential than theoretical—his listening stance. His listening stance will be the fulcrum on which he will seek to balance what he does with what he believes is supposed to lead to therapeutic growth in his patient.

For example, when an analytic author speaks about his mind as an "analyzing instrument" (e.g., Balter et al., 1980; Lasky, 2002), his listening stance is being presented, at least conceptually, as one in which he is using his mind to hear the patient's material as a means of "understanding" him. This "understanding," however, is inherently linked to the analyst's concept of "technique"–the set of rules (whether loosely or rigidly held) for most effectively using his "analyzing instrument" to make and test inferences about what is hidden in the patient's unconscious (see also Levenson, 1972). The idea is to not interfere with the data nor contaminate it with suggestion, while remaining alert to possibilities for intervention in accord with the analyst's "technique."

If the implicit presence of "technique" goes unnoticed–and this is true for analysts of all persuasions–then it generates a listening stance that may be internally consistent with it but will not be open to dyadic scrutiny. Through its impact on an analyst's listening stance, "technique" will shape how the analyst conceptualizes what he hears and how he synthesizes the relationship between what he hears and what he is doing, what he believes is yet to be accomplished, and what factors interfere with the desired outcome. The risk is that all this synthesizing will happen prior to today's negotiation with the patient. I fully grant that among individual analysts there are many who transcend this hidden pitfall, but we are all aware that skilled clinicians have always found a way to work around inhospitable aspects of theory. Reflect on the following passage written by the Norwegian author Per Peterson in his novel, *Out Stealing Horses* (2003).[2]

> People like it when you tell them things, in suitable portions, in a modest, intimate tone, and they think they know you, but they do not, they know *about* you, for what they are let in on are facts, not feelings … not how what has happened to you and how all the decisions you have made have turned you into who you are. *What they do is they fill in with their own feelings and opinions and assumptions, and they compose a new life which has precious little to do with yours, and that lets you off the hook.* (pp. 67–68, emphasis added)

Imagining that the speaker is an analytic patient, I would suggest that a key dimension of the therapeutic relationship lies in the analyst's effort to "catch himself in the act" during those inevitable moments when he is *being* one of the people described above, and that his ability to

---

[2]Many thanks to my new colleague Arne Andreas Døske for introducing me to this inspiring writer.

do this relates directly to the concept of "technique. Why so? Because technique is related to task. Technique, regardless of one's degree of expertise, is something that one applies to a particular task with a hope of command over it, even when one's command is necessarily imperfect. Lawrence Friedman, chairing a 1990 panel that revisited Freud's papers on technique (see Burris, 1995), specified six papers (Freud, 1911, 1912a, 1912b, 1913, 1914, 1915b) as those that Freud intended to stand as a single unit representing the fundamentals of treatment. Following Freud, technique traditionally has been framed by psychoanalysts as a set of rules to guide behavior–a set of rules that organizes an analyst's conduct in a way that, if the rules are followed, should facilitate the development of an authentic analytic process. The creation of an authentic analytic process is the task; rules describing correct technique are the means.

In recent decades, however, a transformation has taken place in psychoanalytic thinking that has profoundly changed how we view the nature of the patient/analyst relationship and what constitutes an authentic analytic process. Since Greenberg and Mitchell's 1983 classic, *Object Relations in Psychoanalytic Theory*, analytic schools of thought increasingly have been debating whether the shift only represents a modification of Freud's theory in a relational direction, or whether it represents something more fundamental–an authentic paradigm shift that is "relational" at its core. The debate, largely between classical and interpersonal/relational positions, has been valuable in creating a lively dialogue between these schools and recently between American relational and British object relational analysts (see, for example, Bass, 2009; Parsons, 2009).

Interpersonal and relational writers largely have endorsed the idea that we are in fact confronted with a paradigm change and have conceptualized it as a transformation from a one-person to a two-person psychology. I feel that this formulation is accurate, and that three central clinical shifts are intrinsic to the conceptual shift: A shift from the primacy of content to the primacy of context, a shift from the primacy of cognition to the primacy of affect, and a shift away from (but not yet an abandonment of) the concept of "technique."

As a group, classical analysts largely have been skeptical about the idea of a relational paradigm shift. They rightly insist that they have always been very aware of the danger of "painting by the numbers." They also insist that although classical technique is framed as a set of rules, classical analysts have demonstrated a long history, arguably beginning with Stone (1961), of dedicatedly thinking about how to apply the rules humanely so that a patient does not feel he is being treated as an object (cf. Bromberg, 1996b). They further argue that technique has served as a baseline of analytic behavior from which certain strategic, but analyzable, departures may be acceptable under predefined conditions with certain patients. Finally, as prescriptions for behavior, the rules of technique also have had the added benefit of allowing the analyst's unconscious deviations from them (counter-transference) to be assessed in terms of their seriousness. And, at a clinical level, classical analysts have tried to refute the notion of a paradigm shift by arguing, justifiably, that by heeding Freud's (1912b) injunction to maintain "evenly hovering attention," they do work with affective experience–their own and their patient's–and thus always have seen the growth context of the analytic relationship as involving both patient and analyst.

The problem with this lattermost argument is that a classical analyst's listening stance, insofar as it is technically defined by Freud's concept of "evenly hovering attention," tends to shape his use of the relationship and his own affective experience in a way that is *experientially* nonrelational. That is, in order to honor Freud's meaning of evenly hovering attention, the classical analyst's listening stance is framed by the observed *content*, and to the degree that the relational context is considered, it is one more aspect of content. The interpersonal/relational analyst's listening stance turns this on its head. The defining quality that clinically distinguishes a relational listening stance from evenly hovering attention is that *the analyst's overarching attunement is to his contextualized perceptual experience.* Verbal content is only one ingredient of a here-and-now field, a field that is shaped by an ever-changing affective dialectic between what is being enacted and what is being said.

The qualitative difference in listening stance has a commanding influence on the relative importance that is attributed to the concept of "technique" in classical analysis and in relational analysis. The reason why this is so becomes clearer once we look more closely at the implications of translating Freud's "evenly hovering attention" into actual clinical process. Freud (1912b) introduced the concept of "evenly hovering attention" when he repudiated what he believed was a forced technique and replaced it with the recommendation of a stance that he considered open-ended listening. The analyst, as far as humanly possible, was to direct his attention to his patient's associations in an unbiased way, allowing unconscious meaning to emerge from the clinical material without the analyst's selective focus on associations to which he attributes special importance because of his personally preferred ideas.

In the classical literature, Freud's recommendation has been discussed in different ways, but rarely more succinctly or fairly than in a 1988 paper by Fred Pine, who observed that "[t]otal uncommittedness is an impossibility," and that "while we may approximate evenly hovering attention ... ordinarily we have in mind a general set of theoretical constructs which dictate what the *potential* meanings are in what we are hearing" (p. 577, emphasis in original). Thus, argues Pine: "Freud's guideline of evenly hovering attention for the listening clinician only makes sense if we recognize its counterpart: the sense-making, *meaning-finding*, ordering tendencies of the human mind" (p. 576, emphasis added). If Pine's observation is accurate, and I believe it is, then the classical analyst's "meaning-finding" is inevitably fueled by a content-driven listening stance, focused on the speaker's associations more than on the speaker (see also Schafer, 1976, 1983), allowing the analyst to choose those theoretical constructs that he feels best match the potential meaning he hears in his patient's associative "material," and to consider how best to then formulate "well-timed" interpretations.

In short, though Freud hoped to arrive at a nondirective stance, generations of analysts have found themselves listening in ways that run counter to the original intent, which intent they still valorized. It was thus predictable that "evenly hovering attention" and "technique" became discrete concepts that divided the clinical situation into two components—how to listen and what to do. The traditional training of classical analysts became similarly shaped around the teaching of a listening stance and the teaching of intervention (i.e., breaking into the flow of associations) as separate entities. Despite efforts to modify it, this division possesses powerful historical roots that persist in the way stated at the 1974 conference of the Committee on Psychoanalytic Education (COPE) of the American Psychoanalytic Association:

> The dual requirements of precise content analysis and of nondefensive utilization of the material should be met in a flexible manner. The constant attuning of the analyst to the ego state and the analytic process, to determine the appropriate dosage of interpretations, etc., may be looked upon as a process parallel to the teaching relationship of the supervisor and student analyst. (Goodman, 1977, p. 36)

Because the concept of "evenly hovering attention" separates what the analyst hears from what he does with what he hears, it requires that the concept of "technique" be packaged alongside it to make sure that what he does allows him to continue to understand the content of what he is hearing in the right way. Not to decide prematurely what content needs to be pursued, though admirable, does not change the fact that one is nonetheless still focused on the content rather than on the dyadic experiential context. The analyst who listens with "evenly hovering attention" is still positioning himself outside the dyad even as he keeps himself open to relational themes as content. Thus, quite apart from whether a given classical analyst claims to work "relationally" with patients, the model that guides him is not experiential and does not describe what is meant by a two-person field.

In an interpersonal/relational listening stance the analyst's overarching state of mind is attuned to his fluctuating, moment-to-moment experience of what it is like for him to be with his patient and for his patient to be with him during the course of a session. It is a stance in which his perception of constantly shifting, multiple perspectives—his own and his patient's—are the source of raw data, the "material." He is not looking for an unconscious fantasy that he tries to piece together inferentially (see chapter 7), nor is he searching for hidden "truth" (see chapter 5). His "material" is an ever-shifting experiential context, the most powerful element of which first reaches him perceptually, not cognitively. Indeed, this experiential context is not immediately available for cognitive processing because it contains elements that are being enacted while other things are being spoken. If the analyst can continue to attend to it perceptually, then, little by little, the enacted experience that links patient and analyst can be felt and then shared. The process of sharing allows the creation of a relational unconscious that can be cognitively and linguistically processed through a *consensual* understanding that is being generated interpersonally by active engagement with each other. It is the quality of active interpersonal engagement that leads Lothane (2009) to argue in favor of the term *language action* rather than Schafer's (1976, 1980) "action language."

I am in no way suggesting that "content" as defined by the conceptual significance of the patient's associations is irrelevant. On the contrary, I am offering a reevaluation of the place of associations in the therapeutic process. I see associations as an aspect of relational experience that are best approached under the sponsorship of perception, a mental process about which I will have more to say before this book concludes.

The Relational Unconscious

Process without Technique

A friend had just returned from a summer vacation at a music camp—a musician's version of the MacDowell Colony—where the applicants were sorted into trios, each member being evaluated on his or her level of musicianship to assure that each trio would comprise individuals of comparable ability. When I asked how this process of evaluation worked out, her reply fascinated me because she is a woman who by nature always sees the cup half full: "I met a lot of people who had good technique but there was no music coming out." When I further asked what she meant by "no music coming out" she shrugged and answered, "It's something hard to describe, but it doesn't get better by learning better technique."

Recently, in an article by Michael Tilson Thomas (2008) about Leonard Bernstein, the same point was made in a different way:

> He knew that musicians could get buried in their parts, looking fixedly at the same notes they had played thousands of times. He wanted the whole band to be out there with him in an experience that felt more like improvisation. He liked fun and a whiff of danger. He thought that a performance should reveal the emotional states the composer had experienced while creating the work. For him that meant being involved emotionally and physically. (p. 25)

Some readers who may feel in tune with this sensibility may also feel that it does not argue against technique and simply illustrates what we already know—that technique alone is not enough. I would agree that this is so with human beings who are doing something together, such as playing music, that intrinsically requires individual mastery of some technical skill, which skill then needs to be infused with relational spontaneity. I firmly believe, however, that the psychoanalytic relationship is inherently different because the "skill" that an analyst must bring to it is not acquired through learned technique, nor is it "applied." It is closer to something that I recall being evaluated on my grade-school report card as "Works and Plays Well with Others." As a kid I could never understand how my teacher arrived at this evaluation without a test, but in retrospect I think she was listening to hear if, while I was working or playing with another child, music was coming out of the duet.

Thomas's idea that Bernstein believed "a performance should reveal the emotional states the composer had experienced while creating the work" is music to *my* ears. It echoes my view (Bromberg, 1999) that the self-state relationship between author and reader similarly illustrates the complex dialectic that links affective experience and verbal language in the analyst/patient relationship. Consider the following lines written by Carlos Ruiz Zafon (2001) in his novel, *The Shadow of the Wind*. Daniel, the protagonist, is suddenly reunited with the most deeply important friend of his childhood, and in the reunion he relives the birth of that friendship:

> It seemed to me that this oversize, solitary boy had constructed his own tin companions and that I was the first person he was introducing them to. It was his secret. I shared mine. I told him about my mother and how much I missed her. When my voice broke, Tomas hugged me without saying a word. We were ten years old. From that day on Tomas Aguilar became *my best–and I his only–friend.* (p. 94, emphasis added)

Through Zafon's brilliant placement of the two em-dashes in the final sentence, he endows "best" and "only" with linguistic unity, and in so doing he evocatively endows the word "friend" with experiential wholeness that transcends our cognitive awareness of each boy's individuality. Even though each adjective remains unique to the personality of just one of the boys, the relational oneness of that friendship is felt as greater than the sum of its parts. The author could have written "Tomas Aguilar became my best friend, and I his only friend" but if he had, separateness would replace oneness; the way Zafon uses language pulls the reader not only into the book but into himself. Individuality and oneness become a single entity in the act of reunion.

So it is in our work as analysts. We have all been aware at some point in our lives that an unanticipated reunion can indeed reawaken "unremembered" *union*. Zafon magically creates state-sharing between author and reader through evoking the experience of two people whose reunion gently brings to life what I call "the nearness of you" (see chapter 8). This for me is the bedrock of what we do as analysts. After all, aren't all those weekly sessions a kind of ongoing process of personal reunion?

In an analytic relationship it is impossible to unravel what is personal from what is professional. I speak of a relationship where the analyst's professional role is subsumed within a shared personal field– a field in which the "royal road to the unconscious" is transformed into a relational unconscious—a *commoner's* road along which the only technical recommendation that can be made is to acknowledge that the unpredictable appearance of potholes is part of the journey. But what am I actually implying when I suggest that the joint creation of a "relational unconscious" takes place while transforming Freud's "royal" road?

David Malouf (2009), in his novel *Ransom*, illustrates my meaning through a brilliant metaphor set during the Trojan War—the transformation of King Priam's self-experience during the course of his journey to ransom from Achilles the body of Hector, his slain warrior son. The meaning of *being* in life rather than traversing the "royal road" as an observer on a boar hunt is discovered by Priam as he was surrendering himself to the mundane act of cooling his feet in a stream, and during an unanticipated moment of *personal* contact with Achilles, a moment that transcended the larger, more "important" purpose of the journey:

> When he set out on this business he had understood quite clearly that he would be exposing himself to things he had not previously encountered. That was the price of the new. But as he sat now with the golden taste of the pancake in his mouth and another drop of wine on his lips, he saw that what was new could also be pleasurable. This sitting with your feet in cooling water, for instance, that ran over them and away. The little fish that came to investigate, and said, No, nothing to be got out of this one. The wheeling and piping of swifts, which grew both in volume and excitement as the day's light thickened. Of course these things were not new in themselves. The water, the fish, the flocks of snub-tailed swifts had always been here, engaged in their own lives and the small activities that were proper to them, pursuing their own busy ends. But until now there had been no occasion to take notice of them. They were not in the royal sphere. Being unnecessary to royal observance or feeling, they were in the background, and his attention was always fixed on what was central. Himself. (p. 122)
>
> He was symbolically at the centre, as form and his own royal dignity demanded, but could have no part in the merely physical business, all panic and sweat, of rushing through the brush to where half a ton of steaming flesh and bone waited to be hacked, and thrust at, and brought crashing to earth. (p. 123)
>
> It was a mystery. Part of a world of ceremony, of high play, that was eternal and had nothing to do with the actual and

immediate, with *this* particular occasion, or *this* boat, or *this* king. Even the landscape it took place in was freed of its particular elements —the kind and colour of the leaves, or whether the day was sunlit or mistily overcast, the earth dry or muddy underfoot. The realm of the royal was representational, ideal. Everything that was merely accidental ... all this was to be ignored, left to fall away into the confused and confusing realm of the incidental and ordinary. His whole life was like that, or had been. But out here, he discovered, everything was just itself. That was what seemed new. (p. 124, emphasis in original)

In an optimal analytic treatment, though the journey along Freud's royal road may indeed start off as "representational, ideal," leaving all that "was to be ignored ... to fall away into the confused and confusing realm of the incidental and ordinary," it must eventually become a commoner's road that cocreates unthinkable not-me self-states into enacted here-and-now events that are lived interpersonally and become part of the patient's overarching configuration of "me." It is then that the frozen aspects of self cease to be a "mystery" because the psychoanalytic relationship ceases being "a world of ceremony, of high play, that was eternal and had nothing to do with the actual and immediate." The nonlinear process of collision and negotiation between the patient's and analyst's self-states slowly fosters recognition of each other's (and one's own) dissociated aspects of self—a dialectic of dissonance and restructuring that, as Priam discovered, was transformational because "everything was just itself. That was what seemed new." But *because* enactments are so perceptually real, they are also so unpredictably messy that I have characterized the analyst's experience as "Stumbling Along and Hanging In." In other words, *if the analyst is not feeling, personally, the impact of the dissociated parts of the patient's self that are trying to find relational existence—if the analyst is not reacting personally to them—the patient's dissociated self-states are robbed of a human context in which they can be recognized and come alive.* For analyst and patient alike, there is nothing more personal than the amalgam of freedom *and pain* entailed in finding a voice to express what had been unspeakable. In the ironic, almost bitter reckoning of C. S. Lewis (1956):

To say the very thing you really mean, the whole of it, nothing more or less or other than what you really mean; that's the whole art and joy of words. A glib saying. When the time comes to you at which you will be forced at last to utter the speech which has

lain at the center of your soul for years, which you have, all that
time, idiot-like, been saying over and over, you'll not talk about
joy of words. (p. 294)

Interpersonal/Relational Technique?

Reciprocal, self-reflective recognition of another's subjectivity (what
we call *intersubjectivity*) has become a topic of great interest to contemporary clinicians, researchers, and theorists representing different analytic schools of thought. A central focus has been on how
best to facilitate the cognitive symbolization of unprocessed affective
experience—experience that Wilma Bucci (1997a, 2003, 2007a, 2007b,
2010) calls *subsymbolic*, Donnel Stern (1997, 2009) conceptualizes as
unformulated, and I see as *dissociated* (Bromberg, 1998a, 2006a).

Jessica Benjamin (1998, 2005, 2007), in her conceptualization of
thirdness, presents a developmental and clinical formulation that is
synchronous with my own work in emphasizing that human relatedness requires the capacity for intersubjective communication in order
to make possible the ability to move beyond polarization of self and
other. As do I (chapters 1 and 3), Benjamin explicates how the development of a transitional mental space and recognition of the other's
subjectivity become achievable through negotiation. She eloquently
argues (Benjamin, 2007) that the experience of internal wholeness
based on recognition

> is the principle that supports the space of thirdness, of shared
> reality. It is the principle constituting the containing space that
> allows realities to be negotiated, failures to be recognized and
> ruptures to be repaired; it is what makes intersubjective meaning
> possible and what allows us to trust the process of knowing and
> being known. (pp. 676–677)

I hope that this clarifies a bit more my assertion that self-growth in psychoanalysis is inherently relational—and why the concept of technique
feels not just unnecessary but a hindrance, or so I would argue.

I consider the basis of therapeutic action in all forms of dynamic
psychotherapy, including psychoanalytic psychotherapy, to be the
development of intersubjectivity in areas of the mind held captive by
dissociative mental structure. A patient's responsiveness to psychoanalytic treatment rests on the ability of humans—as well as certain
other primates—not only to attribute mental states to others, but also

to experience the reciprocal alive responsiveness of others to the existence of their own mental states. There is an experiential continuum in the capacity for relatedness, ranging from what Allan Schore (2003a, pp. 94–97) calls right-brain to right-brain "state-sharing," through what the Boston Change Process Study Group (Lyons-Ruth, 1998, 2006; D. N. Stern et al., 1998) labels *implicit relational knowing*, to what Peter Fonagy (Fonagy et al., 2005) terms *mentalization*. Put simply, the development of intersubjectivity depends on whether an individual is able to experience the "other" as holding him in mind in one way or another, whether lovingly, agreeably, disagreeably, hatefully, or bewilderingly, to name just a few possibilities. Most important, in treatment it depends on reciprocal responsiveness to a shared dissociative field in which the recognition of dissociation in the mental functioning of both analyst and patient facilitates increased self-state permeability as they stumble along together, cocreating a relational unconscious.

The psychologist Seymour Epstein (1994), dealing with the phenomenon of dissociated affect, integrates the cognitive and the psychodynamic unconscious by assuming "the existence of two parallel, interacting modes of information processing: a rational system and an emotionally driven system" (p. 709). He takes the position that no matter how else mental processes are organized, they are also organized according to a supraordinate division of rational and experiential processing. He argues that the striving for expression of the emotionally driven material is not because it has an energy of its own that seeks expression, as proposed by Freud, but because there is a fundamental motive to assimilate representations of affectively significant experiences into a unified, coherent conceptual system. This process, states Epstein, is essentially adaptive, as it promotes accommodation between the two systems and therefore the construction of a coherent model of the world that is consistent with experience.

Epstein goes on to contrast this view of mental functioning with Freud's model of a self-contained energy system. As I survey Epstein's ideas, I find it hard to avoid recognizing the existence of a necessary self/other context (sometimes internal, sometimes external) that organizes what he describes as a fundamental motive to assimilate representations of emotionally significant experiences into a unified, coherent conceptual system.

The implications of this theoretical perspective, however, do not of themselves provide direct clinical support for abandoning the concept of technique. Direct support emerges only from considering how an analyst relates to patients within this frame of reference. To me, it looks something like this: Every time a patient and analyst can each access and openly share their dissociated affective experience of something that is taking place between them—some cognitively unsymbolizable aspect of their mutual experience that is felt but is unthinkable—the process of state-sharing through which this takes place begins to enlarge the domain and fluency of the dialogue. This in turn leads to increasingly integrated and complex content that becomes symbolized linguistically and thus available to self-reflection and potential conflict resolution.

The subjective reality of a patient's unsymbolized states of consciousness, especially with regard to the patient's experience of the analyst, must be felt and, in some useful way, acknowledged by the analyst. Moreover, the analyst's acknowledgment is inherently a process of sharing his personal experience of the here and now while maintaining access to the self-state in which it originated. In psychoanalysis, such sharing is a task that, relationally, requires serious emotional effort because it cannot be known in advance how much sharing is useful and how much is too much. Herbert Rosenfeld (1987) calls it "almost an art form" in which "the analyst has to be prepared to enter into an intense relationship and to retain his function of putting experience into words" (p. 160). I would add that it is the analyst's ongoing and often personally painful effort to struggle with the unpredictable process of sharing his shifting self-state experience that is his greatest contribution to the patient's (and his own) growth. *If there can be said to be an interpersonal or relational analytic technique, it is mainly in the ability of the analyst throughout the course of each analysis to negotiate and renegotiate the meaning of what constitutes useful self-state sharing.*

In the previous chapter I discussed the therapeutic action of analytic growth in terms of a mind/brain process in which the mind's self-state evolution and the brain's synaptic evolution work hand in hand, whereby new combinations of neurons increasingly wire together, allowing self-state evolution to modulate the rigidity of self-state truth. I asserted that insight has been shown to require that the wiring of the brain's synaptic networks, especially those of the right hemisphere, be "transformed by accidental, serendipitous connections" (Lehrer, 2008, p. 43). Current work in the neurobiology of interpersonal experience (e.g. Schore, 1994, 2003a, 2003b; Siegel, 1999) demonstrates that such serendipitous rewirings are facilitated by conscious and nonconscious interactions with other minds in new ways. This is precisely what we seek in an analytic relationship, and, I might add, it is also what we hope for in a personal relationship.

I want to underline this last point by referring to a brief but surprising exchange that took place during an email correspondence with Michel Sanchez-Cardenas, an analyst in France who had just finished reading an earlier version of chapter 5, and to whom interpersonal/relational thinking was relatively unfamiliar. Referring to the genuine interest we each showed in the other's frame of reference despite our areas of divergence, Sanchez-Cardenas wrote the following (personal communication):

> Would you say that here our relation, being authentic and well ruled by the setting, was the new affective, relational, serendipitous experience which allowed this new wiring? I feel this is an important matter because it opens doors allowing us to understand also how other therapies (cognitive ones, for instance) seem also to work.

His use of the phrase "authentic and well ruled by the setting" engaged the affective aliveness between us that had been there all along but had been unaddressed in the email "setting." My immediate response was an experience of feeling deeply "recognized" and I shared that with him. As an enactment of the topic itself, the exchange evoked in me a state of mind that recalled the powerfully simple way Elizabeth Strout (2008), in her novel *Olive Kitteridge,* described her protagonist's experience at such a moment: "[S]he had the sensation that she had been seen. And she had not even known she's felt invisible" (p. 213).

The Growth of the Relational Mind

In terms of philosophy of science, the viewpoint I am presenting draws on the immense contribution of Gestalt psychology, and it does so in two ways: First, Gestalt field theory has demonstrated the centrality of perception, a here-and-now phenomenon, as the organizing factor in cognition. Second, it has emphasized the need to look at phenomena we do not understand, such as personality growth, by specifying the necessary and sufficient conditions for it occur at a given moment within a given field rather than trying to "understand" it conceptually and linearly in terms of abstract cause and effect.

Elizabeth Lloyd Mayer (2007), in a volume that could well hold the future of psychoanalysis between its covers, expands the phenomenon

of intersubjectivity into the domain of what she calls anomalous experience: veridical perceptions that are not compatible with what we
classify as rational. It is beyond the scope of this chapter to address
the full range and significance of her thinking, but I want to excerpt
from her writing because the link between anomalous experience and
perception is highly relevant to what takes place in the psychoanalytic relationship. If a person indeed has many self-states, each with
"a mind of its own," the state-dependency of affective experience will
tend to make an emotionally charged event be perceived as "truth"
and another person's (or another self-state's) differing experience of
the same perceived event be perceived, to one degree or another, as
anomalous. Mayer puts it as follows:

> No matter how useful we might find integrating whatever we've
> learned from seeing one way with whatever we've learned from
> seeing the other, we simply cannot organize our perceptual field
> so that we can see both ways simultaneously. *The relevance of this
> insight is this: The perceptions that characterize potentially anomalous
> experience appear to emerge from a state of mind that is, in the moment
> of perception, radically incompatible with the state of mind in which per-
> ceptions characterizing rational thought are possible.* The mode of per-
> ception ... depends on access to a state of mind in which ordinary
> linear thought is momentarily impossible, literally suspended.
> (p. 137, emphasis in original)

Both states cannot be rational for the same mind at the same time.
Here, Mayer's insight becomes even more luminous. She realizes that
the Gestaltists have shown us that the way to experience anomalous
parts as coexisting is perceptual; the key is

> to become adept at moving between one and the other, holding
> the memory of [one] even as we see the [other]. But that means
> allowing the experience of loss. We have to give up one thing in
> order to see the other. We have to lose what's familiar in order to
> see what's new.... Giving up our habitual grounding in rational
> thought to see something else, even just for a moment–that's any-
> thing but easy for most of us. (p. 138)

For a psychoanalyst, Mayer's most far-reaching insight may be her recognition of loss, the shared loss for both patient and analyst being the

capacity for rational thought, even if only temporarily. For the patient in treatment, however, the loss is more profound and potentially destabilizing because, as she moves toward surrendering her reliance on dissociation, she allows herself to relive, with the analyst, "not-me" areas of developmental trauma, opening herself to the painful physical return of affect dysregulation that had been sequestered as "not-me." To one degree or another, enacted reliving of past developmental trauma is experienced as a threatened loss of self-continuity in the present, and it can be especially destabilizing to mental functioning if it involves a person's attachment-organized core identity–the basic foundation of affective safety. These are the moments in treatment when the analyst's ability to "stumble along and hang in" as a personally engaged partner is all important. Why? Because the maintenance of attachment-based affective safety is *procedural*–concretely tied to a pattern of interaction with an emotionally significant other that is not organized by thought (Ainsworth et al., 1978).

Respecting the patient's need to maintain a procedural attachment is central to the analyst's relational "task" in treatment: helping his patient to stay the same while changing. When the analyst fails at this part of his task he evokes what we have traditionally labeled "resistance"–a phenomenon that I see not as a patient's avoidance of unpleasant insight but as a protest against the analyst's non-negotiated disconfirmation of a dissociated part of the patient's self. Mayer does not talk much about dissociation, but this is because her frame of reference does not lead her to propose a theory of mental functioning. She does not talk about repression either, and neither term is found in her index. However, the word *dissociation* does appear twice in her text, and each time the context is noteworthy. At one point she speaks of the emergence of an anomalous perception as a "dissociative jolt." Mayer's description is intriguingly reminiscent of an analyst's discomfort when he first feels the experience of something anomalous happening between him and his patient, something that, as Mayer (2007) states, "feels utterly different from ordinary knowing."

> A model that aims to contain anomalous cognition has to take into account the feeling of what happens. It has to make room for that unique dissociative jolt, the shock of body, the emotion, and idea erupting into consciousness with knowing that feels utterly different from ordinary knowing. The feeling of what happens is part of the data. (pp. 214–215)

The other time Mayer uses the concept of dissociation, it has the same flavor. One of her colleagues, on listening to a story about an anomalous event that was experienced by another colleague, declared in a state of consternation that she was convinced of its reality and simultaneously found it unbelievable: "How can I think both things at once? It makes no sense! I'm not used to thinking like that—it's almost dissociative" (p. 134). Mayer comments:

> With that statement she was capturing something crucial about how, if we permit them at all, apparently anomalous events enter and register in consciousness, as both expectable and unbelievable. She managed to go back and forth between those two mutually incompatible points of view without rejecting either one or forcing them to "add up." (p. 135)

How does one manage this? Mayer replies that her colleague "accepted a paradox.... If they didn't add up, that in itself became a feature of the data" (p. 135). Mayer here points to the key distinction between paradox and conflict (see also Pizer, 1992, 1998). When one's ability to hold in a single state of mind two experiences that are rationally anomalous because they are incompatible with each other as ways of experiencing oneself, the incompatibility is unresolvable as internal conflict. To hold them in a single state of mind without dissociating, they must be held as paradox, but this is only possible if the level of negative affect is not already felt as so close to dysregulation that it is experienced as a threat to cognitive stability. A person cannot self-reflect when his mind's coherence is felt to be in the throes of destabilization. So what is needed? With exquisite sensitivity, Mayer answers: "Leaving rational thought behind, even momentarily, isn't a loss we easily invite. But if we want access to the state in which anomalous knowing might be possible, *a deliberate invitation might be precisely what is required*" (p. 139, emphasis added).

Mayer is here making an explicit argument that the future of human mental development is not only relational but that it is intersubjective in ways that go beyond what we can now rationally accept as possible. The "invitation" of which she speaks is an invitation from an involved other, an other with whom a shared mental state is potentially possible, a state in which you are each part of a whole that is greater than either of you alone.

Psychoanalytic treatment is functioning at its best when the "invitation" is bidirectional; what is needed is an ongoing process of boundary-negotiation in which analyst and patient are permitting, as well as inviting, increased permeability between their separate selves and are jointly constructing a relational unconscious in which anomalous knowing might be possible. I see the process of treatment as one in which each person more and more feels the other's invitation as safe and allows such a realm to take shape. It is a phenomenon in which self and other become increasingly less anomalous because they are increasingly experienced as part of a greater whole that neither alone defines.

I conclude with an observation by Mayer that touches the heart of what I believe underlies human growth in its broadest sense—the increased ability to stand in the spaces between self-states that would otherwise be alien to each other. It also is the essence of what I believe takes place in a fruitful psychoanalytic relationship. Mayer (2007) captures in one concise paragraph the main reason I am moved to argue that the necessary and sufficient conditions for such a relationship will be optimally facilitated if they are not press-ganged by a model of therapeutic action that because it is wedded to learned technique, thereby interferes with the natural process of therapeutic growth as spontaneous, nonlinear, self–other negotiation.

> To see a view of the world in which anomalous experience happens, we need to temporarily abandon a view of the world in which rational thought happens. Worse, we need to temporarily abandon the state of mind in which we see what rational thought helps us see. And vice versa. Refusing to undergo either loss means refusing the possibility of seeing what the other side sees.... If people on both sides stay lodged in states of mind from which they can't see what the other insists is perfectly visible, why should either side hear the other's truth as reflecting anything but a matter of faith? Why should either find the other's truth remotely plausible? (p. 140)

I suspect that Mayer's understanding involves something so far-reaching that the phenomenon of what I call "standing in the spaces" between self-states will be found to barely scratch the surface of the depth and universality of an ineffable interconnection between entities, the nature of which extends far beyond what we now define as minds or even as life-forms. John Markoff, in a *New York Times* article (November 9, 2010) describing recent quantum-computer research, has in fact discussed what I see as a quantum physics version of "standing in the spaces" between energy particles. "Classic computers are built with transistors that can be in either an 'on' or an 'off' state, representing either a 1 or a 0. But a special particle called a qubit, which can be constructed in different way, can represent 1 and 0 states simultaneously and thus allows them to 'know' each other even though they don't know each other." However, says Markoff:

> There is, of course, a catch. The mere act of measuring or observing a qubit can strip it of its computing potential. So researchers have used *quantum entanglement—in which particles are linked so that measuring a property of one instantly reveals information about the other, no matter how far apart the two particles are.* (p. D2, emphasis added)

As a psychoanalyst, while I am delighted to know of this additional support for what we already know—the need to abandon a one-person model of human psychology—I must confess that I also love the word *entanglement* because physicists seem to be just as befuddled by *how* simultaneity links qubits as analysts are befuddled by *how* patient and therapist "know" each other, implicitly, during enactments, and brain researchers are befuddled by *how* mirror neurons link minds and not just brains. A qubit by any other name...

Coda

In a recent issue of *The Clinical Psychologist* (the Newsletter of the Division of Clinical Psychology of the American Psychological Association), the incoming president of the Division, Dr. Marvin Goldfried, a distinguished researcher and longtime advocate of the need for hard data to justify psychotherapeutic technique, wrote a column titled "Building a Two-way Bridge between Practice and Research" (2010). The author was open-hearted, collegial, and personally forthcoming without making any effort to indoctrinate. This latter quality led him to describe an incident from his personal past that I found so wonderfully thought provoking that I am quoting it here, and commenting on it from my own vantage point:

> A particularly distressing event during my graduate career occurred when Paul Meehl—a very strong advocate of the need for empirical evidence in clinical psychology—visited our program.

> I had read virtually everything he had written. I was particularly
> fortunate to be among the small group of graduate students to
> sit with him at dinner. At one point during the evening, some-
> body asked: "Dr. Meehl, to what extent does research inform
> how you practice clinically?" Without hesitation, Meehl replied:
> "Not at all!" As someone who was aspiring to become a scientist-
> practitioner, I was crushed. Indeed, I continue to be affected by
> this some 50 years (!) later. Depending on your theoretical orien-
> tation, you might say that I am either fixated, continue to have
> unfinished business, or have failed to extinguish my emotional
> response to his comment. (p. 1)

As an interpersonal/relational psychoanalyst I would select the second
of the three choices proposed by Dr. Goldfried– "unfinished business."
In my view, Dr. Goldfried didn't "get" Meehl's point 50 years ago
and still doesn't get it. Meehl was not saying that he, as a clinician,
deemed research irrelevant. He was saying that, when he is *being*
a clinician, research does not explicitly shape who he is while with his
patient. I did not know Meehl, but to the extent my understanding of
his "Not at all!" is accurate, I now have greater appreciation for him
as a clinician quite apart from his legendary valorization of empirical
research.

Meehl's enigmatic comment calls to mind something I once wrote
about the process of supervision (Bromberg, 1984) that is also a way
of looking at the concept of "technique." I proposed that the essential
ingredient of a therapy relationship is spontaneity, and that being an
effective therapist approaches what Theodor Reik (1949) conveyed
when he compared an analyst to an actor:

> The actor should, when he walks out upon the stage, forget what
> he has studied at the academy. He must brush it aside as if it had
> never been there. If he cannot neglect it now, in the moment
> of real performance–if it has not gone deep enough that he
> can afford to neglect it–then his training wasn't good enough.
> (p. 20)

I wrote that for an actor, "deep enough" means being embedded in the
role so that all ongoing experience is processed through it. The saying
of the lines is an expression of what is experienced, not of what has
been learned. And for an analyst, "deep enough" means something
similar but not identical–the ability to hear in such a way that he does

not have to play a role. His interventions are an expression of what he experiences, and what he experiences is an expression of what he has "learned" only as a relational version of the way we understand the aphorism "You are what you eat" –as metaphor.

As both analyst and supervisor my fundamental goal that encompasses all of the others is to help engender a relationship in which "learning *about*" becomes a spontaneous outcome of what is being cocreated experientially. Inasmuch as I am trying to help the student-analyst to look at what he does as an expression of what he experiences in the relationship, it should come as no surprise that I structure much of supervision around a method designed as much to improve his range of experiencing as to teach him whatever principles of clinical psychoanalysis may be useful to know and then, when he is with a patient, forget.

This coda is truly an addendum. My reluctance as a clinician to perpetuate the use of the *concept* of "technique" remains steadfast. As a *clinician*, however, the point I discuss in my coda is one that I support wholeheartedly and without reservation. Meehl's seeming inconsistency is a clinical necessity that I have emphasized in past writing, and that has long shaped and continues to shape my work: There are important things to learn about how to do psychotherapy provided that you can forget them while you are with your patient.

7

"Grown-up" Words
A Perspective on Unconscious Fantasy[1]

CR A group of kindergartners were trying very hard to become accustomed to the first grade. The biggest hurdle they faced was that the teacher insisted on no baby talk. "You need to use 'Big People' words," she was always reminding them. She started by asking Chris, "What did you do over the weekend?"

"I went to visit my Nana."

"No, you went to visit your grandmother. Use 'Big People' words!" She then asked William what he had done.

"I took a ride on a choo-choo."

She said, "No, you took a ride on a train. You must remember to use 'Big People' words." She then asked little Alex what he had done.

"I read a book," he replied.

"That's wonderful!" the teacher said. "What book did you read?"

Alex thought *really hard* about it. Then he puffed out his chest with great pride, and said, "Winnie the shit."

I, too, thought really hard about how to write this chapter. Like Alex, I tried to corral my mind into using "Big People" words, but I fear that some readers might discern a similarity in our developmental level. In writing about the concept of "unconscious fantasy" I tried really hard to use "grown-up" words (i.e., the conceptual language that I learned in my training). But like Alex, I am reluctant to replace the

---

[1]An earlier version of this chapter, "'Grown-up' Words: An Interpersonal/ Relational Perspective on Unconscious Fantasy," was published in *Psychoanalytic Inquiry, 28*, 2008, pp. 131–150.

language of what is observable with the grown-up conceptual language of analytic discourse. I'll be satisfied if my effort to negotiate the two is even half as successful as Alex's was.

The notion of unconscious fantasy is an idea first proposed by Freud in an 1897 letter to Fliess. The formulation evolved to account for the fact that every human being appears to be possessed by an unconscious scenario that is played out repetitively and leads to certain life choices that seem to have a life of their own. For some individuals, these repetitive choices take the form of a drama that shapes the course of their lives in a way that overrides both judgment and memory of past experience. As Langan (1997) has wryly put it: "What is one to do with the fractionating discovery that, as the poet Allen Ginsberg remarked, 'My mind's got a mind of its own'?" (p. 820).

The importance of unconscious fantasy as a foundational element in both Freudian and Kleinian psychoanalytic theory is longstanding. Spelled *phantasy* by Kleinians, the concept has offered clinicians a way of viewing the complex nature of consciousness that has allowed them to make sense of mental phenomena otherwise difficult to comprehend. Despite this, the concept has never appealed to me either conceptually or clinically, and in what follows I'm going to address the question of whether the term *unconscious fantasy* continues to be central or even useful to the theory and practice of psychoanalysis.

I'm going to begin by looking at two fairly recent papers, by myself (2003a) and by James Grotstein (2004), published about a year apart. In these articles each of us addressed the phenomenon of unconscious experience in the same way Albert Goldbarth (2003) spoke about the ineffable subjective experience that takes place in the "incomprehensible lacunae" when "reality blinks." Becoming aware of the gaps in our subjectivity, Goldbarth writes, is to become aware that "we don't know *what* takes place in those betweens" (p. 133). Because we are unable to stare at these gaps too long, "any more than at sunspots," as Goldbarth puts it (p. 133), I suggest that we have found a term—unconscious fantasy—that lets us believe we know more than we do. As Levenson (1983, p. 122) notes, citing Count Alfred Korzybski (1954), "the illusion of clarity increases with the level of abstraction".

The ineffable experience to which I refer is the "ghostly" intrusion into an analyst's subjectivity of a "not-me" presence so difficult to capture in language that Grotstein and I each used poetry to introduce our papers in hope of evoking its essence through metaphor before we attempted to conceptualize it. It is an experience too easily "lost in translation" if we try to make it submit to psychoanalytic explanation.

In my own selection of poetry I favored the lyricism of Emily Dickinson (1863, p. 333) while Grotstein drew upon the more classical imagery of Alexander Pope (1714, pp. 354–364), but we each recognized that the metaphor of being haunted would best communicate the affective presence that led Dickinson to speak of "ourself behind ourself, concealed–." In Pope's words, "Unnumbered spirits around thee fly ... though unseen, are ever on the wing," and in Dickinson's, "One need not be a chamber to be haunted–One need not be a house." Freud saw these "ghosts" as pathological epiphenomena of unconscious fantasy whereas Klein saw these unconscious "phantasies" as developmental necessities that are potentially transformative. Spillius (2001) comments: "Freud and Klein emphasized contrasting aspects of the everyday usage of the word phantasy.... Freud's usage emphasizes the fictitious, wish-fulfilling aspect of the everyday usage, whereas Klein tended to focus on the imaginative aspect" (p. 362).

Spelling the word *fantasy* with a *ph* rather than an *f* has helped analysts to build a bridge between Freudian and Kleinian theory, and also between pathology and creativity. But notwithstanding Bion's seminal contribution to constructing this bridge (1962, 1963, 1965, 1970), the relational heart of the matter doesn't seem yet to have been addressed: Is the concept of unconscious fantasy, no matter how one spells it, a help or a hindrance to comprehending that clinical process is a relational act of meaning-construction?

Grotstein (2004), from a Kleinian/Bionian vantage point, puts his finger on the dilemma by pointing out that no matter what we choose to tell ourselves, all that an analyst can ever truly address with his patient is *conscious* fantasy, which is typically both embedded in and juxtaposed with conscious reality:

> Traditionally, when psychoanalysts interpret unconscious fantasies to analysands, the predominating point of view has always been that of external factual reality, for instance, "When you were in the waiting room and heard me on the phone you thought that I was talking with my mistress" (in fantasy)–implying that, factually, I was not. In other words, phantasies have been understood as the prime cause of pathology, and debunking the phantasy by a safe restoration of reality has been thought to constitute the cure. (pp. 115–116)

The irony in this example, of course, is that what is at stake is not in fact an interpretation of unconscious fantasy but of conscious fantasy (acknowledged by Grotstein's spelling *fantasy* with an *f*) because it is already at the level of thought when the interpretation is made. A truly unsymbolized affective experience, on the other hand, can only reach consciousness through symbolization, and this requires an experiential relational context to organize the meaning of its interpretation. In this regard, consider what R. D. Laing (1967) had to say about fantasy:

> Fantasy is a particular way of relating to the world. It is part of, sometimes the essential part of, the meaning or sense implicit in action. As relationship we may be dissociated from it ... [and] we may ... refuse to admit that our behavior implies an experiential relationship or a relational experience that gives it a meaning. Fantasy ... is always experiential and meaningful; and if the person is not dissociated from it, relational in a valid way. (pp. 31–32)

If Laing is accurate then the concept of unconscious fantasy is a hindrance insofar as it implies buried thought rather than particular ways of relating to the world—what we now refer to under the rubric of "procedural memory." To be sure, my reluctance to embrace the concept of unconscious fantasy involves scruples more clinical than conceptual, though the latter are indeed present. I have made a suggestion (Bromberg, 1989) similar to Laing's: "In a psychoanalysis, patients do not reveal their unconscious fantasies to the analyst. They *are* their unconscious fantasies and live them with the analyst through the *act* of psychoanalysis" (p. 153). This is a way of saying that unconscious fantasy comes to exist while it is being constructed through the interaction of the various and shifting self-states of both patient and analyst. It could therefore be argued that while the same dynamic is enacted again and again during the course of an analysis, within a given analytic relationship what seems to be a patient's "repetition compulsion" doesn't entail a real repetition. Each so-called repetition changes the relationship, and in the same sense that Heraclitus said "one cannot step into the same river twice," it can be similarly said that "one cannot step into the same enactment twice." The point at which the analyst becomes aware that the enactment is a different "river" is the point at which he "wakes up" and recognizes that something is going on *between* them and that he is a partner in its creation. This recognition undermines the analyst's wish to believe that what is taking place is simply a return of material from the patient's past and can be understood solely in terms of the patient's contribution. The necessary conditions are now present to permit a process of interpersonal comparison and interpersonal negotiation between the respective self-states of analyst and patient that were dissociatively engaged with each another in ways that shaped the enactment. Through this interpersonal negotiation between self-states, a similar process of intrapsychic negotiation is facilitated in the patient, whereby self-states that formerly had not been able to coexist, much less communicate, become increasingly able to participate as aspects of a coherent sense of "me" that is now becoming more open to the experience of internal conflict.

Lyons-Ruth and the Boston Change Process Study Group (2001, pp. 13–17) have focused particular attention on this view of therapeutic action, and argue that it may be the next major step in the growth of psychoanalysis. I refer to what they call "a non-linear enactive theory of psychotherapeutic change" whereby "the process of psychodynamic therapy can usefully be thought of as the pursuit of more collaborative, inclusive, and coherent forms of dialogue between the two therapeutic partners."

> If clinical process is affect-guided rather than cognition-guided, [then] therapeutic change is a process that leads to the emergence of new forms of relational organization. New experiences emerge but they are not created by the therapist for the benefit of the patient. Instead, they emerge somewhat unpredictably from the mutual searching of patient and therapist for new forms of recognition, or new forms of fitting together of initiatives in the interaction between them. (p. 17)

Specifically, the Boston Change Process Study Group argues that enlarging the domain and fluency of the dialogue is primary to fostering enduring personality growth in treatment; it is this that leads to increasingly integrated and complex content. This does not mean that content is unimportant; rather, *it is in the relational process of exploring content that the change takes place, not in the discovery of new content per se.* The "content" is embedded in relational experience that embodies what they call "implicit relational knowing"–an ongoing process that is itself part of the content.

Matters are even more complex, however. The patient's implicit relational knowing will be impacted by dissociative mental structure to one degree or another, whereby accessing one way of knowing may cause switching to another set of implicit schemas. And in these switches, what is conscious and what is unconscious, and what is "me" and what is "not-me," will shift and shift back again. It is this issue that I believe creates the strongest argument against retaining the concept of unconscious fantasy. Why? Because if the self is multiple as well as integral, reality is nonlinear and cannot be distinguished from fantasy in absolute terms. The ability of different parts of the self to recognize other parts as "me" is always relative. Consequently, reality for one part of the self will be fantasy to another part. Moreover, what we call *unconscious* will depend on which part of self has access to consciousness at that moment.

Fantasy and Reality

Webster's Unabridged Dictionary (1983) gives three definitions of the word *fantasy* (spelled also *phantasy*) that pertain to its meaning as a psychological event. All three definitions imply a *conscious* mental phenomenon that is either illusory or odd: (1) imagination; (2) an unreal mental image or illusion; (3) in psychology, a mental image as in a daydream, with some continuity. Again, all of these definitions specify qualities that pertain to conscious experience. The concept of *unconscious fantasy* does not actually extend the meaning of the term *fantasy*; it changes its essential nature. To propose that fantasy can be unconscious is to strip the concept of its qualities. If it is unconscious, how do we specify that it is unreal, imaginative, or like a daydream? Conceptually, this is just all a tangle, and I suggest that this tangle is the primary issue that led Arlow (1969) to lament that "it would seem that a concept so well founded clinically and so much a part of the body of our theory would long since have ceased to be a problem for psychoanalysis" (p. 3). I'm not as bewildered by this as Arlow was. The psychoanalytic theory of mind has in general tended to conflate supporting "evidence" with observations based on the theory it is designed to support, simply because its data source has been largely subjective. The concept of unconscious fantasy, not to mention other fundamental principles that are "so much a part of the body of our theory," is less "well founded clinically" than Arlow chose to believe. As an example of what I mean by conflation of "evidence" with observations based on the theory that the evidence is designed to support, Moore and Fine (1990), in their dictionary of psychoanalytic terms and concepts, state: "There is a vast amount of evidence that most mental activity is unconscious. This is especially true of fantasy" (p. 75). Quite a statement if you look at it closely. The first part of the definition offered in these two sentences, that "most mental activity is unconscious," is indeed supported by objective evidence; the second part, sort of slipped under the door, which claims that "this is especially true of fantasy," not only lacks objective support but, as noted before, changes the meaning of the term *fantasy*. What concerns me most, however, is not conceptual but clinical clarity. If the term *unconscious fantasy* permits an analyst to believe that something exists in the patient's mind that is an unconscious replica of what we all know subjectively as fantasy experience, I would wish to retain my view that the term does us more harm than good and should be eliminated from the psychoanalytic vocabulary. But in light of the relational shift taking place in our field from metatheory to clinical theory, I think that a "let's wait and see" attitude might better support the evolution already occurring in analytic thinking at this point in time.

Enactment and Multiplicity of the Self

Lyons-Ruth (2003) has emphasized the major contribution of relational theory to the new understanding of the source of therapeutic action that the Boston Change Process Study Group has lately put forward. She urges that work continue toward developing "a language and structure that moves beyond a narrow focus on interpretation to encompass the broader domain of relational interchanges that contribute to change in psychoanalytic treatment" (pp. 905–906). I believe that the interpersonal/relational emphasis on working with enactment and "not-me" experience constitutes a major step toward providing the language and structure of which she speaks because it encompasses the essence of the interpersonal and intersubjective matrix without losing the focus on the intrapsychic (cf. Levenkron, 2009). When we take that step, the issue of whether the concept of unconscious fantasy is central to the theory and practice of psychoanalysis is brought into high relief.

As an experiential process, enactment considers both partners as an interpenetrating unit. An enactment is a dyadic event in which therapist and patient are linked through a dissociated mode of relating, each in a "not-me" state of his own that is affectively responsive to that of the other. This shared dissociative cocoon has its own imperative; it enmeshes and at least for a time traps the two partners within a "not-me" communication field that is mediated by dissociation. In short, enactment is an intrapsychic phenomenon that is played out interpersonally, and it is through this interpersonal engagement that "not-me" comes to be symbolically processed as "me," a relational aspect of selfhood. I believe this understanding speaks to nothing less than a sea-change paradigm shift from content to process, one that prompted Mitchell (1991), in developing his now seminal view of the mind as relationally organized, to write the following:

> The key transition to postclassical psychoanalytic views of the self occurred when theorists began thinking ... of the repressed not as disorganized, impulsive fragments but as constellations of meanings organized around relationships.... These are versions of the person [that] embody active patterns of experience and behavior, organized around a particular point of view, a sense of self, a way of being, which underlie the ordinary phenomenological sense we have of ourselves as integral.... The result is a plural or manifold organization of self, patterned around different self and object images or representations, derived from different relational contexts. We are all composites of overlapping, multiple organizations and perspectives, and our experience is smoothed out by an illusory sense of continuity. (pp. 127–128)

Similarly, LeDoux (2002) proposes in neurobiological terms that the enigma of brain processes is related to the enigma underlying multiplicity of self:

> Though [the self] is a unit, it is not unitary.... The fact that all aspects of the self are not usually manifest simultaneously, and that their different aspects can even be contradictory, may seem to present a complex problem. However, this simply means that different components of the self reflect the operation of different brain systems, which can be but are not always in sync. While explicit memory is mediated by a single system, there are a variety of different brain systems that store memory implicitly, allowing for many aspects of the self to coexist.... As the painter Paul Klee (1957) expressed it, the self is a "dramatic ensemble." (p. 31)

Fantasy, Affect, and Meaning-Construction

Unconscious fantasy is often linked in the clinician's mind with "insight," the former being the target of the latter. With regard to insight, I agree with Fingarette's (1963) oft-quoted observation that "insight is not like discovering an animal which has been hiding in the bushes. Insight does not reveal a hidden, past reality; it is a reorganization of the meaning of present experience, a present reorientation toward both future and past" (p. 20). With regard to fantasy, I offer the view that what is taken to be evidence of buried unconscious fantasy is an illusion that is inherent to the ongoing development of meaning construction made possible by the interpersonal/relational nature of the analytic process. It is what the patient does *with* the therapist that allows the unsymbolized affect (not fantasy) of each participant to engage in a cocreated process through which the patient's self-narrative is expanded. I would describe this process as brought about by greater and greater ability to hold opposing parts of the self in a single state of consciousness without dissociating, which in turn increases the patient's capacity for self reflection that is affectively safe.

What looks like the "uncovering" of a hidden fantasy is the inch-by-inch development of self-reflectiveness in areas of experience that previously foreclosed reflection and permitted only affective, subsymbolic enactment (Bucci, 1997a, 1997b, 2001, 2002, 2003, 2007a, 2007b, 2010). Self-reflection, as it gradually replaces dissociation as the automatic process safeguarding stability, also underwrites self-continuity (cf. Mitchell, 1991, p. 139) through fostering the illusion of something "emerging" that has been "always known but warded-off." It had indeed been "known" but not thought (cf. Bollas, 1987). We may think of it as an affective imperative that did not belong to what is symbolized as "me." If we are to call this unsymbolized affect a "fantasy," it is essential to specify that it is not a fantasy held by the person but vice versa. The person is possessed by the "fantasy" as by a ghost—a "not-me" experience that is dissociated from self-narrative and from narrative memory.

A haunted person can be seen but a ghost cannot. In a review of Steiner's (2003) edited book, *Unconscious Fantasy*, Rizzuto (2004) pointedly cites Solms's (2003) chapter, "Do Unconscious Phantasies Really Exist?" as underscoring the real danger of speaking about an unconscious fantasy as though it were a perceivable event rather than a theoretical construct. In Rizzuto's words: "Solms examines the role of perception in the grasping of internal and external reality.... As a psychic phenomenon, unconscious fantasy is solely the result of *inference*" (p. 1289). Belief in an unconscious text that is operating on its own perpetuates the myth of uncovering a "buried fantasy" that was too dangerous to be held in consciousness—a kind of daydream that was repressed and is only now being allowed to emerge to the "surface." This myth, by continuing to influence an analyst's clinical stance, stands in the way of allowing the relational nature of analytic growth to be fully utilized on the behalf of patients.

Traditionally, thinking in terms of unconscious fantasy demands from an analyst at least implicit loyalty to the belief that the therapeutic action of psychoanalysis is tied to the process of interpretation, and that a patient must be "analyzable" as a prerequisite. Almost two decades ago (Bromberg, 1993) I offered a challenge to this perspective, my view being that the "shadow and substance of unconscious fantasy" are "captured and reconstructed in a new domain of reality, a chaotic intersubjective field where the collision between narrative memory and immediate perception contains the simultaneous existence of multiple realities and disjunctive self–other representations" (p. 180).

What did I mean by the shadow and substance of unconscious fantasy? I was then, as now, trying to wrestle with the issue of how to understand the mental processes underlying the transition from dissociation to capacity for conflict. To the degree that the capacity for internal conflict begins to develop in those areas where it had been foreclosed or limited, dissociation must first find a negotiable interface with the mind's ability to utilize interpretation. I see the phenomenon of enactment (subsymbolic communication of "not-me") as the interface, and its negotiation between patient and analyst as what fosters capacity for conflict by facilitating the development of intersubjectivity (symbolic communication of a relational "me"). As discussed more extensively in chapter 6, I concur with Epstein (1994) that this involves discrete but overlapping communication channels, not a continuum. It is the cocreation of a relational unconscious–a state of mind that draws on both enactment and symbolic communication but transcends both; a state of mind that contextualizes the development of intersubjectivity in those areas of the personality in which dissociation had made selfhood and otherness rigidly anomalous; "a space uniquely relational and still uniquely individual; a space belonging to neither person alone, and yet, belonging to both and to each; a twilight space in which incompatible selves, each awake to its own 'truth,' can 'dream' the reality of the other without risk to its own integrity" (Bromberg, 1996a, p. 278).

Bonovitz (2004) describes this state in terms of a "transformation of fantasy through play, which in turn shifts psychic structure" (p. 553). He believes, as do I, that the transformation rests upon the fact that "fantasy is elastic in that it serves to generate multiple realities and multiple versions of oneself, versions that one may inhabit and may use to make meaning from experience and work through conflicts" (p. 561). I've offered the view that the very nature of this cocreated playground is that it doesn't stay experientially stable, but changes in the act of relationally symbolizing it, of expressing it in consensually negotiated language. In this twilight space, the generative elasticity of fantasy makes room for the multiple realities and multiple self-states of both patient and analyst, creating and simultaneously symbolizing in the process of creation what analysts have called unconscious fantasy. Through this ever-shifting interface of perception and self-narrative, analysts come to experience the shadow and substance of clinical process and its inseparability from dissociation and enactment. This said, then why retain the concept of unconscious fantasy? In point of fact, I acknowledge that the concept still possesses heuristic power provided it is accepted as coconstructed dissociated experience rather than as symbolized thought (a daydream) that is repressed in the mind of one person. For example, the concept is often useful in making clinical comparisons across cases as in the following:

[E]ach of the three patients, despite dramatic differences in personality, history, and the language they used, seemed to be possessed by the powerful presence of the same unconscious fantasy–largely unsymbolized by language–that permeated and organized their use of imagery, and as it emerged subsequently, informed the enactments played out with their respective analysts. In this dissociated fantasy, some central but unknown aspect of what each felt to be his or her "true" self was being held captive inside of the mind of an other–an other who refuses to know it–and the patient was prevented from attaining his right to the experience of self-wholeness that depends upon the mutual interrelation of psychic and somatic experience as the felt unity that Winnicott (1949) called psyche-soma. (Bromberg, 1998c, pp. 311–312)

As the reader can see, I prefer a more impressionistic view of transitional process than is offered by the hard-edged concept of unconscious fantasy, whether Freudian or Kleinian, but I do occasionally use the term. I suspect that the burgeoning work in neuroscience and cognitive research will inch us closer to an understanding that will bridge classical and postclassical thinking and, as this takes place, I predict that the concept of unconscious fantasy will be among those that will survive insofar as they are revised. Bucci (2002), similarly, has put it that "the goal of psychoanalytic treatment is integration of dissociated schemas" (p. 766) and she maintains that Freud's repression-based conception of the therapeutic action of psychoanalysis is in need of serious reconsideration, a prerequisite for which is that the "concepts such as regression and resistance need to be revised as well" (p. 788).

One of the most persuasive and intriguing lines of thinking in this area can be found in the work of Peter Fonagy and his colleagues, who make the distinction between developmental and conflictual psychopathology. The distinction we both make is between non-interpretable and interpretable experience. They speak to this distinction (Fonagy et al., 1993) in their elaboration of "two aspects of the self: a 'pre-reflective or physical self,' which is the immediate experiencer of life, and a 'reflective or psychological self,' the internal observer of mental life" (p. 472).

Enhancing the functioning of the patient's "reflective self"–what Fonagy and colleagues have called "mentalization"–requires more than simply the accurate mirroring of mental states. The analyst has to move beyond mirroring, and offer a different, yet experientially appropriate re-representation that reflects the analyst's subjectivity as well as the patient's. In other words, the analyst must show his representation of the patient's representation, and to do this the analyst must be himself while being a usable object. In their words:

> A transactional relationship exists between the child's own mental experience of himself and that of his object. His perception of the other is conditioned by his experience of his own mental state, which has in turn been conditioned developmentally by his perception of how his object conceived of his mental world.... Unconsciously and pervasively, the caregiver ascribes a mental state to the child with her behavior, this is gradually internalized by the child, and lays the foundations of a core sense of mental selfhood. (Target & Fonagy, 1996, pp. 460–461)

The role of the analyst, then, is to enhance a patient's ability to symbolize not only his emotional experience of events, but also his capacity to symbolize his experience of his own mental states–"a representation of a mental representation" (Target & Fonagy, 1996, p. 469). This is the underpinning of the so-called "observing ego" that analysts rely upon for interpretation to be a viable mode of communication with a given patient. Whether working with children or with adults, "the greater the unevenness in development," Fonagy and Moran (1991) argue, "the less effective will be a technique which relies solely upon interpretations of conflict, and the greater will be the need to devise strategies of analytic intervention aimed to support and strengthen the ... capacity to tolerate conflict" (p. 16). Similarly, and even more to the point: "Interpretations may remain helpful but their function is certainly no longer limited to the lifting of repression and the addressing of distorted perceptions and beliefs.... *Their goal is the reactivation of the patient's concern with mental states, in himself and in his object*" (Fonagy and Target, 1995, pp. 498–499, emphasis added).

When an analyst wishes to help a patient deepen his emotional experience of an event he is describing, the intervention that is most typically offered is some variation of the question "What did you feel? or "What was the upset-feeling like?" (see chapter 4). Such a question will often evoke a switch to a different self-state or lead to a symptom, either of which can then become an object of attention if it seems potentially useful. It is moments like this that most closely link my clinical vantage point with Fonagy and Target's through our shared recognition that "psychic reality is sensed not only through belief, but also, through perception" (Target & Fonagy, 1996, p. 471). In the face of the typical question, a patient usually tries to "remember" what he felt as a past event in linear time. What I am proposing is a clinical process in which a patient is requested to perceive the moment, not as a narrative to be told, but as a space to be reentered. The term *unconscious fantasy* is, in this regard, misleading insofar as it detracts from the reality of this reentered space.

Perception, Fantasy, and Self-States

What I call the structural shift from dissociation to conflict is clinically represented by the increasing capacity of the patient to adopt a self-reflective posture in which one aspect of the self observes and reflects (often with distaste) upon others that were formerly dissociated. This differs from what classical conflict theory would call the development of an observing ego in that the goal is more than the pragmatic treatment outcome of a greater tolerance for internal conflict. In healthy human discourse, there are always self-states that are not symbolized cognitively as "me" in the here and now of any given moment because they would interfere with routine, normal adaptation. For the most part this creates no problem. It is where self-states are hypnoidally *insulated* from each other as an early-warning system against potentially traumatic dysregulation, that the adaptive fluidity between "me" and "not-me" self-state configurations has been sacrificed, and "not-me" self states are unable to participate in relational discourse. For all patients to different degrees, such is the case. Unsymbolized "not-me" self-states will make themselves known through enactment, signaling the presence of what Fonagy calls developmental pathology and I call noninterpretable pathology.

I thus believe that an intrinsic part of every analytic treatment are moments in which the patient observes and reflects upon the existence of other selves that he or she hates, would like to disown, but can't. This process requires the analyst's willingness to do likewise with his own "not-me" experiences, and, as far as possible, do so aloud. Helped immeasurably by his own affective honesty (Bromberg, 2006b; Levenkron, 2006), the patient discovers in the relationship an opportunity for an internal linking process to take place between her dissociated self-states. During the linking process, fantasy, perception, thought, and language each play their part, providing the patient is not pressured to choose between which self is more "true" (Winnicott, 1960, 1971), and which reality is more "objective" (Winnicott, 1951).

If we think of a person as speaking from different self-states rather than from a single center of self, then the analyst will inevitably become attuned to the multiple voices of himself and his patient. Such listening demands an overarching attunement to the *speaker*, an attunement that addresses the same issue described by Schafer's (1983) "action language" mode of listening and interpreting, in which "the analyst focuses on the action of telling itself … [and] telling is treated as an object of description rather than … an indifferent or transparent medium for imparting information or thematic content" (p. 228). From a nonlinear perspective, this means not only a dedicated receptiveness to the impact that the speaker is having on you at any given moment, but even more so to the shifts in that impact. Ideally, the analyst tries to notice these shifts as close to the time they occur as possible. I look at these shifts as representing shifts in states of self that are to be held by the analyst as an ongoing focus of attention. It is a way of listening different from that of hearing the person feel differently at different moments. The latter takes the switches in states of consciousness as more or less normal background music, unless they are particularly dramatic. The former takes them as the primary data that organize everything else you are hearing and doing; as an analyst it organizes how you approach the issue of unconscious fantasy and the reconstruction of personal narrative.

It is through this process of attending to self-state shifts that relational bridges are built between self-experiences that could not formerly be contained in a single state of mind without leading to dissociation. An analyst, to utilize the frame of reference discussed here, does not have to abandon his or her own school of thought and work in some new way that is incompatible with his present clinical attitude. Historically, the stance of any given analyst has tended to slant toward one of three postures partly organized by differences in preferred metapsychology: interpretation of conflict, detailed inquiry, or empathic attunement. It is striking to observe, however, that regardless of differences in meta-theory, built into each stance is an acceptance of the fact that the transference–countertransference field is where the action takes place. In other words, any analysis that has as its goal enduring and far-reaching characterological growth is grounded in a transference–countertransference understanding, based on its own clinical logic. Why?

Clinically, the transference–countertransference field is characterized by its vividness and its immediacy. But why is this fact so important that it is able to transcend conceptual differences among analysts as to how to best utilize this field? My own answer is that, regardless of a given analyst's metapsychology of therapeutic action, we are all either explicitly or implicitly attempting clinically to facilitate a patient's access to the broadest possible range of consciousness through enhancing perception. Perception is where the action is–and has always been. Josef Breuer, in his theoretical chapter in *Studies on Hysteria* (Breuer & Freud, 1893–1895, pp. 185–251), remarked that in response to trauma, "perception too–the psychical interpretation of sense impressions–is impaired" (p. 201). Echoing this, Enid Balint (1987) wrote: "If the ability to perceive is lacking because it is too traumatic or too alien, can one think of an individual as being truly conscious?" (p. 480).

When psychoanalysis is successful as a method of psychotherapy, the reason is that the process is a dialectic between seeing and being seen, rather than simply being seen "into." That is, analysis simultaneously frees our patients to do unto us, with equivalent perceptiveness, what we are doing unto them, to see us as part of the act of listening to us. I have argued (Bromberg, 1994) that regardless of the analyst's preferred method of inquiry, the utilization of transference creates its analytic impact to the extent the patient is freed to see the analyst while the analyst is seeing him. Enacted domains of self achieve symbolization primarily in a transference–countertransference context because it is the *dyadic* experience that becomes symbolized. The meaning of the symbolization is to be found not in the words themselves but in the dyadic *perceptual* context that the words come to represent. The analyst must play his part by being authentically present as a living part of that context. Speak–that your patient might see you, in order that his dissociated states of mind may find access to the here and now of the analytic relationship and be lived within it.

Of the various mental functions that are compromised by trauma and dissociation, perception is foremost because trauma and dissociation thwart the cognitive capacity to play with images, thus interfering with the use of perception to construct meaning. Perception is a relational process–a personal interaction between the mind of the individual and what is "out there." Dissociative anaesthesia of the personal interactive context upon which perception depends leaves the person with a sensory image of the "thing" itself, but because it cannot be played with cognitively as an interactive event in which the person is participating, sensory experience cannot become perception, personal meaning is thereby absent and the "event" remains excluded from narrative memory. "I 'sort-of know' it happened, and parts of it keep coming back like snapshots, but I can't say I really remember it."

In psychoanalytic treatment, the power of self-truth remains unchanged unless challenged by perception (see chapter 5), which is why enactments hold such powerful therapeutic potential. But for perception to generate "an act of meaning" (Bruner, 1990), a relational context must be constructed that includes the realities of both analyst and patient. Unless this takes place, the immediate perceptual context will only be an enactment of the patient's fixed affective memory system that includes some "other" trying helpfully and logically to extract the person's own reality and replace it with a better one–theirs.

The Human Mind as a Relationally Configured Self-Organizing System[2]

My broadest aim as a psychoanalytic author has been to explore the clinical and conceptual implications of viewing the human mind as a relationally configured, self-organizing system. I've argued that

---

[2]The interested reader is referred here to the seminal contributions of Craig Piers (1998, 2000, 2005, 2007, 2010), whose writings on complex systems theory and its relationship to trauma, mental functioning and character are an invaluable resource and an inspiring read.

personality functioning, normal and pathological, is best understood as an ongoing, nonlinear repatterning of self-state configurations, and that this process is mediated at the brain level by a continuing dialectic between dissociation and conflict. Normal dissociation, a hypnoid brain mechanism that is intrinsic to everyday mental functioning, assures that the mind functions as creatively as possible, selecting whichever self-state configuration is most adaptive to the moment. Johnson (2004) compares this to Edelman's (1989, 1992, 2004) view that the internal mechanisms of both the brain and the immune system run mini-versions of natural selection:

> Think of those modules in your brain as species competing for precious resources—in some cases they're competing for control of the entire organism; in others, they're competing for your attention. Instead of struggling to pass their genes on to the next generation, they're struggling to pass their message on to other groups of neurons, including groups that shape your conscious sense of self. Picture yourself walking down a crowded urban street. As you walk, your brain is filled with internal voices all competing for your attention. At any given moment, a few of them are selected, while most go unheeded. (p. 199)

When dissociation is enlisted as a defense against trauma, the brain utilizes its hypnoid function to limit self-state communication, thereby insulating the mental stability of each separate state. Self-continuity is thus preserved within each state, but self-coherence across states is sacrificed and replaced by a dissociative mental structure that forecloses the possibility of conflictual experience. Clinically, the phenomenon of dissociation, though observable at many points in every treatment, comes into highest relief during enactments, requiring an analyst's close attunement to unacknowledged affective shifts in his own and his patient's self-states. Through the joint cognitive processing of enactments played out interpersonally and intersubjectively between the "not-me" experiences of patient and analyst, a patient's sequestered self-states come alive as a "remembered present" (Edelman, 1989) that can affectively and cognitively reconstruct a remembered past. Because the ability to safely experience conflict is increased, the potential for resolution of conflict is in turn increased for all patients. It allows one's work with so-called "good" analytic patients to become more powerful because it provides a more experience-near perspective from which to *perceptually* engage clinical phenomena that are immune to interpretation, such as "intractable resistance" and "therapeutic stalemate." Further, it puts to rest the notion of "analyzability," and allows analysts to use their expertise with a wide spectrum of personality disorders often considered "difficult" or "unanalyzable," such as individuals diagnosed as borderline, schizoid, narcisstic, and dissociative.

In brief, psychoanalysis must provide an experience that is *perceivably* different from the patient's narrative memory.[3] Sullivan (1954, pp. 94–112), recognizing that self-discordant perceptual data must have an opportunity to structurally reorganize internal narrative for psychoanalysis to be a genuine talking cure, emphasized the powerful relation between personality change and what he called "the detailed inquiry" by the analyst. This latter term refers to the clinical reconstruction of perceptual detail, the recall of affects and interpersonal data that are excluded from the narrative memory of the event as reported to the analyst. A central aspect of this process is that the patient–analyst relationship is itself drawn into the telling of the narrative, and recapitulates aspects of it that are enacted in the here and now as the analysis proceeds. A relationally configured self-organizing system indeed! The patient's old narrative frame is expanded by providing an interpersonal experience that for all its familiarity is perceptibly different. Enactment is the primary perceptual medium that allows this kind change to take place. Expanded, consensually validated narratives containing events and experiences of self/other configurations formerly excluded begin to be constructed because these events and experiences, as I said earlier, are not simply a new way of understanding the past but entail a new symbolization of perceptual reality.

I have offered the view that the concept of unconscious fantasy remains of heuristic value only if the phenomenon to which it refers is acknowledged as a dissociated, affect-driven experience rather than as a form

---

[3]Edgar Levenson, arguably the psychoanalytic wellspring of this increasingly accepted understanding, introduced his 2003 paper, "On Seeing What is Said," with his usual blend of succinctness, clarity and wit: "Harry Stack Sullivan once said that the last thing that happens before you go crazy is that everything becomes clear! Well, I had an epiphany about a year ago when it occurred to me that the detailed inquiry, particularly the deconstructed detailed inquiry, is really visual, not, as one might reasonably expect, verbal, and that, *indeed, the entire psychoanalytic praxis, although annotated in words, actually takes place in a visual-spatial modality*" (p. 233, emphasis added).

of symbolized thought that is repressed. I argue that what is taken to be evidence of buried unconscious fantasy is an illusion created by the interpersonal/relational nature of the analytic process during the ongoing symbolization of unprocessed affect. As cognitive and linguistic symbolization gradually replaces dissociation as the automatic safeguard of a patient's self-stability, increased self-reflectiveness fosters the illusion of something emerging that has been always known but warded off. Thus, if we hypothesize the unconscious existence of something called "fantasy," it is essential to accept that it is not a fantasy possessed by the person but vice versa; the person is possessed by the fantasy—a "not-me" affective experience that is denied self-narrative symbolization. With regard to whether I believe the concept is central to psychoanalytic theory and practice at this point in time, I will end by reiterating my hope that a "let's wait and see" attitude might best support the relational shift from meta-theory to clinical theory already taking place among diverse schools of thought.

PART IV

THE REACH OF INTERSUBJECTIVITY

8

"The Nearness of You"
A Personal Book-end[1]

CR More than 30 years ago, while I was a still a candidate at the William Alanson White Institute, I published what was to be my first piece of analytic writing (Bromberg, 1974). It wasn't actually a paper but a brief introduction to a 1972 symposium that I had organized and chaired as President of the Harry Stack Sullivan Society, the candidate organization. As my first official act, I decided it would be a really appealing idea to hold an "Inter-institute Candidate Symposium" where candidates from some of the major institutes in New York City would present short papers on what it was like to be in training, and then engage each other in discussion.

The word *appealing* didn't turn out to be the best way of characterizing it, but the experience definitely contributed to my later understanding of the advantages and disadvantages of dissociation. I had waded into a hidden swamp of psychoanalytic politics that I managed to feel had nothing to do with *me* because I just knew that my plan,

---

[1]The title, "The Nearness of You," was borrowed from a 1937 song by Carmichael & Washington. This chapter adapts and materially revises an earlier version, "The Nearness of You: Navigating Selfhood, Otherness, and Uncertainty," published in J. Petrucelli (Ed.), *Knowing, Not-Knowing and Sort-of-Knowing: Psychoanalysis and the Experience of Uncertainty* (London: Karnac, 2010, pp. 22–45). It was originally presented April 11, 2008 as a Keynote Address at the 28th Annual Spring Meeting of the Division of Psychoanalysis of the American Psychological Association, New York City.

including the name I chose for the symposium, could never stir up dozing alligators. I naively named it, if you can believe, "The Rational and Irrational in Psychoanalytic Training." Being me, I "knew" that once the leaders of each institute realized how valuable this meeting would be to candidates everywhere, they would all back it wholeheartedly. Amazingly, and despite some grouchy alligators, the meeting took place, with the participation of candidates from different institutes, including two institutes that were affiliated with the American Psychoanalytic Association. That symposium marked the start of my psychoanalytic writing and with it the start of my reputation as someone who didn't seem to get the way things work.

The symposium got published, the gators seemed to go back to dozing, and there it was–in print–including my two-page Introduction which ended by my quoting Allan Wheelis's (1958, p. 154) famously challenging statement:

> Without institutional protection the early discoveries of psychoanalysis might have been diluted or dispersed, never acquiring the usefulness they potentially held. But for such security the price was high. For when the issue is an idea, the institution that protects the infant is likely to stunt the child. (Bromberg, 1974, p. 242)

Overall I learned a few things from the experience, but getting how things work didn't seem to be one of them. Happily unaware that I might have been lucky, I continued going pretty much my own way, more and more enjoying writing, and always puzzled by why I seemed to be raising the eyebrows, and at times the hackles, of some important folks at my own Institute. But I was never blocked from publishing in *Contemporary Psychoanalysis*, the journal published by the White Institute. If anything, I was made welcome by its then Editor, Art Feiner, to whom I will be forever grateful.

I am still not paying a lot of attention to the way things work, and those who have read my writing over the years might have noticed how often I draw on literature that could be considered a bit "edgy" for a psychoanalytic article. Just a few examples are Carlos Castaneda's books (1968, 1971); a Robert Parker (1983) "Spencer" novel; Theodore Sturgeon's (1953) sci-fi classic, *More than Human*; the annotated version of Arthur Conan Doyle's *Sherlock Holmes* (Baring-Gould, 1967); Mary Shelley's (1818) *Frankenstein*; George MacDonald's (1858) *Phantastes*;

Thane Rosenbaum's (2002) *The Golems of Gotham*; and Philip Pull-man's (2007) *His Dark Materials.*[2]

I've always done it without anxiety because I feel that a total com-patibility exists between these authors and certain psychoanalytic authors with whom they share a home in my mind. In "Playing with Boundaries" (Bromberg, 1999), I offered the view that the mind's fundamental ability to shift between different self-states without los-ing self-continuity makes it possible for someone to use another's self-states as part of their own. I suggested that this process of self-state borrowing can also manifest itself within and between a reader and an author, and is what makes certain authors not just an author but *your* author. He becomes yours when the otherness of his words doesn't *feel* other to you—when the affective interplay among his self-states allows the affective interplay among your own self-states to join his. He then becomes *your* author, and you become *his* reader. In the words of Carlos Zafon (2001): "Every book, every volume you see here, has a soul. The soul of the person who wrote it and of those who read it and lived and dreamed with it" (pp. 4–5).

At the neurobiological level Allan Schore (2003a) writes about a right-brain to right-brain channel of affective communication—a chan-nel that he sees as "an organized dialogue" comprised of "dynamically fluctuating moment-to-moment state-sharing" (p. 96). I believe it to be this process of state-sharing that not only allows an author to become your author, but also, in what we call "a good psychoanalytic match," it is what allows an analyst to become *your* analyst. (Although I feel a bit less secure in proposing that the *failure* to develop state-sharing is the thing that most accounts for so-called bad matches between patient and analyst, it is indeed plausible to me that this plays a role of no small significance.)

Sort-of-Knowing

The affect-based, right-brain to right-brain dialogue between self and other, if it lacks a cognitive context for too long a time, leads to

---

[2]I refer the reader to Stephanie Brody's (2009) fascinating psychoanalytic paper written with a similar feel for "edginess" in the work we do. In the article, Brody (pp. 88–89), unbeknownst to me, had there discussed her experience of Pullman's world of "fantasy" and Bromberg's world of psychoanalytic process as representing a shared sensibility that bridges the two domains.

a "sort-of-knowing" and a quality of uncertainty that is basic to the experience.

The terms *knowing* and *not-knowing* are relatively easy to think about because the experiences to which they refer are explicit. *Sort-of-knowing* is different. In its essence, it refers to something that is always at least somewhat dissociative; that is, we are aware of it more implicitly than explicitly. In its everyday manifestation, sort-of-knowing is not a defensive operation but an adaptive process in its own right– a process that among its other uses allows self/other boundaries to become sufficiently permeable to facilitate a transition to knowing. That said, there is a difference between sort-of-knowing as a normal mind/brain process that helps us get through each day with the least amount of stress, and sort-of-knowing as a means of protecting oneself from what may be too much for the mind to bear.

What I mean is nicely captured in a story told to me by a patient about an incident that took place while he was driving his fiancée to pick up her wedding dress (see Chefetz & Bromberg, 2004). He had entered an intersection just as the light was changing from yellow to red, and a policeman pulled him over. He of course told the cop that the light wasn't red yet, and he also asked to be given a break because he was about to get married to the girl sitting next to him. His fiancée suddenly took over and began chastising my patient at length, in front of the cop, about the light really being red and what a bad person he was to lie to a policeman. The cop listened quietly in amazement, and when he finally spoke he told my patient that he wasn't going to give him a ticket because if he was marrying *her* he already had enough trouble. As they drove off, my patient said to her, furiously, "How could you have done that? How could you have been so mean to me?"

"You didn't get a ticket, did you?" she replied.

He, in a state of total consternation, could barely get his words out: "You ... you ... you mean you did that on purpose?"

"Well ... I'm not sure–*Sort of,*" she mumbled.

"Sort of." Oh to have been a fly on the windshield! My guess is that she would have been looking into space as she said "Sort of." Eventually, when my patient's fiancée had come back to what she would call "herself," she acknowledged that she was terribly sorry and ashamed at what she had done, and that she hadn't done it on purpose. She also revealed that since she was a child she had always been terrified of policemen and wasn't "herself" whenever she was around one.

When she was with the policeman, the self-state that organized her "me-ness" was dissociatively trying to control the affect dysregulation caused by her hyperaroused fear. In this context it would be accurate to say that her *brain* "did it on purpose"—as an automatic survival response. The "purpose," however, had no cognitive representation in her *mind.* But later, when she responded to her irate boyfriend "You didn't get a ticket, did you?" the hyperaroused fear had diminished enough for her to inhabit a self-state that was also organized by attachment, making her vituperousness when the cop was present a "not me." At each point, what she did was "right," but in different ways.

To me, what is especially interesting about this vignette is that in her effort to think about whether she "did it on purpose," her reply was not defined totally by either "knowing" or "not-knowing." Her ability to be confused and to symbolize the confusion by the term *sort-of* speaks to a nascent capacity to experience intrapsychic conflict and hold it as a mental state long enough to reflect on what it is like and, to some degree, symbolize it cognitively. To avoid the mental confusion created by a question that required her to consider the possibility that *both* were "me," she was at least able to offer "I'm not sure—*Sort of.*"

By my lights, that's pretty darned good. She didn't automatically switch self-states dissociatively. She was able to hold both states, albeit with confusion, in a single moment of consciousness. The ability to stand in the spaces between the states was not quite in place but she was able to hold both states long enough to experience their presence simultaneously. As a result, time, place, and motive became complex, and confusingly conflictual rather than dissociatively simplified. Because a resolution of the conflict was not yet possible for her, she used the term "sort-of" in order to answer her boyfriend's question; the phrase vividly captures the uncertainty that organized her unfamiliarly complex mental state and its immediate experience of unclarity.[3]

The Reach of Intersubjectivity

When you look at sort-of-knowing in its function as a normal brain process, it is not hard to see why the experience of uncertainty is so relevant to current psychoanalytic thinking, informed as it is by broadening perspectives on the mind's further reaches. Mary Tennes (2007), in a paper titled "Beyond Intersubjectivity," has linked the experience of uncertainty to what she calls "a model of selfhood that resists the need for certainty." As have I, she proposes that "self and other, subject and

---

[3]My thanks to Nina Thomas for recognizing that the presented version did not sufficiently develop this point, which helped me to better clarify the relationship between dissociation and conflict.

object, both are and are not separate" (p. 514). Most centrally, Tennes argues that "as our clinical technique takes us further into intersubjective territory, we are encountering realities for which we have neither language nor context" and that "if we look more closely with less need to fit such experiences into our preexisting framework, we discover that they deconstruct in profound and perhaps destabilizing ways, our notions of self and other" (p. 508).

As with most radically new discoveries about the mind and its undiscovered realms, the new realities that Tennes speaks of were anticipated in the early days of psychoanalysis. Freud himself cast an eye in a similar direction involving subliminal, even telepathic communication, for which he coined the phrase "thought transference," while leaving its implications undeveloped. His diffidence to go forward was based on his estimation of the public's receptiveness to these ideas or the lack thereof. He did not lack personal enthusiasm. In his 1921 paper, "Psychoanalysis and Telepathy," Freud offered the view that

> it no longer seems possible to brush aside the study of … things which seem to vouchsafe the real existence of psychic forces other than the known forces of the human and animal psyche, or which reveal mental faculties in which, until now, we did not believe. The appeal of this kind of inquiry seems irresistible. (cited in Devereux, 1953, p. 56)

Freud, however, was overly optimistic in his prediction. The appeal of this kind of inquiry was quite resistible for the next 75 years among most analysts, even those from the interpersonal and relational communities. Then, Elizabeth Lloyd Mayer (1996), in the *International Journal of Psychoanalysis*, published a now seminal article about the limitation in psychoanalytic thinking with regard to what we call intersubjectivity brought about by our anxiety in straying beyond the narrow range of what we hold to be "legitimate" clinical facts. Freud may have had an enthusiasm for "thought transference," but the fact was, Mayer was discovering that analysts routinely declined to report instances of such phenomena even though they were occurring in their offices. Fully two-thirds of Mayer's paper was devoted to hard research on anomalous experiences and their relationship to so-called paranormal phenomena that are always being encountered by analysts in their day-to-day work with certain patients and subsumed under categories of experience like intuition, empathic attunement, unconscious communication, and if those fail, then "coincidence." It is just such phenomena, Mayer argued, that most demonstrate "the enormous power of the human mind to affect—indeed to create ... what analysts have customarily called *external* reality."

> If we ignore research that significantly recasts our most important concepts, we may find ourselves in a position not unlike the Sufi sage Nasrudin, who searched for his keys at night under a lighted lamp-post not because he'd lost them there, but because there was more light there than where he'd lost them. We need to look wherever we're likely to find what we're actually looking for, whether or not it's bathed in the light of assumptions that are comfortably familiar. (pp. 723–724)

Tennes (2007) cites research by the biologist Rupert Sheldrake (1999, 2003) who developed, Tennes states, "a theory of the 'extended mind,' which he links to already existing field theories in physics, mathematics, and biology. Our minds, he proposes, are not confined inside of our heads, but stretch out beyond them through morphic fields" (p. 508 fn.). Similarly, Neil Altman (2007) in his commentary on Tennes's paper, suggests that holistic field theory is a potentially promising context for comprehending this heretofore unimaginable reach of the mind, and that Mayer's groundbreaking report on Princeton's Anomalies Research Studies has cleared a path toward full acceptance of what we already recognize implicitly—that "people are able to obtain information from remote sources without having any conventional form of contact with the source of information" (p. 529).[4]

---

[4]As a case in point, the prestigious *Journal of Personality and Social Psychology*, in a startling break with its conservative tradition, recently published an article (Bem, 2011) that invites the scientific community to seriously reconsider the heretofore unimaginable reach of the *extended* mind. The article was written by Professor Daryl J. Bem, a distinguished social psychologist at Cornell University, and in a prepublication discussion of it, Burkley (2010) presents the implications of Bem's rigorously researched findings that the brain has the ability to see into the future, the foremost implication being that his evidence is "consistent with modern physics' take on time and space. For example, Einstein believed that the mere act of observing something here could affect something there, a phenomenon he called '*spooky action at a distance*'" (p. 3, emphasis added). "As Dr. Chiao, a physicist from Berkeley once said about quantum mechanics, 'It's completely counterintuitive and outside our everyday experience, but we (physicists) have kind of gotten used to it'. ... *Just because the effect seems 'supernatural' doesn't necessarily mean the cause is.* ... Bem's findings may have a profound effect on what we know and have come to accept as true" (p. 4, emphasis added).

Writing about self/other communication that transcends so-called normal channels has until now been pretty much limited to those who wrote about it as fiction, and to the rare breed of nonfiction authors (including a handful of analysts) for whom such things never were fiction. Thus the powerful link I have long experienced between the science fiction of Theodore Sturgeon, the research on dream telepathy by Montague Ullman and his colleagues at Maimonides Medical Center (1973), and Sándor Ferenczi's (1930) assertion that, especially under the influence of shock, a part of the personality "lives on, hidden, ceaselessly endeavoring to make itself felt," and that sometimes we can "persuade it to engage in what I might almost call an infantile conversation" (p. 122).

In his *Clinical Diary*, Ferenczi (1932), while alone with his own thoughts, privately allowed his prescient "imagination" to envision the future trajectory of this extraordinary assertion and wrote the following—my own resonance with which is discernable throughout this chapter, perhaps most powerfully in the section titled "The Fly Truffler":

> [It] tempts the imagination to suppose that the childish personality is in much closer contact with the universe, and therefore its sensitivity is much greater than that of the adult, crystalized into rigidity. It would not surprise us either if someday it were to be demonstrated that in this early state the whole personality is still resonating with the environment—and not only at particular points that had remained permeable, namely the sense organs. So-called supernormal faculties—being receptive to processes beyond sensory perceptions (clairvoyance), apprehending the communications of an alien will (suggestion from a distance)—may well be ordinary processes, in the same way that animals (dogs) ... possess such apparently supernormal faculties (sense of smell at a colossal distance, the inexplicable adoption of the owners' sympathies and antipathies). (p. 81)

The Reach of Healing

My temperamental compatibility with Ferenczi has fueled my thinking during most of my professional career, but only recently did I become aware that it was personally grounded in a way I could not have anticipated: I discovered that some of the edginess that infiltrates my blending of psychoanalysis and literature has always involved something else—something that although I "sort-of-knew," I did not in fact "know." The way that this sort-of-knowing became knowing was personally amazing, but it is also so illustrative that I'm going to tell the story.

In the Fall 2007 issue of *Contemporary Psychoanalysis* there was a review of my book, *Awakening the Dreamer,* by Max Cavitch—a Professor of English at the University of Pennsylvania. The review was laudatory, but its biggest gift to me was something else. The review was titled "Dissociative Reading: Philip Bromberg and Emily Dickinson" and it was as illuminating about me as it was about its formal topic, dissociative processes and literature. The phenomenon of dissociation is an area of special interest for Cavitch, a quite unusual one for a Professor of English. He is well read in the clinical literature although his special focus is on dissociation as a cultural phenomenon. Unbeknownst to me, Emily Dickinson's verse also happened to be an area of expertise and interest for Cavitch, which in itself would not be unusual were it not for the fact that, as a scholar, he saw these two areas of interest as profoundly related by the phenomenon of trauma, and that as reviewer of my book he experienced this interrelationship as significant not only in my writing, but also in the writer himself—that is to say, in me personally. He noticed that in chapter 8 of my book I had excerpted several lines from one of Dickinson's (1863) poems (poem #670) for use as an epigraph—her poem that begins "One need not be a Chamber—to be Haunted—" (p. 333). In my effort to make the relevance of her lines as clear as possible to my readers I had manifested a lack of concern about the formal rules of literary scholarship by doing something that rendered her verse into (sort-of) prose—so as to better make my point, or so I believed. In Cavitch's words:

> He wants us to get the gist of the poem without having to wrestle too much with her linguistic contortions. Yet this also has the perhaps unconsciously intended effect of evacuating her poem of its uncanny resemblance, in its seemingly unbridgeable gaps and cognitive dissonances, to the very dissociative processes Bromberg wants Dickinson to help him illustrate. He mutes, in other words, the audibility to reflective thought of those places in the poem where dissociative gaps are created. One can point, for example, to his omission of all but one of Dickinson's famous dashes—*her most consistent and visible affront to linear narrative.* (p. 686, emphasis added)

In other words, Cavitch is arguing that it was my elimination of her *unorthodox* use of dashes that was my most manifest affront to Dickinson. As a Professor of English, Cavitch easily could have been critical of me here—but he was not. What he did have to say was both nonjudgmental and perceptive. It also was astonishing, and led to my highly personal reply to his review that was published in the same issue (Bromberg, 2007, pp. 700–705). Cavitch did not experience my obliteration of Dickinson's signature-style of versification as "mere sloppiness" or "unmotivated error" because, as he put it, speaking of Dickinson, "there may be no other writer in the English language who engages readers so relentlessly and so powerfully in the intersubjective experience of dissociative states" (p. 684). Cavitch continues:

> Anyone averse to such biographical speculation need only turn to the poems themselves to encounter an imagination stamped with the imprint of all manner of violence: eyes gauged out, lungs pierced, brains trepanned, bodies subjected to extremes of heat and cold, soldered lips, gushing wounds, dismemberment, rape, torture, hanging, drowning, death in every form. (p. 684)
>
> *To rend, reduce, and suture such a poem, as Bromberg does without comment here, is to seem to participate with the poet in a dissociative enactment*—a transferential encounter, of Bromberg's dissociative immersion in the enactment of the poet's traumatized relation to a flooding of affect in the process of being symbolized. (p. 686, emphasis added)

Cavitch's perceptiveness reached back to a trauma in my own past about which he could not have known but which was always "sort-of-known" by me. I'm referring to the residue of an event that goes back to my days as a doctoral student in English Literature many years ago—an experience that was etched into my psyche when, without warning, I was deliberately shamed in front of the class by a professor who announced that I didn't belong in the field. Why did I not belong? Because I had used the assignment of writing an essay about Shakespeare's play, *Henry IV* (Part I), as an opportunity to discuss Prince Hal's *personality*.

But the professor's words were not the core of the trauma. It was how he did it. Cradling under one arm the class's completed essays, he held between the thumb and forefinger of his other hand a single essay. Silently, he walked slowly among the seated students and stopped at my desk, letting the single essay fall onto it from above. It was then that he spoke his only words: "*We don't do that sort of thing here.*"

This experience, both in spite of and because of its traumatic impact, played an explicit role in my finding a path that led me into the field of psychoanalysis, a field that I experience as my natural home. And, indeed, for many years I continued to use literature freely as part of my psychoanalytic writing, which I took as evidence that the trauma had been processed.

Enter Max Cavitch, stage left. Because of him I was able to recognize that a dissociated residue indeed had remained. I already knew that the trauma had not prevented me from pleasurably immersing myself in literature by using it psychoanalytically, but what I had not seen was the dissociated presence of a determination to never submit to the arbitrary imposition of using literature in some "right" way. Cavitch intuitively sensed this from my interaction with Dickinson. In his eyes, Dickinson and I were comrades in arms. We each refused to bend to orthodoxy. In my use of her lines as an epigraph, I did not simply reduce her poetry to quasi-prose. Dissociatively, I did to her poetry my own version of what she did in writing it. I challenged the system (which for me, now included *her*) by obliterating without acknowledgment an important piece of what had been her own challenge to the system: her signature use of dashes as *her* violation of orthodoxy–a violation that, ironically, "the system" ultimately accepted.

Cavitch surmised that I may have been participating in a dissociative enactment with Dickinson that was being played out as a power struggle, but for both Dickinson and me its traumatic origin was unknown to him. With Dickinson it was kept guarded from the world, and with me no prior personal relationship existed through which I might have made it known either explicitly or through things "about" me that he might have unconsciously experienced. In Dickinson's case, Cavitch wrote: "There is much speculation as to what sort of traumatic experiences Dickinson may have endured that would help explain her famously extreme shyness and virtual self-sequestration in her family's Amherst home" (p. 684). My own trauma, the unanticipated public humiliation by the other English professor, was likewise unknown to him until I shared it as part of my published response to his review.

Through Max Cavitch's not shaming me about my unscholarly behavior, and even more by his appreciating how that behavior led him to a way of understanding a mental process (dissociation) of interest to both of us, he helped me not only professionally, but also personally. This is why my reply to his review was not only a professional expression of gratitude, but was also very personal. In it I recounted to him my experience as a graduate student in English and let him know how much I was benefiting from sharing with him a relational experience that was so personally healing. It was healing because it activated the shadow of the trauma with the other professor, while holding it in a relational context where I felt cared about as a person. What I call a "safe surprise" (Bromberg, 2006a) had been created—and the creation of that safe surprise had taken place without any direct interchange between us. Uncannily, without a direct interchange I was nonetheless able to process a dissociated residue of past trauma—a residue about which I had "sort-of-known" because I knew *about* it, but that I now *knew*, because I knew it personally. I knew it because I relived the original traumatic scenario, but relived it in a manner that did not simply repeat the past. The blend of reliving and processing with Max allowed a new outcome to become part of the reality that defines my sense of self both professionally and personally.[5]

The Fly Truffler

In the remainder of this "personal book-end" I am once again going to draw on literature. When I made that decision, a part of me was saying, "Maybe Cavitch let you off easy; maybe you shouldn't push your luck." But another part was arguing that I should go for it. That latter part prevailed, and so I'm now going to address the theme of "knowing and sort-of-knowing" through sharing self-states with the author of an extraordinary novel, *The Fly Truffler* (Sobin, 1999), a piece of writing that I hope will expand the reader's clinical perspective as much as it has expanded mine.

---

[5]Three years later, in 2010, equally uncannily, an event took place in which I was again befriended by an English Professor, Carola Kaplan, further illuminating my nonlinear awakening as I continued my journey through the lived space unifying trauma, dissociation, psychoanalysis and literature. Interested readers may find our personal/professional dialogue (Kaplan, 2010a, 2010b), (Bromberg, 2010) to be informative in its own right while also enriching their "feel" for what in my earlier encounter with Cavitch I described as illustrating the reach of intersubjectivity and the reach of healing.

It is a book that slowly pulls a reader into a chaotic mix of love, loss, and madness. It allows the reader to feel not just the presence of increasing mental destabilization, but also the simultaneous voice of a potential for relatedness always moving along with it.

Written by an expatriate American poet, Gustave Sobin, the story is set in the rural countryside of Provence where Sobin lived for 40 years until his death in 2005. It is the story of a man in love, Philippe Cabassac, whose mind, slowly but agonizingly, loses the boundary that separates loss of an other from the traumatic loss of self. Simultaneously, Cabassac loses the boundary that separates creative dreaming from autistic thinking as his mind becomes less and less able to hold the reality of the death of his beloved wife Julieta–a young student who disappears from his life as mysteriously as she entered it. To paraphrase Jennifer Reese's (2000) *New York Times* book review, Julieta, out of nowhere, suddenly appears in Cabassac's classroom, taking voluminous notes. Cabassac is a professor of a dying language– Provençal–and she an orphan who has been wandering aimlessly through the fading world of Provence. Now, with Cabassac, she finds words that mystically connect her with her ancestral roots. Julieta moves into Cabassac's farmhouse, conceives a child, marries him, and miscarries. Shortly thereafter she dies. Unable to bear the loss, Cabassac finds his dreams becoming increasingly indistinguishable from waking reality.

Cabassac has hunted for truffles all his life by searching for the swarms of tiny flies that hover over the ground where the truffles are buried in order to lay their eggs in the aromatic earth beneath. Through this miracle of symbiosis, the truffles can be found, and are indeed found by Cabassac, who fries them, eats them, sips herbal tea, and later, when he sleeps, has powerful dreams in which his wife returns to him.

Cabassac was an emotionally isolated man even before Julieta's death; after it, dreams become gradually more real than life. In them Julieta is about to tell him a profound secret but he always awakens before it is revealed. He loses interest in his job as a professor of Provençal linguistics–a job that begins to die just as verbal language itself increasingly dies for him as a medium of communication. He becomes more and more isolated from human relationship and sinks gradually into a state of autistic madness, signing away piece after piece of his family home–the only thing that still connects him to the external world–until all that remains is to search out the flies that lead him to the truffles and in turn to his lost beloved.

The Fly Truffler can be read from many different frames of reference, including as an allegorical portrayal of the Orpheus myth in which the doorway that leads to reunion with a lost beloved lies beneath the ground–and is the doorway to Hell. But what I want to speak to is its ability to evoke the affective experience that makes us aware, sometimes disturbingly aware, of the link between trauma and dissociation and the potential loss of self.

Cabassac's connection to Julieta becomes tied more and more concretely to his being able to experience her as a person who continues to exist as alive; and this Julieta, as even Cabassac senses, is connected to his dead mother in an ineffable way. Sobin's book raises the issue of how to think about people like the protagonist, Cabassac, who are unable to restore themselves as they slide into madness, and how what we term *knowing* and *sort-of-knowing* might be viewed in the context of annihilation dread. Because knowing is dependent on thinking, and thinking is dependent on the degree to which one's capacity for mental representation has not been compromised by trauma, it is worth reflecting anew on Laub and Auerhahn's (1993) famous observation that it is the primary nature of trauma to "elude our knowledge because of both defense and deficit" (p. 288). The deficit is a dissociative gap, by virtue of which sort-of-knowing is recruited from its everyday function into the service of the mind's evolutionary need to protect its stability (and thus functions simultaneously as a defense).

Sobin's work of fiction is simultaneously a work of nonfiction (see also Bromberg, 2010, p. 454). Certain people for whom the early development of intersubjectivity has failed to take place or has been severely compromised are, in times of crisis, especially vulnerable to "uncertainty" about the boundary between selfhood and otherness, and can become unable to navigate this boundary. They become unable to sustain the loss of a needed person as a separate "other." It is these people for whom the potential for annihilation dread is often greatest. For them, the experience of loss can become such a threat to the experience of self-continuity that it results in what we know as insanity.

Self-continuity can of course feel threatened in lesser ways that do not provoke annihilation anxiety. But when the inability to separate self and other is genuinely a possibility, the function of dissociation as a protection against out-of-control affect dysregulation becomes a last-ditch effort to insure brute survival. The mind can no longer assure that one or more parts of the self will continue to engage the world in a way that is functional though limited. Dissociation then becomes the means through which the mind/brain tries to avoid self-annihilation by protecting the inner world from the existence of the outside. Dissociation gradually eliminates the outside world as a *personal* reality by living more and more completely in a nonpermeable, self-contained "dream." One may still know about the outside world but is no longer "of" it.

When the original maternal object is insufficiently differentiated from the self to become a comforting internal "other" that can be remembered later in one's life, a person may appear in one's life—often after one's actual mother has died—who embodies a likeness to the mother in some physically concrete way and who seems totally fixated on the relationship. A passionate attachment to that person then develops a life of its own. In Cabassac's case, in the wake of Julieta's death, this attachment became (borrowing the title of Jules Henry's 1965 classic) a "pathway to madness" that led to a final act done without self-reflection—the act of obliterating what remained of his outside world and his attachment to it. He sold, literally out from under himself, the land and home in which he and his family had lived for generations—a place that until then had been not just his, but *him*. As is made clear by the author, there is an eerie resonance between the increasing loss of personal meaning held by the outside world and an earlier withdrawal into himself during his childhood.

What pushed him over the edge? What was the clincher for Cabassac?[6] My answer would be that he had no one to talk to and no one to listen. Sobin portrays him as having been a loner all his life, and thus especially vulnerable to the horror of self-loss when Julieta disappeared from his external world as suddenly as she appeared in it. His struggle to "stand in the spaces" was unable to prevent his increasing isolation inside himself because he couldn't use the mind of an other to share what he felt. He not only was unable to use a real other, but was unable to use an *imagined* other to heal the loss because imagination

---

[6]I encourage readers to become familiar with recent research by Andrew Moskowitz and his colleagues (e.g., Moskowitz et al., 2008), findings that point powerfully to the centrality of trauma and dissociation in diagnosing psychosis. For example, Moskowitz and Corstens (2007) have affirmed: "Voices heard by persons diagnosed schizophrenic appear to be indistinguishable, on the basis of their experienced characteristics, from voices heard by persons with dissociative disorders or by persons with no mental disorder at all…. [W]e argue that hearing voices should be considered a dissociative experience, which under some conditions may have pathological consequences. In other words, we believe that, while voices may occur in the context of a psychotic disorder, they should not be considered a psychotic symptom" (pp. 35–36).

even in grief requires the simultaneous existence of a separate self that is stable enough to remember a lost other without merging with her.

Cabassac's external environment became more and more undifferentiated from his internal object-world, and could not be sustained as a reality that was *his*. The outside world became grimly limited in what it could offer as a potential grounding for sanity and literally had to be sold off–to be got rid of because it was already starting to take on the presence of a now "malevolent other" threatening to disintegrate the boundary between self and object. Sobin offers a portrayal, both inspiring and chilling, of what trauma can do when there is no one with whom to share it. And to those who might see this novel as somehow representing the consequences of substance abuse (mushrooms and herbal tea), I can only say, "Sorry folks–I don't think so!"

But read on. It's not over yet. There is another message embedded in this novel that is just as important and perhaps even more so. In this remote, sequestered environment of Provence, humans and animals share an intimate relationship that is almost as vital to their evolutionary survival as it was during the Middle Ages, a relationship between species that is inherent in Sobin's very title. A "truffler" is a person who is devoted to a seemingly solitary pursuit. The success of the activity, however, depends on the truffler's interdependence with a nonhuman species that in this area of Provence is a certain type of fly, but most famously is with a pig. Pigs have been used because of both their great sensitivity in being able to sniff out where truffles are hiding beneath the ground and their voracious craving for them which makes a pig fanatical in its search. The problem is that the truffler must remain vigilantly alert to prevent the pig from scarfing down the prize before the truffler gets it, so that more civilized animals (like us) can eat it more slowly. It is not hard to see why the flies in that respect represent an improvement. Looking for flies is clearly an easier, less fraught way to find truffles than by using a hyperaroused pig.

Sobin's wish to open our minds to the interrelationship between animal and human is not limited to fly truffling. Through a powerful and poignant vignette, he expands the scope and depth of this connection to include an *implicit* channel of communication that touches directly on the way we are starting to understand the dialectic between thought and affect, between left and right brain and, in a clinical context, between self-states of the patient and self-states of the analyst. I am suggesting that Sobin, beyond supporting the interdependence of mind/brain systems among humans, may indeed be reflecting in the following vignette the evolutionary status of an intersubjectivity that bridges what is most human and what remains most animal.[7]

In the passage I am going to end with, Sobin narrows the gap between the *internal* worlds of human life and "sort-of-human" life. The passage relates to the breeding of silkworms—an enterprise that for hundreds of years was done in this part of Provence by women, enabling them to survive economically:

> [T]he silkworms, as if on some magical signal, rose into their brushwood uprights and began spinning their cocoons. Rotating their heads continuously so that a thin, spittle-like secretion would run free of a pair of matching glands located on either side of their thorax, these creatures would each spin over a kilometer of precious, opalescent fiber in less than three uninterrupted days of labor. Nothing stopped them either. Nothing aside from unwanted noises. A single thunderclap, for instance, could break the thread, bring their spinning to an end, destroy a whole season's harvest.
>
> When a thunderstorm was seen approaching, the women—in preparation—would gather, begin ringing bells—goat bells, sheep bells—or beating, gently at first, against shovels, frying pans, cauldrons in an attempt to prepare their little nurslings for the far more invasive sounds of the thunderstorm itself. They'd increase the volume of those cacophonous medleys with each passing minute. In response, the silkworms wove all the faster, and their thread, as a result, went unbroken throughout the ensuing thunderstorm. (pp. 83–84)

When I first read this my mouth dropped open. Silkworms? Really??? It seems that even invertebrates can get affectively destabilized when they're subjected to shock—in this case, a sudden noise that is loud beyond their tolerance to bear it. They can no longer function. At this stage of their development—beyond infancy but still pretty vulnerable—that means they stop spinning silk. So the women do what a good therapist would do. To support the continuity of the silkworms'

---

[7]It also perhaps sheds indirect light on the significance of the recent discovery of mirror neurons, the postulation of which, if you will recall, came about through a researcher's fortuitous relationship with a macaque monkey (see Gallese & Goldman, 1998).

developmental maturation, they create conditions that they believe will raise their threshold for affect dysregulation. For a silkworm, developmental maturation at that phase means being able to spin thread, supporting a survival capacity (the creation of a cocoon) that is necessary to their existence. This survival capacity is helped along through a human/animal relationship that, at an affective level, is a plausible analog of what Schore (2003b) calls a conversation between limbic systems. It matters not that the women, like therapists, also reap an economic benefit. A gifted therapist does what he does not just because of a benefit to him but with personal benefit being always a part of it.

Is it a stretch to see an earlier phase of the relationship between the women and the silkworms as similar to an early maternal phase of human infancy? Consider the following description by Sobin that depicts how the women care for the eggs–eggs that the women pour into little sachets which they'd sewn for the very occasion: "Wearing those sachets underneath the warm folds of their skirts or snug between their corseted breasts, they'd incubate those nascent silkworms on nothing more nor less than the heat of their own bodies" (p. 81).

> For ten days running, then, women actually served as agents of gestation for these silkworms-to-be. ... [T]he women would then deposit the freshly hatched larvae in nurseries–kindergartens of sorts–that they'd have meticulously prepared in advance. Temperate, airy, well-lit, these cocooneries became the silkworms' abode, now, as they passed through four successive moltings in as many weeks. Growing from delicate little caterpillars no more than a millimeter long to pale voracious creatures a full sixty times that length, the silkworms required continuous nursing. And nursing they received. (pp. 81–82)

It was after infancy that the silkworms-to-be, now silkworms-that-are, became part of an interactive process. In June "began the moment in which ... the women responded to a need to protect them from thunderstorms" (p. 83). I am offering the view that like the natural presence of thunderstorms in the relationship between a silkworm and its caretaker, the relationship between a patient and a psychoanalyst has its own natural disruptions. But unlike thunderstorms created by the external environment, their psychoanalytic counterparts are not exterior events that intrude into an otherwise safe treatment frame. Because our therapeutic work always involves reliving areas of experience where developmental trauma has left its residue to one degree or another, the analytic relationship is a process of collision and negotiation. It is both the source of potential destabilization and the source of its healing. What patient and analyst do together will always include collisions between subjectivities, some of which will inevitably feel too "loud" to the patient, and it is part of the analyst's job to be alert to signs of this and address it with genuine personal involvement. Threatening "noise" is inherent to the analytic relationship itself–a part of the optimal therapeutic context that I call "safe but not too safe." The therapist's commitment to helping a patient distinguish what is disruptive but negotiable from the dissociated "truth" that "all ruptures in attachment are relationally irreparable" is an essential part of the work. The therapist cannot prevent interpersonal noise from becoming too loud no matter how nonintrusive he or she tries to be. Letting a patient know in an ongoing way that his or her internal experience is being held in your mind *while* you are doing your job is what provides the safety–even though you are not doing it perfectly.[8]

In humans, the ability to strengthen one's readiness to face potential trauma without transforming life itself into an act of interminable vigilance depends on a relationship with an important other who relates to your subjective states as important to him or her–and to whose mental states you can reciprocally relate. Cabassac's capacity to feel that he existed in the mind of an other was so tenuous that the death of his beloved became a loss of selfhood. There was no longer a bridge that could link a stable mental representation of her to a self sturdy enough to maintain self-continuity without her concrete existence having to be part of it. And he had no one with whom to talk.

It is the relationship between patient and analyst that provides a route around the dead-end faced by someone like Cabassac. Similarly, it is the relationship between patient and analyst that provides a way around the problem posed by classical notions of an unconscious as something that can never be observed, only inferred. The problem to which I refer has perhaps never been better captured than by the brilliant and troubled Italian poet Alda Merini (2007)[9] in the aphorism:

---

[8]Margaret Wilkinson (2006) offers a similar perspective from a Jungian vantage point that is both clinically and conceptually compelling. Her chapter, "Un-doing Dissociation" (pp. 94–113), especially, should not be missed.

[9]My gratitude to Kristopher Spring for bringing Merini's aphorism to my attention.

> Psychoanalysis
> Always looks for the egg
> In a basket
> That has been lost. (p. 15)

For over 100 years, psychoanalysts were trained to talk to their patients about an *inferred* basket—an inferred unconscious—through associations and interpretations. Discovering the "egg," which analysts have chosen to term *unconscious fantasy,* has been the endeavor said to demonstrate that even though what is unconscious is lost to direct observation its contents can be pieced together. At this point in the evolution of psychoanalysis, however, it is increasingly recognized that the "egg" can manifestly be brought into palpable existence by accepting that the "egg" is not buried content but the symbolization of a dissociated relational process that is not unearthed, but mutually cocreated through enactment.

The enactment of dissociated experience in psychoanalysis is not comfortable for either patient or analyst. It is characterized not by an experience of confidence in where you are going but by the experience of uncertainty. How do we come to tolerate the ambiguity inherent in not-knowing or, more confusing still, sort-of-knowing? I guess I would say it has to do, sort-of, with the wiring of the brain; sort-of with how much our caretakers were able to affirm the rights of all parts of us to exist; and sort-of being lucky to have someone to talk to at the right times—including someone who can think about you as a silkworm when you most need it.

I'll close by finally making reference to the title of my chapter, which I've not mentioned explicitly even though it is probably clear by now why I chose it. The link between the legendary 1937 song, "The Nearness of You," and what some now call implicit relational knowing needs few words to explain it. And even though I love Allan Schore's concept of conversations between limbic systems, I prefer the wording of Hoagy Carmichael and Ned Washington. When they wrote the "The Nearness of You" they already knew that "It's not your sweet conversation/That brings this sensation, oh no/ It's just the nearness of you."

References

Ackerman, D. (2004). *An alchemy of mind: The marvel and mystery of the brain.* New York: Scribner.

Ainsworth, M., Blehar, M., Waters, E., & Wall, S. (1978). *Patterns of attachment.* Hillsdale, NJ: Lawrence Erlbaum Associates, Inc.

Allen, J. G., Console, D.A., & Lewis, L. (1999). Dissociative detachment and memory impairment: Reversible amnesia or encoding failure? *Comprehensive Psychiatry, 40,* 160–171.

Allen, J. G., & Coyne, L. (1995). Dissociation and vulnerability to psychotic experience: The Dissociative Experiences Scale and the MMPI-2. *Journal of Nervous and Mental Disease, 183,* 615–622.

Allen, J. G., & Fonagy, P. (Eds.) (2006). *The handbook of mentalization-based treatment.* Chichester, UK: Wiley.

Allman, J. M., Watson, K. K., Tetreault, N. A., & Hakeem, A. (2005). Intuition and autism: A possible role for Von Economo neurons. *Trends in Cognitive Sciences, 9,* 367–373.

Altman, N. (2007). Integrating the transpersonal with the intersubjective: Commentary on Mary Tennes's "Beyond intersubjectivity." *Contemporary Psychoanalysis, 43,* 526–535.

Ammaniti, M., & Trentini, C. (2009). How new knowledge about parenting reveals the neurobiological implications of intersubjectivity: A conceptual synthesis of recent research. *Psychoanalytic Dialogues, 19,* 537–555.

Arlow, J. A. (1969). Unconscious fantasy and disturbances of conscious experience. *Psychoanalytic Quarterly, 38,* 1–27.

Balint, E. (1987). Memory and consciousness. *International Journal of Psychoanalysis, 68,* 475–483.

Balter, L., Lothane, Z., & Spencer, J. H. Jr. (1980). On the analyzing instrument. *Psychoanalytic Quarterly, 49,* 474–504.

Barbas, H. (2007). Flow of information for emotions through temporal and orbitofrontal pathways. *Journal of Anatomy, 211,* 237–249.

Barbas, H., Saha, S., Rempel-Clower, N., & Ghashghaei, T. (2003). Serial pathways from primate prefrontal cortex to autonomic areas may influence emotional expression. *BMC Neuroscience, 4,* 25.

Baring-Gould, W. S. (Ed.) (1967). *The annotated Sherlock Holmes: The four novels and the fifty-six short stories complete by Sir Arthur Conan Doyle.* New York: Clarkson N. Potter.

Bass, A. (2003). "E" enactments in psychoanalysis: Another medium, another message. *Psychoanalytic Dialogues, 13,* 657–675.

——— (2009). An independent theory of clinical technique viewed through a relational lens: Commentary on paper by Michael Parsons. *Psychoanalytic Dialogues, 19,* 237–245.

Bem, D. J. (2011). Feeling the future: Experimental evidence for anomalous retroactive influences on cognition and affect. *Journal of Personality and Social Psychology, 100,* 407–425.

Benjamin, J. (1988). *The bonds of love.* New York: Pantheon.

——— (1995). *Like subjects, love objects: Essays on recognition and sexual difference.* New Haven, CT: Yale University Press.

——— (1998). *The shadow of the other.* New York: Routledge.

——— (2005). From many into one: Attention, energy, and the containing of multitudes. *Psychoanalytic Dialogues, 15,* 185–201.

——— (2007). Review of *Awakening the dreamer: Clinical journeys,* by Philip M. Bromberg. *Contemporary Psychoanalysis, 43,* 666–680.

Benowitz, L. I., Bear, D. M., Rosenthal, R., Mesulam, M.-M., Zaidel, E., & Sperry, R. W. (1983). Hemispheric specialization in nonverbal communication. *Cortex, 19,* 5–11.

Bion, W. R. (1962). Learning from experience. In *Seven servants.* New York: Jason Aronson, 1977.

——— (1963). *Elements of psychoanalysis.* London: Heinemann.

——— (1965). *Transformations.* London: Heinemann.

——— (1970). *Attention and interpretation.* London: Maresfield.

Blonder, L. X., Bowers, D., & Heilman, K. M. (1991). The role of the right hemisphere in emotional communication. *Brain, 114,* 1115–1127.

Bogolepova, I. N., & Malofeeva, L. I. (2001). Characteristics of the development of speech areas 44 and 45 in the left and right hemisphere of the human brain in early post-natal ontogenesis. *Neuroscience and Behavioral Physiology, 31,* 349–354.

Bollas, C. (1987). *The shadow of the object: Psychoanalysis of the unthought known.* London: Free Association Books.

Bonovitz, C. (2004). The cocreation of fantasy and the transformation of psychic structure. *Psychoanalytic Dialogues, 14,* 553–580.

Bowden, E. M., & Jung-Beeman, M. J. (1998). Getting the right idea: Semantic activation in the right hemisphere may help solve insight problems. *Psychological Science, 6,* 435–440.

——— (2003). Aha! Insight experience correlates with solution activation in the right hemisphere. *Psychonomic Bulletin & Review, 10,* 730–737.

Bowlby, J. (1969). *Attachment and loss: Vol. 1: Attachment.* New York: Basic
    Books.
_____ (1973). *Attachment and loss: Vol. 2: Separation.* New York: Basic
    Books.
_____ (1980). *Attachment and loss: Vol. 3: Loss.* New York: Basic Books.
Brancucci, A., Lucci, G., Mazzatenta, A., & Tommasi, L. (2009). Asymmetries
    of the human social brain in the visual, auditory and chemical modalities.
    Philosophical Transactions of the Royal Society of London Biological Sciences, 364,
    895–914.
Brenner, C. (1976). *Psychoanalytic technique and psychic conflict.* New York: Inter-
    national Universities Press.
Breuer, J., & Freud, S. (1893–1895). *Studies on hysteria.* In J. Strachey (Ed. &
    Trans.), *The standard edition of the complete psychological works of Sigmund
    Freud* (Vol. 2). London: Hogarth Press, 1955.
Brody, S. (2009). On the edge: Exploring the end of the analytic hour. *Psycho-
    analytic Dialogues, 19,* 87–97.
Bromberg, P. M. (1974). Introduction to "On psychoanalytic training: A sym-
    posium." *Contemporary Psychoanalysis, 10,* 239–242.
_____ (1980). Sullivan's concept of consensual validation and the therapeutic
    action of psychoanalysis. *Contemporary Psychoanalysis, 16,* 237–248.
_____ (1984). The third ear. In L. Caligor, P. M. Bromberg, & J. D. Meltzer
    (Eds.), *Clinical perspectives on the supervision of psychoanalysis and psychotherapy*
    (pp. 29–44). New York: Plenum.
_____ (1989). Interpersonal psychoanalysis and self psychology: A clinical com-
    parison. In *Standing in the spaces: Essays on clinical process, trauma and dis-
    sociation* (pp. 147–162). Hillsdale, NJ: The Analytic Press, 1998.
_____ (1993). Shadow and substance: A relational perspective on clinical proc-
    ess. In *Standing in the spaces: Essays on clinical process, trauma and dissociation*
    (pp. 165–187). Hillsdale, NJ: The Analytic Press, 1998.
_____ (1994). "Speak! That I may see you": Some reflections on dissociation,
    reality, and psychoanalytic listening. In *Standing in the spaces: Essays on
    clinical process, trauma and dissociation* (pp. 241–266). Hillsdale, NJ: The
    Analytic Press, 1998.
_____ (1995a). Psychoanalysis, dissociation, and personality organization. In
    Standing in the spaces: Essays on clinical process, trauma and dissociation (pp.
    189–204). Hillsdale, NJ: The Analytic Press, 1998.
_____ (1995b). Resistance, object-usage, and human relatedness. In *Standing
    in the spaces: Essays on clinical process, trauma and dissociation* (pp. 205–222).
    Hillsdale, NJ: The Analytic Press, 1998.
_____ (1996a). Standing in the spaces: The multiplicity of self and the psy-
    choanalytic relationship. In *Standing in the spaces: Essays on clinical process,
    trauma and dissociation* (pp. 267–290). Hillsdale, NJ: The Analytic Press,
    1998.
_____ (1996b). Discussion of Leo Stone's "The psychoanalytic situation." *Jour-
    nal of Clinical Psychoanalysis, 5,* 267–282.

_____ (1998a). *Standing in the spaces: Essays on clinical process, trauma and dissociation.* Hillsdale, NJ: The Analytic Press.

_____ (1998b). Staying the same while changing: Reflections on clinical judgment. In *Standing in the spaces: Essays on clinical process, trauma and dissociation* (pp. 291–307). Hillsdale, NJ: The Analytic Press, 1998.

_____ (1998c). "Help! I'm going out of your mind." In *Standing in the spaces: Essays on clinical process, trauma and dissociation* (pp. 309–328). Hillsdale, NJ: The Analytic Press, 1998.

_____ (1999). Playing with boundaries. In *Awakening the dreamer: Clinical journeys* (pp. 51–64). Mahwah, NJ: The Analytic Press, 2006.

_____ (2000a). Potholes on the royal road: Or is it an abyss? In *Awakening the dreamer: Clinical journeys* (pp. 85–107). Mahwah, NJ: The Analytic Press, 2006.

_____ (2000b). Reply to reviews by Cavell, Sorenson, and Smith. *Psychoanalytic Dialogues, 10,* 551–568.

_____ (2003a). One need not be a house to be haunted: A case study. In *Awakening the dreamer: Clinical journeys* (pp. 153–173). Mahwah, NJ: The Analytic Press, 2006.

_____ (2003b). Something wicked this way comes: Where psychoanalysis, cognitive science, and neuroscience overlap. In *Awakening the dreamer: Clinical journeys* (pp. 174–202). Mahwah, NJ: The Analytic Press, 2006.

_____ (2006a). *Awakening the dreamer: Clinical journeys.* Mahwah, NJ: The Analytic Press.

_____ (2006b). Ev'ry time we say goodbye, I die a little…: Commentary on Holly Levenkron's "Love (and hate) with the proper stranger." *Psychoanalytic Inquiry, 26,* 182–201.

_____ (2007). Response to reviews of "Awakening the dreamer: Clinical journeys." *Contemporary Psychoanalysis, 43,* 696–708.

_____ (2010). Commentary on Carola M. Kaplan's "Navigating trauma in Joseph Conrad's 'Victory': A voyage from Sigmund Freud to Philip M. Bromberg." *Psychoanalytic Dialogues, 20,* 449–455.

Bruner, J. (1990). *Acts of meaning.* Cambridge, MA: Harvard University Press.

Bucci, W. (1997a). *Psychoanalysis and cognitive science: A multiple code theory.* New York: Guilford.

_____ (1997b). Patterns of discourse in "good" and troubled hours: A multiple code interpretation. *Journal of the American Psychoanalytic Association, 45,* 155–187.

_____ (2001). Pathways of emotional communication. *Psychoanalytic Inquiry, 21,* 40–70.

_____ (2002). The referential process, consciousness, and sense of self. *Psychoanalytic Inquiry, 22,* 766–793.

_____ (2003). Varieties of dissociative experience: A multiple code account and a discussion of Bromberg's case of "William." *Psychoanalytic Psychology, 20,* 542–557.

_____ (2007a). Dissociation from the perspective of multiple code theory–Part I: Psychological roots and implications for psychoanalytic treatment. *Contemporary Psychoanalysis, 43*, 165–184.

_____ (2007b). Dissociation from the perspective of multiple code theory–Part II: The spectrum of dissociative processes in the psychoanalytic relationship. *Contemporary Psychoanalysis, 43*, 305–326.

_____ (2010). The uncertainty principle in the psychoanalytic process. In J. Petrucelli (Ed.), *Knowing, not-knowing, and sort-of knowing: Psychoanalysis and the experience of uncertainty* (pp. 203–214). London: Karnac.

Buchanan, T. W., Tranel, D., & Adolphs, R. (2006). Memories for emotional autobiographical events following unilateral damage to medial temporal lobe. *Brain, 129*, 115–127.

Buck, R. (1994). The neuropsychology of communication: Spontaneous and symbolic aspects. *Journal of Pragmatics, 22*, 265–278.

Burke, E. (1757). *A philosophical enquiry into the origin of our ideas of the sublime and the beautiful.* London: Penguin, 1998.

Burkley, M. (2010). Have scientists finally discovered evidence for psychic phenomena? *Psychology Today* blog. Retrieved October 11, 2010 from www. psychologytoday.com/blog/the-social-thinker/201010/have-scientists-finally-discovered-evidence-psychic-phenomena.

Burns, R. (1786). To a louse: On seeing one on a lady's bonnet at church. In R. Bentman (Ed.), *The poetical works of Burns: Cambridge edition* (pp. 43–44). Boston: Houghton Mifflin, 1974.

Burris, B. L. (1995). Classics revisited: Freud's papers on technique. *Journal of the American Psychoanalytic Association, 43*, 175–185.

Caligor, E., Diamond, D., Yeomans, F. E., & Kernberg, O. F. (2009). The interpretive process in the psychoanalytic psychotherapy of borderline personality pathology. *Journal of the American Psychoanalytic Association, 57*, 271–301.

Canestri, J. (2005). Some reflections on the use and meaning of conflict in contemporary psychoanalysis. *Psychoanalytic Quarterly, 74*, 295–326.

Castaneda, C. (1968). *The teachings of Don Juan: A Yaqui way of knowledge.* New York: Ballentine Books.

_____ (1971). *A separate reality: Further conversations with Don Juan.* New York: Simon & Schuster.

Cavell, M. (1998). Triangulation, one's own mind and objectivity. *International Journal of Psychoanalysis, 79*, 449–467.

_____ (2000). Review essay: Self-reflections. *Psychoanalytic Dialogues, 10*, 513–529.

Cavitch, M. (2007). Dissociative reading: Philip Bromberg and Emily Dickinson. *Contemporary Psychoanalysis, 43*, 681–688.

Cerqueira, J. J., Almeida, O. F. X., & Sousa, N. (2008). The stressed prefrontal cortex. Left? Right! *Brain, Behavior, and Immunity, 22*, 630–638.

Chefetz, R. A. (1997). Special case transferences and countertransferences in the treatment of dissociative disorders. *Dissociation, 10,* 255–265.

_____ (2000). Disorder in the therapist's view of the self: Working with the person with dissociative identity disorder. *Psychoanalytic Inquiry, 20,* 305–329.

Chefetz, R. A., & Bromberg, P. M. (2004). Talking with "me and not-me": A dialogue. *Contemporary Psychoanalysis, 40,* 409–464.

Chiron, C., Jambaque, I., Nabbout, R., Lounes, R., Syrota, A., & Dulac, O. (1997). The right brain hemisphere is dominant in human infants. *Brain, 120,* 1057–1065.

Ciardi, J. (1959, 21 March). Robert Frost: Master conversationalist at work. *Saturday Review,* pp. 17–20.

Cunningham, M. (1998). *The hours.* New York: Farrar, Straus & Giroux.

Decety, J., & Chaminade, T. (2003). When the self represents the other: A new cognitive neuroscience view on psychological identification. *Consciousness and Cognition, 12,* 577–596.

Devereux, G. (1953). *Psychoanalysis and the occult.* New York: International Universities Press.

Dickinson, E. (1862). Poem 599. In T. H. Johnson (Ed.), *The complete poems of Emily Dickinson* (p. 294). New York: Little, Brown, 1960.

_____ (1863). Poem 670. In T. H. Johnson (Ed.), *The complete poems of Emily Dickinson* (p. 333). New York: Little, Brown, 1960.

Dobbing, J., & Sands, J. (1973). Quantitative growth and development of human brain. *Archives of Diseases of Childhood, 48,* 757–767.

Dutra, L., Bureau, J.-F., Holmes, B., Lyubchik, A., & Lyons-Ruth, K. (2009). Quality of early care and childhood trauma: A prospective study of developmental pathways to dissociation. *Journal of Nervous and Mental Disease, 197,* 383–390.

Edelman, G. M. (1989). *The remembered present: A biological theory of consciousness.* New York: Basic Books.

_____ (1992). *Bright air, brilliant fire.* New York: Basic Books.

_____ (2004). *Wider than the sky: The phenomenal gift of consciousness.* New Haven, CT: Yale University Press.

Enriquez, P., & Bernabeu, E. (2008). Hemispheric laterality and dissociative tendencies: Differences in emotional processing in a dichotic listening task. *Consciousness and Cognition, 17,* 267–275.

Epstein, S. (1994). Integration of the cognitive and psychodynamic unconscious. *American Psychologist, 49,* 709–724.

Ferenczi, S. (1930). The principles of relaxation and neo-catharsis. In M. Balint (Ed.), *Final contributions to the problems and methods of psychoanalysis* (pp. 108–125). New York: Brunner/Mazel, 1980.

_____ (1932/1988). *The clinical diary of Sándor Ferenczi* (J. Dupont, Ed., M. Balint & N. Z. Jackson, Trans.). Cambridge, MA: Harvard University Press.

Fingarette, H. (1963). *The self in transformation: Psychoanalysis, philosophy, and the life of the spirit.* New York: Basic Books.

Fonagy, P., & Moran, G. S. (1991). Understanding psychic change in child psychoanalysis. *International Journal of Psychoanalysis, 72*, 15–22.

Fonagy P., Moran, G. S., & Target, M. (1993). Aggression and the psychological self. *International Journal of Psychoanalysis, 74*, 471–485.

Fonagy, P., & Target, M. (1995). Understanding the violent patient: The use of the body and the role of the father. *International Journal of Psychoanalysis, 76*, 487–501.

——— (1996). Playing with reality: I. Theory of mind and the normal development of psychic reality. *International Journal of Psychoanalysis, 77*, 217–233.

Fonagy, P., Gergely, G., Jurist, E. L., & Target, M. (2005). *Affect regulation, mentalization, and the development of the self.* New York: Other Press.

Freud, S. (1897). Letter 69 (September 21, 1897). Extracts from the Fliess papers (1950 [1892–1899]). In J. Strachey (Ed. & Trans.), *The standard edition of the complete psychological works of Sigmund Freud* (Vol. 1, pp. 259–260). London: Hogarth Press, 1966.

——— (1911). The handling of dream-interpretation in psycho-analysis. In J. Strachey (Ed. & Trans.), *The standard edition of the complete psychological works of Sigmund Freud* (Vol. 12, pp. 89–96). London: Hogarth Press, 1958.

——— (1912a). The dynamics of transference. In J. Strachey (Ed. & Trans.), *The standard edition of the complete psychological works of Sigmund Freud* (Vol. 12, pp. 97–108). London: Hogarth Press, 1958.

——— (1912b). Recommendations to physicians practising psycho-analysis. In J. Strachey (Ed. & Trans.), *The standard edition of the complete psychological works of Sigmund Freud* (Vol. 12, pp. 109–120). London: Hogarth Press, 1958.

——— (1913). On beginning the treatment (Further recommendations on the technique of psycho-analysis, I). In J. Strachey (Ed. & Trans.), *The standard edition of the complete psychological works of Sigmund Freud* (Vol. 12, pp. 121–144). London: Hogarth Press, 1958.

——— (1914). Remembering, repeating and working-through (Further recommendations on the technique of psycho-analysis II). In J. Strachey (Ed. & Trans.), *The standard edition of the complete psychological works of Sigmund Freud* (Vol. 12, pp. 145–156). London: Hogarth Press, 1958.

——— (1915a). The unconscious. In J. Strachey (Ed. & Trans.), *The standard edition of the complete psychological works of Sigmund Freud* (Vol. 14, pp. 159–205). London: Hogarth Press, 1957.

——— (1915b). Observations on transference-love (Further recommendations on the technique of psycho-analysis III). In J. Strachey (Ed. & Trans.), *The standard edition of the complete psychological works of Sigmund Freud* (Vol. 12, pp. 159–171). London: Hogarth Press, 1958.

——— (1921). Psychoanalysis and telepathy (Original English translation by G. Devereux). In G. Devereux (Ed.), *Psychoanalysis and the occult* (pp. 56–68). New York: International Universities Press, 1953.

_____ (1933). New introductory lectures on psychoanalysis. In J. Strachey (Ed. & Trans.), *The standard edition of the complete psychological works of Sigmund Freud* (Vol. 22, pp. 1–182). London: Hogarth Press.

Friedman, L. (1988). *The anatomy of psychotherapy*. Hillsdale, NJ: The Analytic Press.

Frost, R. (1939). The figure a poem makes. In E. C. Lathem & L. R. Thompson (Eds.), *The Robert Frost reader: Poetry and prose*. New York: Henry Holt, 2002.

_____ (1942). The secret sits. In E. C. Lathem (Ed.), *The poetry of Robert Frost* (p. 362). New York: Henry Holt, 1979.

Gaddini, E. (1992). *A psychoanalytic theory of infantile experience*. London: Routledge.

Gainotti, G. (2006). Unconscious emotional memories and the right hemisphere. In M. Mancia (Ed.), *Psychoanalysis and neuroscience* (pp. 2045). Milan: Springer.

Gallese, V., & Goldman, A. (1998). Mirror neurons and the simulation theory of mind-reading. *Trends in Cognitive Science, 2*, 493–501.

Gaudillière, J.-M. (2010). Psychoanalysis and the trauma(s) of history. Online colloquium of the International Association for Relational Psychoanalysis and Psychotherapy. 5–19 December.

Goldbarth, A. (2003). *Pieces of Payne*. Saint Paul, MN: Graywolf Press.

Goldfried, M. (2010). Building a two-way bridge between practice and research. *The Clinical Psychologist: Newsletter, Div. 12, American Psychological Association, 63*(1), 1–3.

Goodman, S. (Ed.) (1977). *Psychoanalytic education and research: The current situation and future possibilities*. New York: International Universities Press.

Greenacre, P. (1969). *Trauma, growth and personality*. New York: International Universities Press.

Greenberg, J. R., & Mitchell, S. A. (1983). *Object relations in psychoanalytic theory*. Cambridge, MA: Harvard University Press.

Grotstein, J. S. (2004). "The light militia of the lower sky": The deeper nature of dreaming and phantasying. *Psychoanalytic Dialogues, 14*, 99–118.

Gupta, R. K., Hasan, K. M., Trivedi, R., Pradhan, M., Das, V., Parikh, N. A., & Narayana, P. A. (2005). Diffusion tensor imaging of the developing human cerebrum. *Journal of Neuroscience Research, 81*, 172–178.

Hansel, A., & von Kanel, R. (2008). The ventro-medial prefrontal cortex: A major link between the autonomic nervous system, regulation of emotion, and stress reactivity? *BioPsychoSocial Medicine, 2*, 21.

Happaney, K., Zelazo, P. D., & Stuss, D. T. (2004). Development of orbitofrontal function: Current themes and future directions. *Brain and Cognition, 55*, 1–10.

Harris, A. (2004). The relational unconscious: Commentary on papers by Michael Eigen and James Grotstein. *Psychoanalytic Dialogues, 14*, 131–137.

_____ (2009). "You must remember this." *Psychoanalytic Dialogues, 19*, 2–21.

Hatfield, E., Cacioppo, J. T., & Rapson, R. L. (1992). Primitive emotional contagion. In M.S. Clark (Ed.), *Emotion and social behavior* (pp. 151–171). Newbury Park, CA: Sage.

Helmeke, C., Ovtscharoff, W., Poeggel, G., & Braun, K. (2001). Juvenile emotional experience alyters synaptic inputs on pyramidal neurons in the anterior cingulate cortex. *Cerebral Cortex, 11,* 717–727.

Helton, W. S., Dorahy, M. J., & Russell, P. N. (2010). Dissociative tendencies and right-hemisphere processing load: Effects on vigilance performance. *Consciousness and Cognition.*

Henry, J. (1965). *Pathways to madness.* New York: Random House.

Hermans, H. J. M., Kempen, H. J. G., & van Loon, R. J. P. (1992). The dialogical self: Beyond individualism and rationalism. *American Psychologist, 47,* 23–33.

Hesse, E., & Main, M. (1999). Second-generation effects of unresolved trauma in nonmaltreating parents: Dissociated, frightened, and threatening parental behavior. *Psychoanalytic Inquiry, 19,* 481–540.

Hilgard, E. R. (1965). *Hypnotic susceptibility.* New York: Harcourt, Brace & World.

——— (1977). *Divided consciousness: Multiple controls in human thought and action.* New York: Wiley.

Howell, E. F. (2005). *The dissociative mind.* Hillsdale, NJ: The Analytic Press.

Hutterer, J., & Liss, M. (2006). Cognitive development, memory, trauma, treatment: An integration of psychoanalytic and behavioural concepts in light of current neuroscience research. *Journal of the American Academy of Psychoanalysis and Dynamic Psychiatry, 34,* 287–302.

Ischlondsky, N. D. (1955). The inhibitory process in the cerebrophysiological laboratory and in the clinic. *Journal of Nervous and Mental Disease, 121,* 5–18.

Iturria-Medina, Y., et al. (2011). Brain hemispheric structural efficiency and interconnectivity rightward asymmetry in humans and nonhuman primates. *Cerebral Cortex, 21,* 56–67.

James, W. (1892). *Psychology: Briefer course.* London: Macmillan.

Janet, P. (1907). *The major symptoms of hysteria* (1st ed.). New York: Macmillan.

Johnson, S. (2004). *Mind wide open: Your brain and the neuroscience of everyday life.* New York: Scribner.

Kalsched, D. (2005). Hope versus hopelessness in the psychoanalytic situation and Dante's *Divine Comedy. Spring, 72,* 167–187.

Kaplan, C. M. (2010a). Navigating trauma in Joseph Conrad's *Victory:* A voyage from Sigmund Freud to Philip M. Bromberg. *Psychoanalytic Dialogues, 20,* 441–448.

——— (2010b). Navigating trauma: Reply to "Commentary." *Psychoanalytic Dialogues, 20,* 456–458.

Keenan, J. P., Rubio, J., Racioppi, C., Johnson, A., & Barnacz, A. (2005). The right hemisphere and the dark side of consciousness. *Cortex, 41,* 695–704.

Kestenberg, J. (1985). The flow of empathy and trust between mother and child. In E. J. Anthony & G. H. Pollack (Eds.), *Parental influences in health and disease* (pp. 137–163). Boston, MA: Little Brown.

Khan, M. (1971). "To hear with the eyes": Clinical notes on body as subject and object. In *The privacy of the self* (pp. 234–250). New York: International Universities Press, 1974.

—— (1979). Secret as potential space. In S. A. Grolnick, L. Barkin, & W. Muensterberger (Eds.), *Between reality and fantasy: Transitional objects and phenomena* (pp. 259–270). New York: Jason Aronson.

Kihlstrom, J. (1987). The cognitive unconscious. *Science, 237*, 1445–1452.

Klauber, J. (1980). Formulating interpretations in clinical psychoanalysis. *International Journal of Psychoanalysis, 61*, 195–201.

Klee, P. (1957). *The diaries of Paul Klee, 1898–1918.* Berkeley, CA: University of California Press.

Korzybski, A. (1954). *Time-binding: The general theory.* Lakeville, CT: Institute of General Semantics.

Kounios, J., Frymiare, J. L., Bowden, E. M., Fleck, J. I., Subramaniam, K., Parrish, T. B., & Jung-Beeman, M. J. (2006). The prepared mind: Neural activity prior to problem presentation predicts solution by sudden insight. *Psychological Science, 17*, 882–890.

Kounios, J., Fleck, J., Green, D. L., Payne, L., Stevenson, J. L., Bowden, E. M., & Jung-Beeman, M. J. (2008). The origins of insight in resting-state brain activity. *Neuropsychologia, 46*, 281–291.

Laing, R. D. (1962). Confirmation and disconfirmation. In *The self and others* (pp. 88–97). Chicago: Quadrangle Books.

—— (1967). *The politics of experience.* New York: Pantheon Books.

—— (1969). *The politics of the family.* New York: Vintage Books, 1972.

Lane, R. D., Ahern, G. L., Schwartz, G. E., & Kaszniak, A. W. (1997). Is alexithymia the emotional equivalent of blindsight? *Biological Psychiatry, 42*, 834–844.

Langan, R. (1997). On free-floating attention. *Psychoanalytic Dialogues, 7*, 819–839.

Lanius, R. A., Williamson, P. C., Bluhm, R. L., Densmore, M., Boksman, K., Neufeld, R. W. J., Gati, J. S., & Menon, R. S. (2005). Functional connectivity of dissociative responses in posttraumatic stress disorder: A functional magnetic resonance imaging investigation. *Biological Psychiatry, 57*, 873–884.

Lasky, R. (2002). Countertransference and the analytic instrument. *Psychoanalytic Psychology, 19*, 65–94.

Laub, D., & Auerhahn, N. C. (1993). Knowing and not knowing massive psychic trauma: Forms of traumatic memory. *International Journal of Psychoanalysis, 74*, 287–302.

Lazarus, R. S., & McCleary, R. A. (1951). Autonomic discrimination without awareness: A study of subception. *Psychological Review, 58*, 113–122.

LeDoux, J. E. (1989). Cognitive-emotional interactions in the brain. *Cognition & Emotion, 3*, 267–289.

—— (1996). *The emotional brain.* New York: Touchstone.

—— (2002). *The synaptic self.* New York: Viking.

Lehrer, J. (2008, 28 July). Annals of science: The eureka hunt. *The New Yorker*, pp. 39–45.

Levenkron, H. (2006). Love (and hate) with the proper stranger: Affective honesty and enactment. *Psychoanalytic Inquiry, 26*, 157–181.

—— (2009). Engaging the implicit: Meeting points between the Boston Change Process Study Group and relational psychoanalysis. *Contemporary Psychoanalysis, 45*, 179–217.

Levenson, E. A. (1972). *The fallacy of understanding.* New York: Basic Books.

—— (1983). *The ambiguity of change.* New York: Basic Books.

—— (2003). On seeing what is said: Visual aids to the psychoanalytic process. *Contemporary Psychoanalysis, 39*, 233–249.

Lewis, C. S. (1956). *Till we have faces: A myth retold.* New York: Harcourt Brace Jovanovich.

Loewenstein, R. J. (1996). Dissociative amnesia and dissociative fugue. In L. K. Michelson & W. J. Ray (Eds.), *Handbook of dissociation: Theoretical, empirical, and clinical perspectives* . New York: Plenum.

Lothane, Z. (2009). Dramatology in life, disorder, and psychoanalytic therapy: A further contribution to interpersonal psychoanalysis. *International Forum of Psychoanalysis, 18*, 135–148.

Lynd, H. M. (1958). *On shame and the search for identity.* New York: Harcourt Brace.

Lyons-Ruth, K. (1998). Implicit relational knowing: Its role in development and psychoanalytic treatment. *Infant Mental Health Journal, 19*, 282–289.

—— (2003). Dissociation and the parent–infant dialogue: A longitudinal perspective from attachment research. *Journal of the American Psychoanalytic Association, 51*, 883–911.

—— (2006). The interface between attachment and intersubjectivity: Perspective from the longitudinal study of disorganized attachment. *Psychoanalytic Inquiry, 26*, 595–616.

Lyons-Ruth, K., & Boston Change Process Study Group (2001). The emergence of new experiences: Relational improvisation, recognition process, and non-linear change in psychoanalytic therapy. *Psychologist-Psychoanalyst, 21*, 13–17.

MacDonald, G. (1858). *Phantastes.* Grand Rapids, MI: Wm. B. Eeerdmans, 1981.

Main, M., & Morgan, H. (1996). Disorganization and disorientation in infant strange situation behavior: Phenotypic resemblance to dissociative states. In L. Michelson & W. Ray (Eds.), *Handbook of dissociation: Theoretical, empirical, and clinical perspectives* (pp. 107–138). New York: Plenum.

Malouf, D. (2009). *Ransom.* New York: Pantheon.

Markoff, J. (2010, 9 November). Quantum computing reaches for true power. *New York Times Science Section*, p. D2.

Maroda, K. J. (2005). Show some emotion: Completing the cycle of affective communication. In L. Aron & A. Harris (Eds.), *Relational psychoanalysis, vol. II. Innovation and expansion* (pp. 121–142). Hillsdale, NJ: The Analytic Press.

Mayer, E. L. (1996). Subjectivity and intersubjectivity of clinical facts. *International Journal of Psychoanalysis, 77*, 709–737.

____ (2001). On "Telepathic Dreams?" An unpublished paper by Robert J. Stoller. *Journal of the American Psychoanalytic Association, 49*, 629–657.

____ (2007). *Extraordinary knowing: Science, skepticism, and the inexplicable powers of the human mind.* New York: Bantam Books.

McGilchrist, I. (2009). *The master and his emissary: The divided brain and the making of the western world.* New Haven, CT: Yale University Press.

Meares, R. (2001). What happens next? A developmental model of therapeutic spontaneity. *Psychoanalytic Dialogues, 11*, 755–769.

Merini, A. (2007). From "Aphorisms" (D. Basford, Trans.). *Poetry, 191*, 18.

Minagawa-Kawai, Y., Matsuoka, S., Dan, I., Naoi, N., Nakamura, K., & Kojima, S. (2009). Prefrontal activation associated with social attachment: Facial-emotion recognition in mothers and infants. *Cerebral Cortex, 19*, 284–292.

Mitchell, S. A. (1991). Contemporary perspectives on self: Toward an integration. *Psychoanalytic Dialogues, 1*, 121–147.

____ (1993). *Hope and dread in psychoanalysis.* New York: Basic Books.

Moore, B. E., & Fine, B. D. (Eds.) (1990). *Psychoanalytic terms and concepts* (3rd ed.). New Haven, CT: American Psychoanalytic Association & Yale University Press.

Morris, J. S., Ohman, A., & Dolan, R. J. (1999). A subcortical pathway to the right amygdala mediating "unseen" fear. *Proceedings of the National Academy of Sciences of the United States of America, 96*, 1680–1685.

Morris, J. S., & Dolan, R. J. (2004). Dissociable amygdala and orbitofrontal responses during reversal fear conditioning. *NeuroImage, 22*, 372–380.

Moskowitz, A., & Corstens, D. (2007). Auditory hallucinations: Psychotic symptom or dissociative experience? *Journal of Psychological Trauma, 6*, 35–63.

Moskowitz, A., Schafer, I., & Dorahy, M. J. (Eds.) (2008). *Psychosis, trauma and dissociation: Emerging perspectives on severe psychopathology.* Chichester, UK: Wiley.

Nagel, T. (1979). What is it like to be a bat? In *Mortal questions* (pp. 165–180). Cambridge, UK: Cambridge University Press.

Nijenhuis, E. R. S. (2000). Somatoform dissociation: Major symptoms of dissociative disorders. *Journal of Trauma & Dissociation, 1*, 7–32.

Ogden, P. (2007, 3 November). A psychology of action: The role of movement and mindfulness in the treatment of trauma, attachment and affect dysregulation. Paper presented at the conference on "Affect Regulation: Development, Trauma, and Treatment of the Brain–Mind–Body," Mt. Sinai Medical Center, New York.

Ogden, P., Minton, K., & Pain, C. (2006). *Trauma and the body: A sensorimotor approach to psychotherapy.* New York: Norton.

Osborne, J. W., & Baldwin, J. R. (1982). Psychotherapy: From one state of illusion to another. *Psychotherapy, 19,* 266–275.

Papeo, L., Longo, M. R., Feurra, M., & Haggard, P. (2010). The role of the right temporoparietal junction in intersensory conflict: Detection or resolution? *Experimental Brain Research, 206,* 129–139.

Parker, R. B. (1983). *The widening gyre: A Spenser novel.* New York: Dell.

Parsons, M. (2009). An independent theory of clinical technique. *Psychoanalytic Dialogues, 19,* 221–236.

Peterson, P. (2003). *Out stealing horses.* New York: Picador.

Phillips, A. (1993). *On kissing, tickling, and being bored.* Cambridge, MA: Harvard University Press.

Piers, C. (1998). Contemporary trauma theory and its relation to character. *Psychoanalytic Psychology, 15,* 14–33.

____ (2000). Character as self-organizing complexity. *Psychoanalysis and Contemporary Thought, 23,* 3–34.

____ (2005). The mind's multiplicity and continuity. *Psychoanalytic Dialogues, 15,* 229–254.

____ (2007). Emergence: When a difference in degree becomes a difference in kind. In C. Piers, J. P. Muller, & J. Brent (Eds.), *Self-organizing complexity in psychological systems* (pp. 83–110). New York: Jason Aronson.

____ (2010). David Shapiro's characterology and complex systems theory. In *Personality and psychopathology: Critical dialogues with David Shapiro* (pp. 223–246). New York: Springer.

Pine, F. (1988). The four psychologies of psychoanalysis and their place in clinical work. *Journal of the American Psychoanalytic Association, 36,* 571–596.

Pizer, S. A. (1992). The negotiation of paradox in the analytic process. *Psychoanalytic Dialogues, 2,* 215–240.

____ (1998). *Building bridges: The negotiation of paradox in psychoanalysis.* Hillsdale, NJ: The Analytic Press.

Pope, A. (1714). The rape of the lock. In L. I. Bredvold, A. D. McKillop, & L. Whitney (Eds.), *Eighteenth century poetry and prose* (pp. 354–364). New York: Ronald Press, 1939.

Porges, S. W. (1997). Emotion: An evolutionary by-product of the neural regulation of the autonomic nervous system. *Annals of the New York Academy of Sciences, 807,* 62–77.

Porges, S. W., Doussard-Roosevelt, J. A., & Maiti, A. K. (1994). Vagal tone and the physiological regulation of emotion. *Monographs of the Society for Research in Child Development, 59,* 167–186.

Pullman, P. (2007). *His dark materials.* New York: Knopf.

Putnam, F. W. (1992). Discussion: Are alter personalities fragments or figments? *Psychoanalytic Inquiry, 12*, 95–111.

Rather, L. (2001). Collaborating with the unconscious other: The analyst's capacity for creative thinking. *International Journal of Psychoanalysis, 82*, 515–532.

Raz, A. (2004). Anatomy of attentional networks. *Anatomical Records, 281B*, 21–36.

Recordati, G. (2003). A thermodynamic model of the sympathetic and parasympathetic nervous systems. *Autonomic Neuroscience: Basic and Clinical, 103*, 1–12.

Reese, J. (2000, 11 June). Black magic. *New York Times.*

Reik, T. (1949). *Listening with the third ear.* New York: Farrar, Straus.

Ringstrom, P. (2001). Cultivating the improvisational in psychoanalytic treatment. *Psychoanalytic Dialogues, 11*, 727–754.

_____ (2007a). Scenes that write themselves: Improvisational moments in relational psychoanalysis. *Psychoanalytic Dialogues, 17*, 69–99.

_____ (2007b). Principles of improvisation relevant to relational psychoanalysis. Paper presented at meeting of International Association for Relational Psychoanalysis and Psychotherapy (IARPP), Rome.

Rizzuto, A.-M. (2004). Book review of R. Steiner, "Unconscious fantasy." London: Karnac. *Journal of the American Psychoanalytic Association, 52*, 1285–1290.

Rogers, R., & Hart, L. (1940). "It never entered my mind." From the show *Higher and higher.*

Rosenbaum, T. (2002). *The golems of Gotham.* New York: HarperCollins.

Rosenfeld, H. (1987). *Impasse and interpretation.* London: Routledge.

Ross, E. D., & Monnot, M. (2008). Neurology of affective prosody and its functional-anatomic organization in right hemisphere. *Brain and Language, 104*, 51–74.

Rule, R. R., Shimamura, A. P., & Knight, R. T. (2002). Orbitofrontal cortex and dynamic filtering of emotional stimuli. *Cognition, Affective, & Behavioral Neuroscience, 2*, 264–270.

Salberg, J. (2010). *Good enough endings: Breaks, interruptions, and terminations from contemporary relational perspectives.* New York: Routledge.

Schafer, R. (1976). *A new language for psychoanalysis.* New Haven, CT: Yale University Press.

_____ (1980). Action language and the psychology of the self. *Annual of Psychoanalysis, 8*, 83–92.

_____ (1983). *The analytic attitude.* New York: Basic Books.

Schore, A. N. (1994). *Affect regulation and the origin of the self.* Hillsdale, NJ: Lawrence Erlbaum Associates, Inc.

_____ (2000). Attachment and the regulation of the right brain. *Attachment and Human Development, 2*, 23–47.

_____ (2001). The effects of relational trauma on right brain development, affect regulation, and infant mental health. *Infant Mental Health Journal, 22*, 201–269.

_____ (2002). Dysregulation of the right brain: A fundamental mechanism of traumatic attachment and the psychopathogenesis of posttraumatic stress disorder. *Australian & New Zealand Journal of Psychiatry, 36*, 9–30.

_____ (2003a). *Affect dysregulation and disorders of the self.* New York: Norton.

_____ (2003b). *Affect regulation and the repair of the self.* New York: Norton.

_____ (2007). Review of *Awakening the dreamer: Clinical journeys,* by Philip M. Bromberg. *Psychoanalytic Dialogues, 17*, 753–767.

_____ (2009a). Attachment trauma and the developing right brain: Origins of pathological dissociation. In P. F. Dell & J. A. O'Neil (Eds.), *Dissociation and the dissociative disorders: DSM-V and beyond* (pp. 107–141). New York: Routledge.

_____ (2009b). Relational trauma and the developing right brain: An interface of psychoanalytic self psychology and neuroscience. *Annals of the New York Academy of Sciences, 1159*, 189–203.

_____ (2009c). Right brain affect regulation: An essential mechanism of development, trauma, dissociation, and psychotherapy. In D. Fosha, D. Siegel, & M. Solomon (Eds.), *The healing power of emotion: Affective neuroscience, development, & clinical practice* (pp. 112–144). New York: Norton.

_____ (2009d, August 8). The paradigm shift: The right brain and the relational unconscious. Invited plenary address, 2009 Convention of the American Psychological Association, Toronto, Canada. Retrieved September 16, 2009 from http://www.allanschore.com/pdf/APA%20Schore%20Plenary%20Final%2009.pdf

_____ (2010). Relational trauma and the developing right brain: The neurobiology of broken attachment bonds. In T. Baradon (Ed.), *Relational trauma in infancy* (pp. 19–47). London: Routledge.

_____ (2011). The right brain implicit self lies at the core of psychoanalysis. *Psychoanalytic Dialogues, 21*, 75–100.

_____ (in preparation). *The science of the art of psychotherapy.* New York: Norton.

Schore, J. R., & Schore, A. N. (2008). Modern attachment theory: The central role of affect regulation in development and treatment. *Clinical Social Work Journal, 36*, 9–20.

Schutz, L. E. (2005). Broad-perspective perceptual disorder of the right hemisphere. *Neuropsychology Review, 15*, 11– 27.

Shakespeare, W. (1599–1601). Hamlet, prince of Denmark. In W. A. Neilson & C. J. Hill (Eds.), *The complete plays and poems of William Shakespeare* (pp. 1043–1092). Cambridge, MA: Riverside, 1942.

Sheldrake, R. (1999). *Dogs who know when their owners are coming home.* New York: Three Rivers Press.

_____ (2003). *The sense of being stared at.* New York: Crown.

Shelley, M. (1818). *Frankenstein.* New York: Bantam Books, 1991.

Siegel, D. J. (1999). *The developing mind: Toward a neurobiology of interpersonal experience.* New York: Guilford.

Sim, T.-C., & Martinez, C. (2005). Emotion words are remembered better in the left ear. *Laterality, 10*, 149–159.

Sobin, G. (1999). *The fly truffler: A novel.* New York: Norton, 2000.

Solms, M. (2003). Do unconscious phantasies really exist? In R. Steiner (Ed.), *Unconscious phantasy* (pp. 89–106). London: Karnac, 2003.

Spiegel, D., & Cardeña, E. (1991). Disintegrated experience: The dissociative disorders revisited. *Journal of Abnormal Psychology, 100,* 366–378.

Spillius, E. B. (2001). Freud and Klein on the concept of phantasy. *International Journal of Psychoanalysis, 82,* 361–373.

Spitzer, C., Wilert, C., Grabe, H.-J., Rizos, T., & Freyberger, H. J. (2004). Dissociation, hemispheric asymmetry, and dysfunction of hemispheric interaction: A transcranial magnetic approach. *Journal of Neuropsychiatry and Clinical Neurosciences, 16,* 163–169.

Spitzer, C., Barnow, S., Freyberger, H. J., & Grabe, H. J. (2007). Dissociation predicts symptom-related treatment outcome in short-term inpatient psychotherapy. *Australian and New Zealand Journal of Psychiatry, 41,* 682–687.

Stechler, G. (2003). Affect: The heart of the matter. *Psychoanalytic Dialogues, 13,* 711–726.

Stein, G. (1937). *Everybody's autobiography.* Cambridge, MA: Exact Change, 1993.

Steiner, R. (Ed.) (2003). *Unconscious phantasy.* London: Karnac.

Stern, D. B. (1996). Dissociation and constructivism. *Psychoanalytic Dialogues, 6,* 251–266.

—— (1997). *Unformulated experience: From dissociation to imagination in psychoanalysis.* Hillsdale, NJ: The Analytic Press.

—— (2004). The eye sees itself: Dissociation, enactment, and the achievement of conflict. *Contemporary Psychoanalysis, 40,* 197–237.

—— (2009). *Partners in thought: Working with unformulated experience, dissociation, and enactment.* New York: Routledge.

Stern, D. N., Bruschweiler-Stern, N., Harrison, A. M., Lyons-Ruth, K., Morgan, A. C., Nahum, J. P., Sander, L., & Tronick, E. Z. (1998). The process of therapeutic change involving implicit knowledge: Some implications of developmental observations for adult psychotherapy. *Infant Mental Health Journal, 19,* 300–308.

Sterne, L. (1762). *The life and opinions of Tristram Shandy, gentleman.* New York: Modern Library, 2004.

Stone, L. (1961). *The psychoanalytic situation: An examination of its development and essential nature.* New York: International Universities Press.

Strout, E. (2008). *Olive Kitteridge.* New York: Random House.

Sturgeon, T. (1953). *More than human.* New York: Carroll & Graf.

Sullivan, H. S. (1953). *The interpersonal theory of psychiatry.* New York: Norton.

—— (1954). *The psychiatric interview.* New York: Norton.

Sullivan, R. M., & Dufresne, M. M. (2006). Mesocortical dopamine and HPA axis regulation: Role of laterality and early environment. *Brain Research, 1076,* 49–59.

Sun, T., Patoine, C., Abu-Khalil, A., Visvader, J., Sum, E., Cherry, T. J., Orkin, S. H., Geschwind, D. H., & Walsh, C. A. (2005). Early asymmetry of gene transcription in embryonic human left and right cerebral cortex. *Science*, *308*, 1794–1798.

Symonds, L. L., Gordon, N. S., Bixby, J. C., & Mande, M. M. (2006). Right-lateralized pain processing in the human cortex: An fMRI study. *Journal of Neurophysiology*, *95*, 3823–3830.

Target, M., & Fonagy, P. (1996). Playing with reality: II. The development of psychic reality from a theoretical perspective. *International Journal of Psychoanalysis*, *77*, 459–479.

Tennes, M. (2007). Beyond intersubjectivity: The transpersonal dimension of the psychoanalytic encounter. *Contemporary Psychoanalysis*, *43*, 505–525.

Thomas, M. T. (2008, 21 September). Performance of his life: He composed himself. *New York Times* (Arts and Leisure Section), pp. 1, 25.

Tronick, E. Z. (2003). "Of course all relationships are unique": How co-created processes generate unique mother–infant and patient–therapist relationships and change other relationships. *Psychoanalytic Inquiry*, *23*, 473–491.

Tronick, E. Z., & Weinberg, M. K. (1997). Depressed mothers and infants: Failure to form dyadic states of consciousness. In L. Murray & P. Cooper (Eds.), *Postpartum depression and child development* (pp. 54–81). New York: Guilford, 1997.

Tsakiris, M., Costantini, M., & Haggard, P. (2008). The role of the right tempero-parietal junction in maintaining a coherent sense of one's body. *Neuropsychologia*, *46*, 3014–3018.

Ullman, M., Krippner, S., & Vaughn, A. (1973). *Dream telepathy*. New York: Macmillan.

Untermeyer, L. (1964). *Robert Frost: A backward look*. Ann Arbor, MI: University of Michigan Library.

van der Kolk, B. A. (1995). The body, memory, and the psychobiology of trauma. In J. A. Alpert (Ed.), *Sexual abuse recalled* (pp. 29–60). Northvale, NJ: Jason Aronson.

van der Kolk, B. A., Pelcovitz, D., Roth, S., Mandel, F. S., McFarlane, A., & Herman, J. L. (1996). Dissociation, somatization, and affect dysregulation: The complexity of adaptation to trauma. *American Journal of Psychiatry*, *153*, 83–93.

Webster's new universal unabridged dictionary, second edition (1983). New York: Simon & Schuster.

Wheelis, A. (1958). *The quest for identity*. New York: Norton.

Wilkinson, M. (2006). *Coming into mind: The mind–brain relationship: A Jungian perspective*. New York: Routledge.

Winnicott, D. W. (1949). Mind and its relation to the psyche-soma. In *Collected papers: Through paediatrics to psychoanalysis* (pp. 243–254). London: Tavistock, 1958.

_____ (1951). Transitional objects and transitional phenomena. In *Collected papers: Through paediatrics to psychoanalysis* (pp. 229–242). London: Tavistock, 1958.

Winnicott, D. W. (1958). The capacity to be alone. In *The maturational processes and the facilitating environment* (pp. 29–36). New York: International Universities Press, 1965.

—— (1960). Ego distortion in terms of true and false self. In *The maturational processes and the facilitating environment* (pp. 140–152). New York: International Universities Press, 1965.

—— (1963). Communicating and not communicating leading to a study of certain opposites. In *The maturational processes and the facilitating environment* (pp. 179–192). New York: International Universities Press, 1965.

—— (1965). *The maturational processes and the facilitating environment.* New York: International Universities Press.

—— (1971). *Playing and reality.* New York: Basic Books.

Wittling, W. (1997). The right hemisphere and the human stress response. *Acta Physiologica Scandinavica, 640*(Suppl.), 55–59.

Wittling, W., & Schweiger, E. (1993). Neuroendocrine brain asymmetry and physical complaints. *Neuropsychologia, 31*, 591–608.

Young, W. (1988). Psychodynamics and dissociation. *Dissociation, 1*, 33–38.

Zafon, C. R. (2001). *The shadow of the wind* (L. Graves, Trans.). New York: Penguin, 2004.

Zakharov, L. V. (2008, 8 March). Featured response to "Who said poetry is what gets lost in translation?" *Packingtown Review.*

Index

parasympathetic nervous system,
xxi, xxxi
parasympathetic vagal systems,
xvii–xviii
Parker, R. B., 168
perception, xv, xxiii, 52, 157,
159–160
"anomalous" experience, 71, 138
Gestalt psychology, 137
personality disorders, xxv, xxvi,
xxxiii, 26–27, 76, 162
Peterson, P., 125
Phillips, A., 102–103
Piers, C., 160n2
Pine, F., 128
play, 18, 20, 65, 154
poetry, 2–4, 146–147
Pope, A., 147
Porges, S. W., xv, xviii, 100
positive affect, xiii
post traumatic stress disorder
(PTSD), xx, xxv
prefrontal cortex, xx–xxi, xxii
"pretend mode" of reality, 65–66
projective identification, xxx
psyche-soma, xxiv, 54, 110, 155
"psychic death", xxiii
"psychic equivalent mode" of reality,
65–66
psychoanalysis, 53, 92–93, 168, 186.
See also therapeutic relationship
aim of, 102, 121, 156
boundary-negotiation, 140–141
interpersonal/relational, x, xxvii,
67–68, 103–104, 126–127,
129, 134, 136, 151–152
Laing's concept of, 105
perception, 160
technique, 24, 123–129, 130, 144
unconscious fantasy, 148, 154
psychosis, xxv, 181n6
psychotherapeutic change, x, xxxii–
xxxvi, 53, 57, 149
PTSD. See post traumatic stress
disorder
Pullman, P., 169
Putnam, F. W., 100

R

Rather, L., 102
reactive attachment disorder, xxv
reality, 65–66, 97, 147, 150, 173
Reese, J., 179
reflective function, 15, 47
Regulation Theory, x, xii, xxvi,
xxvii–xxviii, xxxvi
Reik, T., 143
the relational mind, growth of, ix, 6,
8, 137–142
relational (developmental) trauma,
xvi, xix–xx, xxvi, xxxvi, 14
attachment patterns, 27, 76, 99
brain processes, xxiii, 98–99
disconfirmation of self, 57–58
Hamlet, 31, 32
impact of, 4–5, 6
infant's responses to, xvii
nonrecognition, 69
processing of, 120
reliving, 139, 184–185
relational unconscious, 72, 94, 97,
123, 129, 131–132, 154
relational/interpersonal
psychoanalysis, x, xxvii, 67–68,
103–104, 126–127, 129, 134,
136, 151–152
reliving, 17, 23–24, 78–80, 139,
184–185. See also enactment
repression, 24, 49, 101, 139, 156
resistance, 75–76, 78, 102, 103,
139
right brain hemisphere, xiii, xxxvii
affect regulation, xxxiii, xxxiv
attachment, xv, xviii
autonomic arousal, xiv–xv
consciousness, 79
dissociation, xix, xx–xxi, xxiv,
26–27
hyperarousal, xvii
impact of abuse on, xx
implicit self, xxii
integration tasks, xxxiv–xxxv
relational change mechanism, x,
xxxvi